Debates in Economic History

Edited by Peter Mathias

The Standard of Living in Britain in the Industrial Revolution

GW00374114

The Standard of Living in Britain in the Industrial Revolution

edited with an introduction by
ARTHUR J. TAYLOR

METHUEN & CO LTD
11 NEW FETTER LANE LONDON EC4

First published in 1975 by Methuen & Co. Ltd
Introduction © 1975 by Arthur J. Taylor
Printed in Great Britain by
Richard Clay (The Chaucer Press), Ltd,
Bungay, Suffolk

ISBN 0 416 08250 5 hardbound
ISBN 0 416 08260 2 paperback

Distributed in the USA by
HARPER & ROW PUBLISHERS, INC.
BARNES & NOBLE IMPORT DIVISION

Contents

Contents

Preface

The standard of living debate in the Industrial Revolution has proved, from contemporaries living through the experience up to our own days, the most sustained single controversy in British economic history. It shows no sign of slackening; indeed we are probably now at the beginning of a new range of inquiries. The debate has even begun a new life as a subject for study as an historical phenomenon in its own right, being an intellectual sequence illustrating the tug-of-war between the growth of new knowledge, methodological issues and value judgments in a social science, irrespective of the underlying truth which is at stake. Becoming a contribution to the sociology of knowledge is surely the ultimate fate for any intellectual debate – and a *trahison des clercs*. By being transposed into an end in itself for significance, it ceases to be a dialogue followed in pursuit of some elusive final judgment about historical reality.

Some justification is perhaps needed for reprinting again some much reprinted material. The present volume seeks to present a wide representative view of the debate: new contributions by both Dr Hartwell and Professor Hobsbawm provide re-assessments of their position at the present time while Professor Taylor's introduction surveys the debate as a whole, as the position now stands, just as his earlier article (in *History*, XLV (1960)) provided a detached assessment of the earlier position.

The principal reasons explain the sustained life, past, present and future, which this controversy has enjoyed, apart from its intrinsic historical importance. The first is that there seems no possibility of an unchallengeable answer to such a diffuse, many-sided question; the second that the debate has always been suffused with current political values. Essentially it has been a judgment on capitalism, about the social consequences of the operation of the free-market economy. As long as this remains a theme for current political controversy I have no doubt that reflected interest will keep debate alive about living standards during the Industrial Revolution – however much the actual grounds of contention have changed in the interim and however misleading the analogues between what constituted 'capitalism' in the second half of the twentieth century and the first half of the nineteenth.

Integral with this conflict over current political values has been the importance which this topic assumed for the radical tradition in British historiography. Economic history developed as a subject in the latter decades of the nineteenth century much embattled with conflicts over current economic policies of free-trade versus protection and other orthodox liberal economic assumptions versus critiques of the free market. As a subject it became a congenial base for the radical tradition – though never a united orthodoxy – for formal and informal Marxist positions and particularly for the Fabians. Indeed, with the work of the Webbs, the Hammonds, R. H. Tawney, G. D. H. Cole and Raymond Postgate it seemed that economic history had been mobilized to defend for the faithful the historical flank of those eternal political truths which the Fabian Society was propagating for the present and future. In the new phase of the controversy which is now beginning the radical tradition in British historiography seems to be being driven out of economic history by quantification and the dictates of neo-classical economic theory to find a sympathetic new base in a revitalized social history. Professor Hobsbawm and Mr Edward Thompson are marching off this particular battlefield under a banner which reads 'Thou shalt not judge by real wage indexes alone'. They are concerned with all the non-quantifiable aspects of the way of life which industrialization and urbanization brought with them: the smell of drains, a deteriorating urban environment affecting a rising percentage of the population; human dissatisfactions are not caught in the nets wielded by economists concerned with movements of money wages and prices.

Paradoxically enough, this is a conclusion explicitly drawn by the Hammonds in 1934, when they wrote in the introduction to *The Bleak Age* (about Clapham's and Silberling's conclusions): 'Statisticians tell us that when they have put in order such data as they can find, they are satisfied that earnings increased and that most men and women were less poor when this discontent was loud and active than they were when the eighteenth century was beginning to grow old in a silence like that of autumn. The evidence, of course, is scanty, and its interpretation not too simple, but this general view is probably more or less correct. If, then, there is for the first time systematic and widespread discontent, the explanation must be sought outside the sphere of strictly economic conditions.' The protean nature of this controversy is shown by the fact that this same conclusion can be sustained forty years later, after two generations' further work of increasing precision on the economic aspects of the case. The scene of the conflict is now changing, but no less controversy is in prospect for the future upon these less quantifiable social and cultural dimensions of living standards which social historians are bringing into the discussion.

It should also be said that, even within the strictly economic variables governing movements in real wages, a decade of research is needed at the local and regional level to give precision to such data: local retail price indexes (as distinct from the wholesale prices featured in the records of institutions mainly in the south of England built into aggregative national indexes); costs of living indexes based upon actual patterns of spending of the social groups in question; family earnings (as distinct from formal wage rates), and quantifying local variations in unemployment. In a period of rapid structural change, with much regional concentration of industrial development, with the economy increasingly affected by short-term fluctuations, evidence needs to be precisely related to its context of time, locality and economic sector. There is possibly less national uniformity (save in price movements) during this first century of industrialization than either in previous centuries, when there was the greater uniformity produced by a less differentiated economy, or after 1850 with greater national institutional and economic unity in the country. With a balanced sample of such local and regional studies (some of which are now emerging) a surer national picture can be built up.

Generalizations need to be made at the national level because it is the fate and fortune of the nation which is in question. Such extrapolations suggest a long and vigorous life for this already long-lived and vigorous debate.

All Souls College, Oxford   PETER MATHIAS
16 August 1974

Acknowledgements

The editor and publishers wish to thank the following for permission to reproduce the articles listed below:

The American Statistical Association for 'Real Wages of Artisans in London, 1729–1935' by R. S. Tucker (*Journal of the American Statistical Association*, XXXI, 1936); the Economic History Association for 'The Standard of Life of the Workers in England, 1790–1830' by T. S. Ashton (*Journal of Economic History*, supp. IX, 1949); Victor Gollancz Ltd for E. P. Thompson's 'Standards and Experiences' (from chapters 6 and 10 of *The Making of the English Working Class*, 1963); Dr R. M. Hartwell for 'The Rising Standard of Living in England, 1800–50' (*Economic History Review*, 2nd series, XIII, 1961); Professor E. J. Hobsbawm for 'The British Standard of Living, 1790–1850' (*Economic History Review*, 2nd series, X, 1957); R. S. Neale for 'The Standard of Living, 1780–1844: a Regional and Class Study' (*Economic History Review*, 2nd series, XIX, 1966); the *Review of Economics and Statistics* for 'The Cost of Living and Real Wages in Eighteenth-Century England' by E. W. Gilboy (*Review of Economic Statistics*, XVIII, 1936).

Editor's Introduction[1]

I

The origins of the modern controversy about the standard of life in Britain may be traced to the publication in 1926 of the first volume of J. H. Clapham's *Economic History of Modern Britain* and the appearance four years later of J. L. Hammond's essay on 'The Industrial Revolution and Discontent'.[2] It was the renewal of a debate which had been virtually quiescent for over half a century. In the years between 1825 and 1850, when the pressures of expanding industry on a long-established social order were growing yearly in intensity, contemporaries so various as Andrew Ure, Edwin Chadwick and G. R. Porter on the one side and Friedrich Engels, Benjamin Disraeli and John Stuart Mill on the other were expressing themselves vigorously on the Condition of England question. Yet the debate so firmly and fully joined failed to survive the middle of the century. It was, it has been suggested, like Chartism, killed by Free Trade, the railways and prosperity. When discussion of the subject was revived in the last quarter of the nineteenth century liberal optimists like Robert Giffen – Porter's successor at the Board of Trade – and social critics like Thorold Rogers and Arnold Toynbee were alike disposed, from their very different standpoints, to cast an unfavourable eye on the early years of the century.

[1] In an earlier essay ('Poverty and Progress in Britain, 1780–1850: a Reappraisal', *History*, XLV (1960), pp. 16–31) I attempted to survey the course of the debate on living standards as it had developed down to 1960. My primary purpose was not to present my own views but to summarize the main issues and arguments in the debate. This present essay has a similar purpose although, more particularly in the final sections, I have gone beyond the stage of 'summing-up' to that of 'delivering a verdict' on the evidence as I see it at present. Differences of interpretation and emphasis between this essay and its predecessor reflect in part the progress of the debate and in part my own changing opinions.

[2] J. H. Clapham, *An Economic History of Modern Britain*, vol. I (Cambridge, 1926: 2nd edn 1939); J. L. Hammond, 'The Industrial Revolution and Discontent', *Economic History Review*, 1st series, II (1930), pp. 215–28.

Clapham's approach was distinctive not only in the conclusions to which it pointed but also in the quantitative methods which it involved. Though his evidence was diverse, at the core of his argument lay calculations based on wage data brought together at the turn of the century by G. H. Wood and A. L. Bowley, and a price index more recently constructed by N. J. Silberling. From these the conclusion emerged that the purchasing power of the average industrial worker had increased by some 60 per cent between 1790 and 1850 and that of the agricultural labourer by a similar amount.[1] Hammond's reply came first in a review essay and then in his article in the *Economic History Review*. In this, although he made some attempt to meet Clapham on his own statistical ground, Hammond rested his case on the basic arguments of Rogers and Toynbee and the assertion that more food and better clothing were no substitute for the qualities of life which industrialism had destroyed. There the argument largely rested. The antagonists had not so much agreed to differ as each to keep to his own end of the field.

While these leisurely exchanges were proceeding the discussion was further advanced by the investigations of two American historians. Rufus Tucker attempted to plot the course of the real wages of London artisans over a period of two centuries from 1729 to 1935, and Elizabeth Gilboy pursued similar inquiries, more restricted in time but covering a wider area, into living standards in three major regions of England in the eighteenth century.[2] Though their findings could be, and in due course were, pressed into service by protagonists on both sides of the developing debate, the first concern of both Tucker and Mrs Gilboy was with evidence rather than argument. The conclusions to which their evidence pointed were in fact only slowly assimilated into the mainstream of historical discussion. By the end of the 'thirties the standard

---

[1] Clapham, op. cit., pp. 128, 561. Clapham, however, speaks of 'statistical difficulties which prevent its being taken as an exact index of the course of events'.

[2] R. S. Tucker, 'Real Wages of Artisans in London, 1729–1935', *Journal of the American Statistical Association*, XXXI (1936), pp. 73–84; E. W. Gilboy, *Wages in Eighteenth-Century England* (Cambridge, Mass., 1934), and 'The Cost of Living and Real Wages in Eighteenth-Century England', *Review of Economic Statistics*, XVIII (1936), pp. 134–43.

of living controversy had not yet found its way into the general text-books.

In retrospect the 'forties can be seen as a watershed in the debate. By 1950 both Clapham and Hammond were dead and E. J. Hobsbawm and R. M. Hartwell, the two central figures of the post-war controversy, were still at the threshold of their academic careers. Bridging the two generations was T. S. Ashton. Ashton was at many points Clapham's heir. He came to economic history out of economics and, like Clapham, he was a quantifier and a meliorist. Yet his first service to the standard of living debate was the removal of the main plank on which Clapham had rested his argument. Specifically Ashton questioned the validity of the Silberling index of wholesale prices on which Clapham had based his own calculations of the movement of real wages. He subjected the work of Tucker and Mrs Gilboy to similar close and critical scrutiny and reached the general conclusion 'that it is not possible to compare the welfare of two groups of people separated widely in time and space'.[1] Ashton's own conclusions, however, based on Lancashire evidence and on more general considerations, were firmly meliorist – that among the working classes those who by 1830 had profited outnumbered those who had failed to profit by the coming of factory industry.

In the early 'fifties the debate remained in a formative stage. There was as yet no direct confrontation. While meliorists took their stand on a consideration of changes in the conditions of material existence, deteriorationists were primarily concerned with the quality of life and argued in terms of happiness and misery rather than of the level of real wages. The entry into the debate in 1957 of E. J. Hobsbawm, therefore, was of major significance to its development. For the first time meliorist and deteriorationist met on the same ground. Hobsbawm criticized 'the extreme feebleness'[2] of Hammond's reply to Clapham and sought to demonstrate that not only the quality of life but also the material standard of existence of the working classes was

[1] T. S. Ashton, 'The Standard of Life of the Workers in England, 1790–1830', *Journal of Economic History*, supp. IX (1949), p. 33.

[2] E. J. Hobsbawm, 'The British Standard of Living, 1790–1850', *Economic History Review*, 2nd series, X (1957), p. 49.

adversely affected by the coming of industrialization. Though accepting the argument that in the long run increasing productivity in industry had brought an overall improvement in living standards, he maintained that in the period of the Industrial Revolution such improvement had not been experienced by the mass of the population. Following Ashton, Hobsbawm rejected Clapham's thesis of rising real wages on the ground that it was founded on an unsuitable and deficient price index. He explored questions of mortality rates and unemployment both of which he maintained provided evidence 'to throw doubt upon the less critical statements of the optimistic view, but not to establish any alternative view'.[1] The main weight of his argument, however, was thrown on to a discussion of changing food consumption and it was on this that the case for deterioration, or at most minimal improvement, was substantially based.

Hobsbawm's article provoked an early reply from R. M. Hartwell. His first venture into the field in 1959 was cast in general terms but the reply direct to Hobsbawm came two years later in 'The Rising Standard of Living in England, 1800–50'.[2] A major part of this article was given over to the deployment of evidence and argument in refutation of that produced by Hobsbawm, but Hartwell also introduced a further important element into the debate in raising the question of the changing size and distribution of the national income. In this he made use of recent work on the growth of the national income carried out by Phyllis Deane and on income distribution by Simon Kuznets, and he also injected a measure of theory into a debate from which it has hitherto been largely absent.

The debate was now fully joined. On the question of the national standard of life the three major lines of inquiry – into the level of real wages, changing patterns of consumption and the size and distribution of the national income – had all been set in train and the principal combatants had declared themselves. Yet, on the surface at least, the divisions in the debate

[1] Hobsbawm, op. cit., p. 57.

[2] R. M. Hartwell, 'Interpretations of the Industrial Revolution in England: a Methodological Inquiry', *Journal of Economic History*, XIX (1959), pp. 229–49; 'The Rising Standard of Living in England, 1800–50', *Economic History Review*, 2nd series, XIII (1961), pp. 397–416.

seemed narrow. Hobsbawm had committed himself no further than to say that there was 'no strong basis for the optimistic view, at any rate for the period from *c.* 1790 or 1800 on until the middle 1840s. The plausibility of, and the evidence for, deterioration are not to be lightly dismissed'.[1] Likewise Hartwell hedged his fundamentally meliorist position. 'To say that the standard of living was rising is *not* to assert that it was high, *nor* is it to affirm that it was rising fast, *nor* that there was no dire poverty, and cyclical fluctuations and technological unemployment of a most distressing character.'[2] A newcomer to the discussion faced with these two statements might well have been pardoned for wondering what the debate was all about. But a closer reading of the two essays to which these statements formed the conclusion makes evident the fact that the division, if narrow, was also deep. How deep became apparent in the further interchange of fact and argument which took place between the two disputants in the *Economic History Review* of 1963.[3] The lines of battle were now tightly drawn. Each combatant stood entrenched behind his own array of argument and evidence, and what had begun under Clapham and Hammond as a leisurely free-flowing encounter had become a bitter war of attrition in which no quarter was asked or given.

This second phase of the Hobsbawm–Hartwell debate not surprisingly showed diminishing returns in terms of evidence. The antagonists were most closely at grips over the issue of food consumption, but while Hartwell set this in the context of parallel arguments about the movement of real wages and the distribution of the national income, Hobsbawm invoked arguments about the quality of life – 'imponderables' which he had dismissed from his case in his earlier article.[4] He now asserted that 'to compare the pre-industrial with the industrial age in purely quantitative terms is to play *Lear* without the king'.[5]

---

[1] Hobsbawm, op. cit., p. 60.

[2] Hartwell, 'The Rising Standard of Living', p. 413 (Hartwell's italics).

[3] E. J. Hobsbawm and R. M. Hartwell, 'The Standard of Living during the Industrial Revolution: a Discussion', *Economic History Review*, 2nd series, XVI (1963), pp. 120–48.

[4] Hobsbawm, 'The British Standard of Living', p. 47.

[5] Hobsbawm, 'Standard of Living during the Industrial Revolution', p. 128.

With the appearance of these 1963 essays Hobsbawm and Hartwell each rested his case and the field lay open for others. In the early stages the weight of further publication was more in terms of argument than evidence. The standard of living issue was now a controversy of major interest to economic historians and it had come to occupy a prominent place in the new generation of 'text-books' which appeared in the 'sixties.[1] Though the primary contribution to the debate of this spate of publication was assimilative, the controversy itself was advanced by authoritative presentation and analysis. The most extensive contribution to the discussion in these years, however, was made by E. P. Thompson. As Ashton was the heir to Clapham, so Thompson stood in the direct line of the Hammonds. Like Hammond, Thompson felt the obligation to meet the quantifiers on their own ground. His chapter on 'Standards and Experiences' in *The Making of the English Working Class*[2] opens with a discussion of patterns of consumption and statistics of morbidity but quickly moves into the world of the Bluebooks and the literature of protest on which Hammond had drawn so extensively.

The debate was therefore coming full circle. In its course it had brought into focus much relevant evidence about working-class life in late eighteenth- and early nineteenth-century Britain; but, to the less committed, evidence had seemed to become increasingly subservient to argument. If from this point the discussion were to go forward fruitfully it could hardly do so effectively except on the basis of new material.

This new phase of the discussion had already begun in 1966 with R. S. Neale's investigation of the changing living standards of workers in Bath.[3] In answer to Ashton's plea for 'not a single index but many, each derived from retail prices, each confined to a short run of years, each relating to a single area,

---

[1] S. G. Checkland, *The Rise of Industrial Society in England 1815–85* (London, 1964); Phyllis Deane, *The First Industrial Revolution* (Cambridge, 1965); S. Pollard and D. W. Crossley, *The Wealth of Britain, 1085–1966* (London, 1968); E. J. Hobsbawm, *Industry and Empire* (London, 1968); P. Mathias, *The First Industrial Nation* (London, 1969); H. Perkin, *The Origins of Modern English Society, 1780–1880* (London, 1969).

[2] E. P. Thompson, *The Making of the English Working Class* (London, 1963).

[3] R. S. Neale, 'The Standard of Living, 1780–1844: a Regional and Class Study', *Economic History Review*, 2nd series, XIX (1966), pp. 590–606.

perhaps to a single social or occupational group within an area,'[1] he produced evidence covering the experiences of workers both agricultural and non-agricultural in the City of Bath over the periods 1780–1812 and 1832–44. Bath, of course, neither is nor was the whole of England, and the essence of Neale's argument was that it should not be so regarded. While, therefore, he reached his own clear conclusions about the experience of Bath, Neale made no attempt to give them national application. But his work pointed the way to the resumption of a neglected approach to the standard of living question, modest in its immediate product but significant in long-term possibility.

A similar investigation, into a community closer to the mainstream of industrial development, was made by T. R. Gourvish in his study of changes in the cost of living in early nineteenth-century Glasgow. Gourvish laid particular emphasis on the collection and collation of data relating to the movement of prices and the cost of living in the years between 1810 and 1831. The changed temper of this new phase of the debate is evident in his conclusion that 'the results may give some comfort to the pessimists in the standard of living debate, but the most important conclusion emerging is the suggestion of considerable regional diversity in price and wage experience and the need for considerable work on a regional basis before we can make sound generalizations of any kind'.[2]

The value of these and similar studies to the resolution of the questions in the general debate will grow in proportion as their number increases. At present their principal service must be to provide controls against which current generalizations may be tested. Alongside such regional and district investigations are to be set other detailed studies of diet[3] and housing[4]

---

[1] Ashton, 'The Standard of Life', p. 33.

[2] T. R. Gourvish, 'The Cost of Living in Glasgow in the early nineteenth century', *Economic History Review*, 2nd series, XXV (1972), pp. 65–80. See also G. J. Barnsby, 'The Standard of Living in the Black Country during the nineteenth century', *Economic History Review*, 2nd series, XXIV (1971), pp. 220–39, though this relates mainly to the second half of the century.

[3] J. Burnett, *Plenty and Want* (London, 1966); T. C. Barker, J. C. McKenzie and J. Yudkin, *Our Changing Fare* (London, 1966).

[4] S. D. Chapman (ed.), *The History of Working-Class Housing: a Symposium* (Newton Abbot, 1971).

and of particular occupational groups.[1] The immediate impression given by such studies is of variety and diversity rather than of common experience, but out of the proliferation of such inquiries there should emerge a more detailed and perhaps a more coherent picture of the economic condition of the working class in the period of early industrialization.

II

The debate whose progress has now been briefly sketched has been inconclusive in the sense that no generally accepted answers have as yet been found to the questions at issue. The areas of dispute, and the extent of disagreement, have at some points been more clearly defined but the major issues – whether there was deterioration or improvement, and to what extent – remain unresolved. The reasons for this are threefold: (1) disagreement and confusion about definitions and terms of reference; (2) limitations of, and disagreements about, the validity of evidence; and (3) differences of interpretation. These may be usefully considered in turn.

Disagreements about definitions and terms of reference arise at three major points. The first of these has already been given some consideration. What meaning is to be attached to the concept of the standard of life? Both Hobsbawm and Hartwell, and before them Hammond and Clapham, were prepared to make a distinction between the conditions of material existence and the qualitative aspects of life, described by Hobsbawm as the 'moral and other non-material territories'.[2] Though meliorists have consistently made this distinction, deteriorationists have been less ready to accept it. (What, it may well be asked, does the quality of life mean to a family living close to subsistence level?) Even when the distinction is accepted in principle there still remains the problem of defining the boundary between the two areas. Purchasing power, the ability to buy food and clothing, the cost and quality of housing, health and the expectation of life are all clearly to be comprehended within the sphere of material existence. Equally the comparative virtues of

---

[1] E.g. D. Bythell, *The Handloom Weavers* (Cambridge, 1969).
[2] Hobsbawm, 'The British Standard of Living', p. 49.

rural and urban life and the psychological effects on individuals of the transition from country to town belong to Hobsbawm's 'non-material territories'. But between these two lies a wide and significant borderland in which the conditions of material existence and the quality of life are closely interwoven, frequently to the point of inseparability.

More immediately tangible and resolvable is the definition of the physical area covered by the debate. There seems to be a general disposition on both sides of the argument to leave Ireland out of the debate and to concentrate attention on the single island of Great Britain. This is a welcome simplification though it is possible to question its validity. As Giffen said, treatment of the United Kingdom as an entity is called for not only for political reasons but also because for a major part of the nineteenth century 'the English labour market' was itself 'largely recruited . . . from other parts of the United Kingdom'.[1] The importance of the distinction between Great Britain and Ireland is made evident by a consideration of the course of average money wages in the two countries. Whereas between 1790 and 1850 money wages in Britain have been calculated as *increasing* by some 40 per cent, in Ireland over the same period they *declined* by 7 per cent.[2]

No less important than the establishment of national boundaries for the debate is the consideration whether the controversy relates to the experience of the whole working community or to that part of it which was more immediately affected by the processes of industrial change. Both Hobsbawm and Hartwell, as much by their methodology as by their conclusions, established their frame of reference as the whole working community. This has been less evidently the case with other participants in the debate. Deteriorationists from Engels to Thompson have tended to concentrate attention on the conditions of life and work in the new industrial areas. This has created a debate within a debate. Mrs Gilboy and, more recently, Neale and Gourvish have demonstrated the considerable divergencies which existed in both money wages

[1] R. Giffen, *Essays in Finance, Second Series* (2nd edn, London, 1887), p. 445.
[2] B. R. Mitchell and P. Deane, *Abstract of British Historical Statistics* (Cambridge, 1962), p. 343.

and prices in different parts of the country. Such differences, however, were not only regional. They were also present within a locality and indeed within a single industry. Prosperity for one group could and did coincide with adversity for another. How then is the progress of the working classes to be measured? Is it to be calculated in terms of the *medium* or the *mean*? In terms of a notional average working man or by balancing those who gained from industrialization against those who lost? Both approaches have been attempted. Hobsbawm and Hartwell – and before them Clapham – in laying emphasis on national aggregates have tended to look to the mean. Ashton, on the other hand, and more recently Harold Perkin have essayed the other route. Both methods are valid and each is necessary if we are to see the economic and social experience of the period in its full dimensions; but there is no reason in theory or practice why they should give coincident answers to the basic question of the debate.

More controversial than the definition of area or of occupational groups has been that of boundaries of time. The chronology of the Industrial Revolution has long been a matter of dispute among economic historians. In discussing the origins and causes of industrial growth historians have considered various dates between 1740 and 1780 as the point of 'take-off' for the revolutionary changes of the eighteenth century. There has been less dispute about a terminal date. Ashton chose to end his study of the Industrial Revolution at 1830, but almost without exception other historians have allowed themselves more elbow room and found 1850 a convenient if imprecise terminal date.

If for the general economic historian precise dating of the Industrial Revolution has lost meaning and purpose, it still has significance for the standard of living debate. A single example will illustrate this. Tucker's index of real wages for London artisans shows a *decline* in real wages of 11 per cent between the years 1780 and 1840 but an *increase* of 25 per cent between 1790 and 1850.[1] Comparisons involving single years inevitably produce distortions of this kind and it is therefore essential that, wherever possible, moving averages covering periods of

[1] Tucker, op. cit., pp. 78–9.

up to a decade should be used rather than the statistics for individual years. Beyond this the historian must be prepared to make his comparisons over varying periods of time and draw the appropriate conclusions from the diverse results which such comparisons will produce. There is certainly no warrant for the assumption that 'the debate is *entirely* about what happened in a period which ended, *by common consent*, some time between 1842 and 1845'.[1]

The problems presented by deficiencies of evidence are, of course, not peculiar to students of the standard of living. In general the further back the historian travels the less satisfactory are his sources both in quality and in quantity. Evidence, particularly of a quantifiable character, relating to industry and society in pre-Industrial Revolution Britain is meagre; even for the period of the Industrial Revolution itself there are important lacunae. At the most basic level there are no population returns before 1801 and no satisfactory general occupational returns before 1841. The civil registration of births, marriages and deaths, indispensable for the accurate calculation of birth and death rates, begins only in 1837. The position in relation to material bearing directly on the standard of life – wages, prices, rents, house-building, etc. – is even less satisfactory. In the absence of official statistics the historian must make his bricks with what straws of evidence he can find. The sources often stop short at the point where they could become most valuable. There is more evidence about wage-rates than about earnings, about wholesale than about retail prices and about employment than about unemployment. The lesser source must often supply the deficiencies of the greater. Thus the Smithfield market returns have been pressed into service to indicate trends in general meat consumption and the excise on bricks to indicate the changing level of house-building. It is not surprising that evidence of this general quality has only served to feed the fires of controversy. Where evidence is fragmentary and disputable, argument can be readily sustained but agreed conclusions rarely reached.

[1] Hobsbawm, 'The Standard of Living during the Industrial Revolution', p. 123 (my italics).

These differences, ambiguities and deficiencies of evidence go far to explain the continuity and indecisiveness of the debate, but they do not account for its temper. Differences of interpretation are essential to the advance of scholarship but they can be experienced at different levels. The more general and fundamental their nature, the more intractable they prove themselves to be.

The Industrial Revolution in Britain was marked by the parallel emergence of three distinct but interpenetrating phenomena: industrialization itself, urbanization and industrial capitalism. Each, both at the time of its emergence and subsequently, has been the subject of impassioned debate. In its attack on the factory system Blake's 'dark Satanic mills' is the forerunner of Chaplin's *Modern Times*, and Cobbett's castigation of urban life and values anticipates the twentieth-century criticism of Lewis Mumford and his followers. Both these elements are present in the debate about living standards but overriding them is the central issue of industrial capitalism. Clapham was an economic liberal, Hammond a socialist; Ashton reprinted his article on 'The Standard of Life of the Workers in England' in a volume on *Capitalism and the Historians*[1] and prefaced it with an essay on 'The Treatment of Capitalism by the Historians'. The undertones of ideological strife were never far below the surface of the debate. Hartwell made them explicit in his essay on 'Interpretations of the Industrial Revolution in England'. Hobsbawm declared himself at the outset to be concerned 'primarily with fact and not with accusation, exculpation or justification'[2] but the forensic character of the argument which followed, the method and language of debate and the tenacity with which positions were defended on both sides suggest that in the controversy something more than the elucidation of fact was felt to be at stake. One recent deteriorationist at least is as clear as Hartwell in stating where the crux of much of the argument has lain. After setting on record his view that 'changes in the quality of life of most town and village labourers in the Industrial Revolution period were demonstrably for the worse', Brian Inglis proceeds

---

[1] Ed. F. A. Hayek (London, 1954).
[2] Hobsbawm, 'The British Standard of Living', p. 47.

to argue that 'where the Pessimists have been wrong is in attributing the deterioration to "capitalism" '.[1]

The recent work of Neale, Gourvish and others has, at least temporarily, lifted the controversy out of the arena of ideological debate. For historians concerned primarily with investigating the standard of life the ideological debate must remain secondary. This is in no way to minimize the achievement of Hobsbawm and Hartwell in focusing attention on a critical phase of British social and economic development nor is it to deny the relevance of the standard of living controversy to the wider and more fundamental debate about the merits and limitations of different social and economic systems. But the order of precedence is clear. 'Sentence first – verdict afterwards' or, more exactly, 'verdict first – evidence afterwards' is poor counsel for the historian.

III

The essays which make up this volume have been chosen to illustrate the varying and changing facets of the debate. For this reason they are reprinted in the order of their original publication. *Post hoc*, of course, does not necessarily mean *propter hoc*. Nevertheless, in broad terms the order of publication represents the development of the debate through its three principal movements – real wages, patterns of consumption and national income distribution – with the underlying contrapuntal theme of the quality of life.

The most direct approach to the problem of changing living standards is through the measurement of real wages. Attempts to establish a satisfactory index of real wages have largely foundered because of the lack of relevant data of acceptable quality. Yet the alternative approaches to the problem have

---

[1] B. Inglis, *Poverty and the Industrial Revolution* (London, 1971): Foreword to paperback edn (1972), p. 31. It seems somewhat ingenuous of Hobsbawm to brush aside as 'hardly worthy of comment' my earlier observation ('Progress and Poverty in Britain', p. 30) that 'the retardation of living standards in the early stages of industrialisation has revealed itself as the experience of socialist as well as of capitalist societies'. If the debate is indeed fundamentally about the achievements and shortcomings of capitalism as Marxist deteriorationists – and some others – have tended to make it, then such comparisons are highly relevant.

encountered no less intractable obstacles and it is therefore at least necessary to see the areas of agreement and disagreement which the varied real wage computations have established.

Computations of real wage movements within the period 1790–1850 all begin with the index of money wages constructed by G. H. Wood at the end of the nineteenth century.[1] In some instances this index has been modified by splicing into it an index of agricultural wages based on data collected by A. L. Bowley. The modification is at no point substantial and over the whole period it merely alters the span of the index from 72–102 to 70–100. To this common wage index various price indices have been applied. S. G. Checkland, and following him S. Pollard and D. W. Crossley, have used Wood's own retail price index and from this calculated that real wages increased by some 18 per cent between 1816 and 1850.[2] Deane and Cole using the Gayer–Rostow–Schwarz index of wholesale prices have estimated that real wages rose by about 25 per cent between 1800 and 1824 and by a further 40 per cent between 1824 and 1850 – 75 per cent in all.[3] Perkin makes use of the Gayer–Rostow–Schwarz index and also the Rousseaux wholesale price index, the latter showing an increase in real wages of some 95 per cent between 1800 and 1850 and of 22 per cent between 1824 and 1850.[4]

The explanation of these wide divergencies lies in part in the dates chosen as points of reference, in part in the different price indices used to deflate the single wage index. A fuller comparison is provided by the tables on p. xxv.

Except after 1840 and to a lesser extent before 1800 the three central indices in Table I show strong mutual conformity. The movement of London bread and meat prices between 1840 and 1850 suggests that Wood's calculation of an 8 per cent decrease in retail prices over the decade may well err seriously on the low

[1] G. H. Wood, 'The Course of Average Wages between 1790 and 1860', *Economic Journal*, IX (1899), pp. 588–92.

[2] Checkland, op. cit., p. 228; Pollard and Crossley, op. cit., p. 203.

[3] P. Deane and W. A. Cole, *British Economic Growth 1688–1959* (Cambridge, 1962), pp. 25–6. My own calculation from the same data used by Deane and Cole shows an increase in real wages between 1800 and 1850 not of 75 per cent but of 115 per cent. The Gayer–Rostow–Schwarz and Rousseaux indices can most conveniently be seen in Mitchell and Deane, op. cit., pp. 470–3.

[4] Perkin, op. cit., p. 137.

side. The difference is a significant one as calculations of real wage movements based on those indices show (Table II).

TABLE I   *Real wages computed from Wood–Bowley money wages index*

and (1) *Wood Retail Prices Index*

(2) *Gayer–Rostow–Schwarz Wholesale Prices Index*

(3) *Rousseaux Wholesale Price Index of Agricultural Products*

(4) *Index of London Bread Prices*

$$(1840 = 100)$$

	Wood–Bowley money wages	Real wages			
		(1)	(2)	(3)	(4)
1790	70	95	80	—	100
1800	95	73	65	71	62
1816	117	97	92	108	70
1831	101	105	109	113	101
1840	100	100	100	100	100
1850	100	108	140	143	148

TABLE II   *Movements of real wages*

	(1) *Wood R.P. Index*	(2) *Gayer–Rostow–Schwarz*	(3) *Rousseaux*
1790–1850	+14%	+ 75%	—
1790–1840	+ 5%	+ 25%	—
1800–50	+48%	+115%	+101%
1800–40	+37%	+ 54%	+ 41%
1816–50	+10%	+ 52%	+ 32%

On general grounds, for purposes of real wages assessment, an index of retail prices is to be preferred to one based on wholesale prices. The Gayer–Rostow–Schwarz index is a highly sophisticated compilation based upon much detailed and well-sifted information, and carefully weighted; but it contains many substantial elements far removed from any household budget. The Rousseaux index, based on the prices of agricultural products, is to be preferred on this score but, like the

Gayer–Rostow–Schwarz index, it has the major deficiency of making no allowance for varying distribution and middlemen's costs. The Wood index escapes these disadvantages but has deficiencies of its own. All we know of it is that it is intended to represent 'the average course of retail prices in ten large towns corrected by the average cost of articles composing a typical workman's budget of the period 1831'.[1] Beyond this bare statement there is no way of assessing its quality or validity. Over and above this it invites criticism in that it is concerned with single years of greatly varying prosperity.

Wood's money wages index – even when modified to give a greater weighting to agricultural wages – is also open to objection. In this instance more is known of its provenance. The index is based on wage data collected in twenty-four towns and districts in the United Kingdom. In each town 'all trades for which data were procurable have been included, the results being obtained by the use of simple unweighted averages in every case'.[2] A similar process of unweighted averaging is employed in bringing together the results from the twenty-four towns and this involves equal emphasis being given to places so diverse as London, Manchester, Macclesfield and Monimail (Fife), a procedure which Wood justifies by referring to his local statistics as 'representative' of larger areas. The original index was light on agriculture and thin overall for certain years and, though it related to fourteen years in all well scattered between 1790 and 1850, it has the major deficiency which is inescapable in selective computations of this kind. Though wages in general were less volatile than prices they could and did move sharply from year to year, and the combination of contrary movements of the two variables could produce major short-term changes in real wages, significantly affecting long-term comparisons.

These calculations and explanations make clear both the fragility of arguments that rest solely or largely on aggregate real wage data, and the significance which attaches to the precise bench-marks adopted for purposes of comparison.

---

[1] G. H. Wood, 'The Course of Average Wages between 1790 and 1860', *Report of the British Association for the Advancement of Science*, section F (1899), pp. 829–30.

[2] Wood, 'The Course of Average Wages', *Economic Journal*, IX (1899), p. 589.

Moreover, as indicators of changes in the standard of living, such indices are deficient in at least four further respects: (i) they are concerned solely with wages and not with earnings; (ii) they make no allowance for unemployment; (iii) they take no account of changes in the balance of occupations within the economy; and (iv) they do not allow for changing wants and needs as expressed through family budgets.

These deficiencies do not all operate in the same direction. To the extent that real wage computations ignore movement between occupations, they tend to understate improvements in living standards. The demands of industry for skilled and semi-skilled labour and the growth of tertiary occupations, together with the movement from low-paid agricultural to more highly remunerated industrial employment, implies an upward drift of wage expectation. On the other hand, it has been suggested, it is necessary to discount the increase in real wages by a figure allowing for the incidence of unemployment in this period which Hobsbawm has described as 'extremely high', 'abnormal', 'in times of crisis catastrophic' and 'much higher' before than after the middle 'forties.[1]

Unemployment was by no means unknown before the Industrial Revolution and it did not disappear in 1850. It is important to see what, if any, special characteristics belonged to the unemployment of the first half of the nineteenth century. Chronic unemployment, largely in the form of underemployment in rural England, existed in the seventeenth century[2] and the increase in population throughout the eighteenth and early nineteenth centuries did nothing to lessen its incidence. Industrialization, though basically employment-creating, brought severe increases in unemployment in two important areas – in the form of technological and of cyclical unemployment. An economy in a state of rapid transition inevitably creates short-term frictional or technological unemployment. The handloom-weavers and the framework-knitters are the most notorious examples of this but there are other less frequently

[1] Hobsbawm, 'The British Standard of Living', pp. 52–7; 'The Standard of Living during the Industrial Revolution', p. 121.

[2] D. C. Coleman, 'Labour in the English Economy of the seventeenth century', *Economic History Review*, 2nd series, VIII (1956), pp. 280–95.

cited examples. The transition from a textile industry based on the country mill to an industry mainly located in towns created short-term rural unemployment, and the declining use of the canal in the face of railway competition had similar consequences. These were not, however, difficulties peculiar to the early nineteenth century; in some respects indeed they multiplied after 1850 as the pace of technological change itself intensified.

More serious was the unemployment which came on the ebb of the business cycle. No one would wish to minimize the poverty, deprivation, ill-health and misery which such unemployment brought with it, and it was the more severely felt by the urban unemployed who lacked the palliatives and social supports which eased the burden on the workless of the countryside. But the intensity of such cyclical unemployment – and indeed of unemployment in general – is difficult to assess. Judgments on its magnitude have been strongly influenced by the experiences of the depression year of 1842. Of the depth of depression in that year and its consequence in terms of unemployment there can be no question. The epicentre of the profound economic disturbance was the cotton district of southeast Lancashire and Cheshire, and especially Bolton and Stockport, but the shock waves were felt in places so far separated as Greenock, Newcastle upon Tyne and Birmingham.[1] 1842, the last of four years of deepening depression, was however a wholly exceptional year.[2] There were other notably bad years – 1816 and 1819, for example – but none which, in the minds of those who lived through the period, ranked in adversity with 1842; and against such black years are to be set years of high prosperity like 1835 when 'every man who was able and willing to work readily obtained employment at full wages; every loom was filled, every anvil was at work'.[3] Moreover, if comparison is attempted with the second half of the century, long periods present themselves in the 'seventies

[1] R. C. O. Matthews, *A Study in Trade-Cycle History* (Cambridge, 1954), p. 164.

[2] Even in 1842 unemployment was very uneven in its incidence. In London, for example, building activity was greater in 1840–2 than at any time since 1825. Cf. H. A. Shannon, 'Bricks – a Trade Index, 1785–1849', *Economica*, new series, I (1934), p. 309.

[3] G. R. Porter, *The Progress of the Nation* (London, 1851 edn), p. 543.

and 'eighties in which depression was no less continuous than between 1839 and 1842 and in which there were also years of exceptionally heavy unemployment, most notably 1879 and 1886.

Present evidence, therefore, does not seem sufficient to establish the view that the movement of the business cycle produced more unemployment before 1850 than subsequently. From another standpoint, however, it can be suggested that the substratum of chronic unemployment, and more particularly underemployment, was more substantial in the first than the second half of the nineteenth century and may have been greater in the period of the Industrial Revolution than previously. It has already been suggested that the underemployment characteristic of much of the rural economy of pre-Industrial Revolution England may well have been aggravated and increased by the rapid population increase of the eighteenth and nineteenth centuries. This relative abundance of labour was not confined to the southern counties and it may have increased the tendency to underemployment even in the industrial north. Over the longer period, the economy adjusted itself to its conditions of labour supply. To the extent that labour was abundant and relatively cheap, investment in labour-saving and unemployment-creating machinery was restricted, but it is at least possible that during the early nineteenth century the provision of labour through population growth was tending to run ahead of investment demand. Whether, however, this unemployment was 'extremely high' or 'abnormal' in comparison with what had gone before or what followed must be regarded as, at the least, a matter of doubt.

The abortiveness of the debate about real wages had by 1963 led Hobsbawm to concentrate increasing attention on the subject of food consumption. This had been a major theme of his 1957 article and it had brought forth a response in kind from Hartwell four years later. Unfortunately, though the evidence on foodstuffs and other necessaries is relatively plentiful, the statistical data is no more general and no less contentious than in the case of wages and prices.

At the national level the only series of statistics relating to food consumption are those contained in the Customs and

Excise Returns.[1] They include four items of general working-class consumption – tea, coffee, sugar and beer – but the returns for beer end in 1830 and those for tea and coffee are much affected by their interchangeability as beverages as well as by the distorting effect of changing and diverging rates of duty. For sugar, however, there was virtually no substitute. 'Without being one of the necessaries of life,' said G. R. Porter, 'long habit in this country has led almost every class to the daily use of it.'[2] During the eighteenth century sugar consumption had risen appreciably, though not necessarily to the same degree among all classes. The extent to which this tendency continued in the nineteenth century might therefore be regarded as affording a sensitive indication of the general movement in food consumption.

On the surface, at least, the record of sugar consumption in Britain tells a clear story. *Per capita* consumption has been calculated as follows:[3]

Sugar Consumption Per Capita

Annual average in lb.			
1800–9	19·12	1840–9	18·45
1810–19	18·06	1850–9	30·30
1820–9	17·83	1860–9	53·90
1830–9	17·59	1870–9	68·09

Even when allowance has been made for shortcomings in the earlier (pre-1815) statistics, these figures point clearly to near-stationary levels of consumption down to the 1840s and a sharp and continuing rise thereafter. This interpretation requires some qualification, however. Though the decennial figures may suggest otherwise, demand for sugar among the mass of the population in early nineteenth-century England was highly elastic. Porter, who as a one-time sugar-broker was well-

---

[1] Reprinted in Mitchell and Deane, op. cit., pp. 355–8.

[2] Porter, op. cit., p. 541. Arthur Young and Adam Smith regarded sugar as a luxury; Huskisson in 1829 saw it as an ordinary article of consumption; Henry Parnell a year later called it 'a luxury in universal use' (*vide* S. Dowell, *A History of Taxation and Taxes in England*, vol. IV [London, 1884], pp. 23–4).

[3] As averaged by Mathias, op. cit., p. 453.

informed on the matter, suggested that, while among 'the families of the rich and middle ranks' the annual consumption of sugar maintained a constant average of 40 lb. per head, consumption by the masses varied sharply.[1] The main determinant of this fluctuating demand seems to have been less the prosperity of the consumer than the price of the product, and this in its turn was determined in part by conditions of supply and in part by variations in the level of duty. In the 'thirties adverse supply conditions, resulting largely from the abolition of slavery, forced up prices and reduced consumption, whereas in the 'forties the reduction of duty brought down prices and stimulated sales.

The sensitivity of the ordinary consumer to capricious changes in price makes sugar an unsatisfactory indicator of *short-run* changes in working-class standards of consumption. In the *long run* it is also unsatisfactory to the extent that even major shifts in consumption are not necessarily a measure of a general increase in working-class prosperity but may simply reflect a change in the price of sugar relative to other commodities. In the event the price of sugar (including duty) fell by 30 per cent between 1840 and 1850 and by a further 25 per cent in the succeeding twenty years. Nevertheless the fact that sugar, along with tea and coffee, failed before the 1840s to break out of the circle of semi-luxuries into that of necessities may in itself be accounted a measure of the slowness of advance of working-class consumption standards in the first half of the nineteenth century.

Significant as the evidence on sugar may be, it relates to an item which even at the end of the century occupied only a small place in any householder's budget. Data of a comparable kind about the more central elements of working-class dietary and expenditure, and in particular bread and meat, are non-existent for this period.

On bread it seems probable that in the closing years of the eighteenth century there was a tendency for demand to outrun supply. Earlier in the century, between 1730 and 1750, a run of good harvests had reduced grain prices and lowered the cost of bread; but towards the end of the century the pressure of a

[1] Porter, op. cit., pp. 544–5.

population expanding at an unprecedented rate was changing England from a corn-exporting to an importing country and forcing up the price of bread. During the French Wars, the pressure of population on available supplies was at its height and an increasing acreage of land came under cultivation. Beyond 1815 such limited quantitative evidence as is available to the historian suggests that, overall, output and population kept pace with one another.[1] Porter would seem to have fairly assessed the position as it had emerged by the 1840s. 'Unless in years of scarcity,' he said, 'no part of the inhabitants of England except perhaps in the extreme north, and there only partially, have now recourse to rye or barley bread, but a larger and increasing number are in a great measure fed upon potatoes.'[2] The one condition was for many a mark of improvement, the other evidence of deterioration.

The potato had, of course, made its way extensively in Ireland but its cultivation and consumption in England had intensified in the years of high grain prices at the end of the eighteenth century. At that time it was regarded as a poor substitute for bread – the 'lowest species of human food' as Caird later described it.[3] In the south it continued to have a low reputation and its increased use was properly regarded as a mark of a lower standard of living; but this was not the case in the expanding industrial north where the potato was appreciated, then as now, as a useful variant in the common diet and the valued constituent of a hot cooked meal, whether that meal was distinguished as Irish stew or Lancashire hotpot. It would seem unwise, therefore, to draw general conclusions either for advance or deterioration from the case of bread and the potato.

On meat the evidence is equally elusive and ambiguous. The only major statistical data are the returns of sheep and cattle brought to Smithfield and the excise returns relating to the

[1] See especially M. J. R. Healy and E. L. Jones, 'Wheat yields in England 1815–59', *Journal of the Royal Statistical Society*, series A, CXXVI (1962), pp. 574–9; S. Fairlie, 'The Corn Laws and British Wheat Production, 1829–76', *Economic History Review*, 2nd series, XXII (1969), pp. 88–116.

[2] Porter, op. cit., p. 538.

[3] Quoted by R. N. Salaman, *The History and Social Influence of the Potato* (Cambridge, 1949), p. 531.

production of hides and skins. The record of beasts brought for sale at Smithfield is continuous from 1730 and, if taken as an indication of general meat consumption, suggests that for long periods of the eighteenth and early nineteenth centuries meat consumption lagged behind population increase. But as general indicators the Smithfield returns are deficient at many points. They relate only to London and to one market in the metropolitan area, they take no account of the changing size of animals and they provide no information about pig-meat, a highly important item in working-class diet. More weight may be attached to the evidence on hides and skins. The statistics relate to England and Wales and, therefore, offer wider coverage than the Smithfield returns, but the leap from a count of hides to an estimate of meat consumption is not without its hazards. Nevertheless Deane and Cole, who have made a particularly careful scrutiny of the data, are firm in the conclusion that 'in the second half of the eighteenth century, and still more at the beginning of the nineteenth, the supply of beef failed to keep pace with population'.[1] By the time of the French Wars, however, England was importing beef in large and increasing quantities from Ireland. Whether this was sufficient to make good – or indeed to exceed – the shortfall of home production is an unresolvable question; and discussion on the basis of the excise returns becomes impossible with their termination in 1828. Beyond this quantitative data, the evidence on meat consumption is fragmentary and at many points contradictory; though it seems possible that consumption may have increased in the industrial north and declined in the agricultural south.

If it is impossible to give any precision to changes in the consumption of such basic commodities as meat and bread, this is even more the case with other commodities.[2] In relation to quickly perishable commodities like fresh vegetables and milk it seems probable that, as towns grew, so no less did difficulties of supply until the advent of the railway produced a new and rapidly improving situation. The worst years were those between 1820 and 1840 before the railway had established

[1] Deane and Cole, op. cit., p. 74.
[2] For a wider treatment of this subject see Burnett, op. cit., and Barker, McKenzie and Yudkin, op. cit., *passim*.

itself and when, under the twin pressures of industrialization and population growth, town boundaries were being steadily extended, farming land was being absorbed and the distance between producer and consumer was constantly increasing. But this is no more than inferred probability and its measurement in terms of the price and consumption of milk and vegetables is beyond determination. Equally, as urban life placed an increasing number of intermediaries between the farmer and the housewife, quality was put in jeopardy and food adulteration became more prevalent.[1]

Food was the major item of working-class expenditure. Few if any working-class households spent less than half their income on food and many necessarily spent much more. Nevertheless there were other inescapable items of expenditure, in particular housing, fuel and clothing. Here, as in the case of food, conditions varied greatly from place to place. Much has been written about the quality of urban housing in the age of the Industrial Revolution, less about the housing conditions of the farm labourer – or indeed of the poorer town-dweller – of an earlier period. Nor has any systematic survey been made of rents. Though comparisons from place to place are possible – rents were higher in London than in provincial towns and higher in towns than in the countryside where the tied-cottage system was prevalent – little evidence is available on which to base comparisons over time or to estimate whether the cost of housing took proportionately more or less of working-class incomes towards the middle of the century. Recent investigations by a number of historians suggest some improvement in the general quality of urban working-class housing – if not of the urban environment – in England in the second quarter of the nineteenth century; and this view is supported by the census returns which show a steady diminution in the density of occupation per house. But there were considerable local variations on this theme of progress and, as in Nottingham, some sections of the working class benefited more than others.[2]

[1] On adulteration, see especially Burnett, op cit., pp. 72–90.

[2] For a comprehensive annotated bibliography see A. Sutcliffe, 'Housing in nineteenth-century Britain; a review of recent research', *Bulletin of the Society for the Study of Labour History*, 24 (1972), pp. 40–51. See also S. D. Chapman (ed.), *History of Working-Class Housing* (1971), pp. 133–64.

As with food and housing so even more with fuel there were considerable local variations in supply and price. But here time worked clearly to the consumer's advantage. Down to the end of the seventeenth century a large proportion of the inhabitants of England seldom if ever saw a coal-fire. The gathering of wood (or in some places peat) cost time and labour rather than money. But as wood became scarcer coal became more accessible and cheap. The canal, the railway and the removal of the coastal duties all had worked to this common end by the middle of the nineteenth century. The price of coal in London in 1850 was one-third of what it had been in 1815. Nearer the coalfields the reduction in price, though not on the same scale, was also significant for working-class budgets and working-class comfort.

With clothing we move into a different area of working-class expenditure. If economy had to be practised by a household this was the point at which it could be most readily achieved. Not surprisingly, therefore, this is the item which shows most variation in working-class budgets. At the same time this was pre-eminently the area of consumption which the manufacturers of the new industrial Britain were best equipped and most eager to serve. The industrial effort of the new society might have its roots in the mining of coal and the manufacture of iron but its development and expansion depended on the growing output and consumption of mass-produced articles of common use. These came in ever-increasing quantities from the textile factories of the north of England, the potteries of Staffordshire and the metal-works of Birmingham and the Black Country. Much of this produce went abroad in exchange for supplies of raw material and food – and, to the extent that the terms of trade moved against Britain throughout the 'twenties and 'thirties, this implied a limitation of the return to British capital and labour – but a large and increasing quantity of goods was retained for home consumption. Between 1820 and 1845 the proportion of British cotton goods entering the home market remained fairly constant at 40 per cent of total production but the weight of material had increased fivefold.

It has been suggested that the last to benefit from the new products was the class by whose labour they were produced.

'The advantages derived from the vast increase of wealth have principally fallen into the hands of those by whose enterprise and industry the interests of our manufacturing power have mainly been directed . . . On every hand the sides of the hills are adorned with the commodious dwellings of the master manufacturers manifesting wealth and comfort.'[1] The place was Lancashire and the witness Henry Ashworth, himself a Bolton manufacturer. More recently Harold Perkin has pointed to the 'fashionable new muslins and printed cottons . . . Wedgwood's "ornamental ware" . . . and Fothergill's Birmingham "toys" and the best ironmongery, furniture and gadgets of the new creation',[2] which the new industry provided for the benefit of the upper and middle classes. There can be no question that the advantages of the new industrialism in terms not only of wealth but of access to new manufactured articles was first experienced by the wealthier classes, but already by the early years of the nineteenth century such luxury wares were no longer the typical products of the consumer-goods industries. Fine muslins, whose manufacture had so benefited Samuel Oldknow and his handloom weavers, soon lost their ascendency to coarser calicoes as manufacturers sought a more extensive market for their goods, and increasing numbers of the working class were able to buy the new and cheap material. The counterpart of the fivefold increase in output by weight between 1820 and 1845 was an increase of no more than 60 per cent in the value of goods produced; in relation to weight goods consumed at home had fallen in price by 65 per cent between 1820 and 1845.[3] The consequence of this reduction in price – and an accompanying rise in quantity – was, as Porter saw it, 'that few indeed [were] now so low in the scale of society as to be unable to provide themselves with decent and appropriate clothing',[4] though among the unfortunate exceptions were domestic workers such as the weavers of Spitalfields.

Cotton is an outstanding case in the extent of its contribution to improving living standards but it is in no way unique in

[1] H. Ashworth, 'Statistical Illustrations of the Past and Present State of Lancashire', *Journal of the Statistical Society of London*, V (1842), p. 255.

[2] Perkin, op. cit., p. 141.

[3] T. Ellison, *Cotton Trade of Great Britain* (London, 1886), p. 59.

[4] Porter, op. cit., p. 452.

kind. What was true of cotton was also true to a lesser extent of other textiles and of a widening range of household commodities. Not all the working classes shared immediately or equally in these benefits, but industrialization, as by 1840 it existed in the English north and midlands, in the Scottish lowlands and in the Lagan valley, could not have maintained itself if it had not established for itself a considerable working-class market. How extensive that penetration was at different times and in different places, how large a place expenditure on the 'new' commodities occupied in the budget of the average working-class household, and to what extent, if any, it involved sacrifices at other points of expenditure are questions to which no present answers can be given; but the buoyancy of the mass-production industries suggests that, in respect of such items at least, working-class standards of consumption were rising with each decade.

While the controversy about patterns of consumption was at its height a further substantial item was added to the agenda of the main debate. During the 1950s Miss Phyllis Deane had produced estimates of national income for Great Britain covering each of the census years between 1801 and 1851. Subsequently J. E. Williams[1] used Deane and Cole's index of total real output in the eighteenth century to calculate gross national income in England and Wales between 1751 and 1791. By dividing these estimates by the population in the census years – or by estimates of population before 1801 – it was possible to make decennial estimates of income per head.

The reservations which must be attached to these final estimates are evident. Their acceptability depends in the first instance on the accuracy of calculation of their prime components, and beyond this on the validity of assumptions about the apportionment of the national income in terms both of use and of distribution among various sections of the community. For the eighteenth century it is doubtful whether the statistics can pass even the first of these tests. Deane and Cole did not go even so far as to put forward gross national income estimates, and Williams' *per capita* income calculations must be regarded

[1] J. E. Williams, 'The British Standard of Living, 1750–1850', *Economic History Review*, 2nd series, XIX (1966), pp. 581–9.

as something of a *jeu d'esprit*. His calculations for England and Wales indicate a growth of 15–20 per cent in *per capita* income between 1751 and 1791. This is a plausible estimate but the margin of error implicit in the calculation could well double or eliminate the figure.

Beyond 1800 the prime estimates become firmer – firm enough indeed to encourage Deane and Cole themselves to make calculations of *per capita* national income. From these it can be deduced that income per head rose fourfold in the course of the century and by 85 per cent between 1801 and 1851. Of the three major variables involved in the calculation – population, national income at current prices and the ratio of current to 'constant' prices – population may be taken as firmly established from the census of 1801. The estimates of national product at current prices are open to, and have received, detailed criticism, but they have received the general blessing of economic historians as basically valid within the limitations imposed by the available evidence. Certain specific points of criticism are to be noted, however, in the context of their use in the present debate.

Pollard and Crossley[1] have drawn attention to the implications for the national income estimates of changes in the terms of trade. After showing considerable fluctuations in the war years, the net barter terms of trade turned downwards after 1815 and continued to run adversely until 1840 when they levelled off for the remainder of the half-century. The consequence of this was, as Matthews observes, that 'the benefit obtained from investment expenditure which increased the productivity in British industry accrued in some measure to the foreigner instead of bringing benefit to the country where the investment was undertaken'.[2] The issue, however, is complex. To a large extent the worsening of the terms of trade was an inevitable concomitant of industrial growth in the period before large-scale capital exports opened up and thereby cheapened the world's supply of raw material and food resources. Yet, as Ashton has argued, net barter terms of trade do not take account of changes in the *quality* as distinct from the *quantity* of the product exported.[3] In this connection the change

---

[1] Pollard and Crossley, op. cit., p. 202. [2] Matthews, op. cit., p. 223.
[3] Ashton, 'The Standard of Life', pp. 25–8.

of emphasis in the Lancashire cotton industry from finer quality goods produced mainly for the American and European markets to coarser fabrics destined for the markets of India and the Levant is of particular significance. Moreover, foreign trade, important as it was, yet made only a minority contribution to the national income. For most of the first half of the nineteenth century exports amounted to no more than 10 per cent of the national product so that the effect of any deterioration in the terms of trade was necessarily limited.

Pollard and Crossley's second *caveat* relates to activities like brewing, baking, market-gardening and dressmaking which in the pre-industrial era had largely been undertaken as domestic pursuits but which in the nineteenth century became increasingly institutionalized. In the former state they escape and in the latter gain inclusion in the national income estimates; and to this extent there is a bias in favour of growth in the later figures. The point has undoubted validity yet it is questionable whether the transition was fast enough before 1850 greatly to affect the national income estimates. If allowance were to be made for it, the alteration called for would be no more than marginal.

A more substantial weakness in the chain of argument leading to the *per capita* income estimates comes at the point of conversion of current into 'constant' prices. To effect this conversion Deane and Cole have made use of the Rousseaux wholesale price indices; and it has been suggested that, from the standpoint of the householder buying in the retail market, this tends to exaggerate the fall in prices after 1815. The absence of any acceptable retail price index makes any general adjustment impracticable, but it is possible in the case of bread to suggest the relative movements of wholesale and retail prices in the course of the first half of the nineteenth century. A comparison between *national* average prices of wheat and *London* bread prices shows that between 1790–9 and 1840–9 the margin between wholesale and retail prices increased by between 13 and 14 per cent. It would obviously be unwise to generalize from this figure – in the case of coal, by contrast, the margin between pit-head and retail prices was shrinking to the obvious benefit of the consumer – but it suggests the presence of a significant diversifying element of which account must be taken in any attempted quantification of changes in the size of the *per capita* national income.

There remains the important problem of determining the changing distribution of the national income between land, capital and labour. On this Hartwell, drawing on theory and more recent experience, puts forward the view that in periods of industrial growth wage incomes tend to rise at least as rapidly as incomes arising out of investments. Hobsbawm, on the other hand, argues that 'the early stages of industrialization are likely to make the distribution of the national income *less* even to allow for larger savings and more investments'.[1]

In the years immediately following the second world war, when economic historians were increasingly interesting themselves in problems of economic growth, it was the generally accepted view that the substantial need for investment capital in the early stages of industrialization could only be met out of that part of the national product which had hitherto been available for immediate consumption. W. W. Rostow, a major exponent of this thesis, suggested that during the period of 'take-off' into industrial growth the rate of effective investment might rise from 5 to 10 per cent of the national income and that in the next stage of growth – the 'drive to maturity', approached by Britain in the second quarter of the nineteenth century – this would be again increased from 10 to 20 per cent.[2] More recent estimates of domestic capital formation in Britain, however, have suggested that these figures are too high. It is now estimated that investment rose from 3 to 4 per cent of the national income at the beginning of the eighteenth century to a possible 7 per cent a century later and that even by 1850 it did not exceed 10 per cent.[3] Even allowing for the fact that some of this investment was slow-yielding and therefore gave little benefit to the generation at whose expense it was made, these estimates suggest that the diversion of resources from consumption to investment, though not negligible, was far from substantial.

[1] Hartwell, 'The Rising Standard of Living', p. 402; Hobsbawm, 'The Standard of Living during the Industrial Revolution', p. 122 (Hobsbawm's italics).

[2] W. W. Rostow, *The Stages of Economic Growth* (Cambridge, 1960), pp. 7–9.

[3] Deane and Cole, op. cit., pp. 259–64.

The only two attempts made to quantify the changing distribution of the national product point to very different conclusions. Deane and Cole, after surveying a mass of relevant data, estimated that the share of employment incomes (wages *and* salaries) of the national income rose from 44 per cent in *c.* 1801 to 49 per cent in 1860–9.[1] Perkin, on the other hand, using evidence largely derived from the income-tax returns but supported by corroborative price and wage data, reached the conclusion that the first half of the nineteenth century saw a 'considerable shift in income distribution towards the rich and the well-to-do'.[2] He used tax returns for 1801 and 1848 to demonstrate that the wealthiest section of the population (1·14 per cent with incomes over £130 in 1801 and 1·18 per cent with incomes over £200 in 1848) increased its share of the national income from 25·4 per cent in 1801 to at least 34·9 per cent in 1848. Two reservations should be attached to these calculations. There is the distinct possibility of differential understatement affecting the relative accuracy of the 1801 return and thereby exaggerating the difference between the two years; and there is necessarily an assumption of accuracy in the national income totals to which the taxable incomes are related. As they stand, however, these figures give strong support to Perkin's thesis that there was a marked movement of income away from the wage-earning to the property-owning and investing classes. Even if it is assumed that the redistribution stopped at this high level of income, the implication is that there was a *relative* decline of 14 per cent in the size of workers' money incomes over the half century.

Two important addenda, however, must be attached to this conclusion. To infer that there was a shift of income from the wage-earner is not to suggest that it was a persistent and constant movement. Under the inflationary conditions of the French Wars, the pressure on wages was at its most intense. Agricultural rents moved up sharply and there were windfall profits for many, though not all, industrialists. But for the working classes this was in general a time when prices led and wages lagged behind. After the war agricultural, though not urban, rents fell back, if not perhaps as far or as rapidly as they had risen. In

[1] Ibid., p. 301.   [2] Perkin, op. cit., pp. 135–6.

the 'thirties and early 'forties competition among industrialists also intensified leading to reductions in profit margins and diminished returns on investments. The overall tendency of the share of wages in the national income to fall, therefore, conceals an early period when the downward movement was at its most precipitous and a later, longer period in which the process was certainly slowed and may well have been halted. Furthermore, substantial as the shift may have been, its effect was in no sense to eliminate but rather to trim back sharply – perhaps to the extent of a quarter – the rise in living standards flowing from increased productivity.

IV

Each of the three major approaches to the problem of changes in the standard of living, therefore, would seem to lead not so much to a dead end as to country so open that no wholly satisfying answers suggest themselves to the main questions of the debate: Did living standards rise or fall? If so, to what extent and with what chronology? There are too many imprecise variables in the computations both of aggregate real wages and *per capita* national income to make either of these a reliable indicator of changing living standards; and, the excisable commodities apart, the evidence on consumption offers little that is quantifiable. Yet, by bringing together the three lines of inquiry and calling into account other relevant evidence, it may at least be possible to define somewhat more closely the persisting areas of disagreement in the general debate.

For the years before the French Wars, the period of incipient industrialization, there are no national aggregates of wages or of national income though there is available Tucker's carefully constructed index of prices. It is still in fact pre-eminently the work of Tucker and Mrs Gilboy on which reliance has to be placed for a broad view of the movement of living standards in the eighteenth century. The second half of the century saw the emergence of the cotton industry and the opening up of the Black Country, but even more significant in determining the movement of living standards in this period were the unprecedented growth in population and the expansion of agricultural production. The period down to 1795 was one in which a growing population pressed increasingly on the means of subsistence. As a result the price of food in general and of bread in particular increased, at first slowly and then with growing rapidity. In London, where the four-pound loaf had averaged 5*s*. 3*d*. in the 1750s, it had risen to 6*s*. 6*d*. in the 1780s and jumped to 9*s*. 6*d*. in 1795. More particularly in the later years wages in London and in the south of England generally failed to keep close company with this rise in the cost of living. This was not the case in the industrial north, however. The expanding industries on both sides of the Pennines provided increasing incomes both in cash and in real terms for working-class households and the benefits of this growing prosperity spread widely beyond the towns among the rural labouring classes. By 1795 the weekly wages of agricultural labourers in the six northern counties, which thirty years earlier had been among the lowest in England, were higher than in any other region; and to a lesser degree these favourable conditions had also been experienced by labourers in those midland counties – Derbyshire, Nottinghamshire, Leicestershire and Staffordshire – which had been most directly affected by early industrialism.[1] The exact balance of gain and loss implied by these varying experiences is impossible to determine. Where there was loss, however, it can be fairly attributed not to industrialization but to the independent pressures of population growth.

The years of the French Wars have been generally regarded as a time of retreat in working-class living standards. 'The demand for labour', asserted Porter, 'can only increase with the increase of capital destined for the payment of wages; and we have seen that capital was so far from being suffered to accumulate that it was dissipated by Government expenditure more rapidly than it could be accumulated by individuals.'[2] Most economic historians have endorsed this conclusion, at least in general terms. Yet the real wage calculations of both Wood and Deane and Cole indicate significant increases in real wages over the period 1795–1816. It would be unwise to build an

[1] A. L. Bowley, *Wages in the United Kingdom in the Nineteenth Century* (Cambridge, 1900), p. 25 ff.

[2] Porter, op. cit., p. 470.

argument on such limited and fragile statistical data but it at least suggests that the orthodox view of the war as a time of retrogression in living standards should not be accepted uncritically. The considerable increase in government spending, financed largely by borrowing and indirect taxation, sharply regressive in character, induced inflationary tendencies which benefited the property-owner and the manufacturer rather than the working-man. At the same time investment was diverted from the consumer-goods industries and into the capital-goods and war-production industries. The question remains, however, to what extent the losses experienced in terms of income transfers of this kind were balanced by the compensations arising from overall economic growth. Industry continued to expand during, and in part because of, the war. Iron led the way, doubling its output in ten years between 1796 and 1806 and serving primarily the interests of war itself; cotton, notwithstanding the considerable disturbance of its markets, enjoyed a fourfold expansion between 1793 and 1815; and there were modest but appreciable increases in the output of commodities so varied as woollen cloth, paper, soap and, not least important, coal. These advances brought employment and increasing earnings; but if incomes rose so no less did prices, particularly when after 1805 a series of poor harvests reinforced more general inflationary tendencies. Some workers, profitably employed in war industries, were no doubt able to keep their earnings moving abreast of rising prices but the majority almost certainly failed to do so. What the war did provide, however, was a quantity of capital equipment which could be put to profitable use thereafter and which, in the disinflationary conditions then obtaining, contributed to a revival in real incomes for the working class.

The conclusion that the purchasing power of the average working-class household declined during the years of war, therefore, seems not unwarranted, but the detailed evidence is too conflicting to permit any reliable assessment of its extent. For the years between 1815 and 1850, on the other hand, the national aggregates, however assessed and interpreted, all point to a rise in living standards. The central questions of debate are less whether there was an increase in purchasing power than how soon this increase was achieved, what was its size and how widely was it shared.

On the chronology of living standards there are significant differences of opinion. Where Deane and Cole speak of a 'positive increase in real wages' before 1825 and 'an unprecedently rapid improvement in the second quarter' – albeit with the first possibly outweighed, and the second modified, by the effects of unemployment – Hobsbawm sees the 'twenties and 'thirties as a time of 'at best, relative stagnation in real wages' and only the years beyond 1842–5 as a period of undisputed growth.[1]

The view that living standards moved more sharply upward in the 'forties than in the two previous decades is not without justification. Indicators of improving standards such as tea and sugar consumption, wheat yields and bread prices, and mortality rates show significant ameliorative tendencies in this decade. By contrast the 'thirties had ended in even deeper depression than they began, with unemployment rising and real wages little if any higher than at the beginning of the decade. Yet it is as wrong to suggest the improvement was concentrated after 1842 as it would be to contend that it had all taken place by 1836, a year in which economic activity in general and working-class purchasing power in particular reached hitherto unprecedented heights. These two years, the one of deep depression, the other of high prosperity, offer wholly different perspectives on the achievements of the half-century. Over-concentration on the great trough which touched its deepest point in 1841–2 gives as distorted a view of the half-century – and indeed of the two decades between 1830 and 1850 – as would similar over-emphasis on the boom of 1835–6 or of 1844–5. Nor is it right to assume that from the 'forties growth became continuous and rapid. The 'fifties, if reliance may be placed upon the now more sophisticated indices of Wood and Bowley, exhibit a varying pattern of real wages with decline evident in the middle years and an appreciation over the decade of no more than 3–5 per cent.

What these figures make clear is that there was no consistent

[1] Deane and Cole, op. cit., p. 27; Hobsbawm, 'The British Standard of Living', p. 49.

upward movement in living standards. Though the long-term trend was upward, progress was intermittent and there were years of retreat as well as advance. Macaulay perhaps put the matter too optimistically when he said that 'a single breaker may recede, but the tide is evidently coming in', but the analogy is wholly pertinent. The tide was undoubtedly rising but it was not flowing fast and the breakers were of uneven size – sometimes indeed the waves rolled back further than they advanced. Though a man could reasonably expect that his children would in due time enjoy a higher standard of life than he had known, he himself could have no certainty that next year would be better than this – it might well be worse. The short-term future was as unpredictable as the weather under whose influence it so largely lay. Over the decade 1810–19 Gourvish's Glasgow bricklayer improved his spending power by 10 per cent but this increase was achieved through five years in which his real income rose and five in which it declined. Over the next two decades the purchasing power of Tucker's London artisan ran a more regular but no less interrupted upward course; while the real wages of Neale's Bath labourer moved irregularly downward through the 'thirties before moving sharply and steeply upward after 1841.

The explanation of these irregular and vigorous short-term variations is not difficult to find. They derive in part from the movement of the business cycle but still more from changes in the supply of basic foodstuffs, particularly bread. Because, said Porter, 'there can be no permanence or steadiness in the prices of articles dependent for their abundance or scarcity upon the seasons, it must often happen under our present [protective] system that the bulk of the people will be exposed to violent alternations of plenty and misery'.[1] Since food prices tended to be more volatile than wages and since the latter were influenced at least as much by the ebb and flow of industrial prosperity as by the size and quality of the harvest, short-term variations in purchasing power tended to be considerable. When, as in 1825, industrial and commercial prosperity coincided with high food prices, the one largely mitigated the other; when on the other hand prosperity and a good harvest came together as in 1835 or

[1] Porter, op. cit., p. 442.

depression was joined by high grain prices as in 1847 the working class knew the divergent experiences of relative affluence and deep misery.

The strong influence which food, and especially grain, prices exerted on working-class living standards is made evident in the second half of the century. Of the 80 per cent increase in real wages which Wood attributes to this period more than three-quarters belongs to the years after 1870 when the influx of foreign grain was steadily reducing the price of bread and of animal feeding-stuffs. These same influences were also working between 1815 and 1850 but in a less regular and consistent manner. Following the steep rise during the French Wars grain prices fell sharply down to 1820, then ran a fairly even course for twenty years – broken only by a period of lower prices from 1833 to 1837 – before falling again in the 1840s. In so far as wages were generally stickier than prices this would tend to confirm the view that overall this was a period of tangible if uneven advance in working-class purchasing power.

Opinions differ widely about the extent of this advance and it is easier – as well as more prudent – to point to the deficiencies of the existing estimates than to add to their number. The evidence on consumption, fragmentary and unsatisfactory as it is, is relevant here. Because for most of this period the price of agricultural products was falling more slowly than that of manufactured goods, increased working-class purchasing power tended to express itself more in the acquisition of clothing and household goods than of food. Nevertheless, the fact that positive evidence of a marked upward shift in food consumption in this period is so meagre and that the known growth in consumption in the following decades is so large suggests that the rate of growth in purchasing power before 1850 was appreciably lower than it was to become in the later years of the century.

To say that real wages were rising is not, of course, to imply that they rose equally for all or indeed that there were not some – possibly even a majority – who lost rather than gained in these years of intensive industrialization. One approach to the main standard of living debate is to try to determine the proportion of the working population who fell into the two categories. Few detailed attempts have been made to achieve this, partly no doubt because of the intractability of the material. Ashton, however, advanced the general proposition that by 1830 'the number of those who were able to share in the benefits of economic progress was larger than the number of those who were shut out from these benefits, and that it was steadily growing'.[1] By contrast, Perkin, on the basis of a more detailed analysis, has suggested the possibility that 'until the steep decline in handloom weaving and other dying domestic trades after 1840 and the absolute decrease of agricultural labour after 1851, the number of those who suffered exceeded those who benefited'.[2]

Perkin's view rests on a consideration of the occupational structure of the working force towards the middle of the nineteenth century. He lists as gainers under the new industrial order (i) older craftsmen (e.g. printers, blacksmiths, joiners and other building craftsmen) whose work had not been mechanized and whose services were increasingly required by the developing economy; (ii) new craftsmen (e.g. iron puddlers, fine spinners, railway-engine drivers, etc.); (iii) factory-workers; (iv) miners, transport workers, iron-shipbuilders, etc. The losers fall principally into three categories: (i) displaced craftsmen (e.g. woolcombers, calico-printers); (ii) domestic workers (handloom-weavers, framework-knitters, nail- and chain-makers, boot- and shoe-makers, etc.); and (iii) farm-labourers. It would be difficult to quarrel with the general principles of this division, yet the categorization invites further scrutiny in part for its omissions and in part for its inevitable simplifications. The most conspicuous omissions are the vast and increasing army of domestic servants, already numbering over one million by 1841, and the no less rapidly growing body of white-collar and distributive workers, ranging from clerks and warehousemen to publicans and shop-keepers. Of the first it can only be said that it is at least possible that their living standards – low as they frequently were – improved in some measure as the wealth of their employers increased. The second multifarious group presents a somewhat different problem for

---

[1] Ashton, 'The Standard of Life', p. 38.   [2] Perkin, op. cit., p. 148.

it includes many who, by their own designation, were moving out of the working class; but in so far as industrialization took men and women out of manual employment and in so doing raised their real incomes, these must be counted a section of the labouring classes who were gainers in the process of industrial change.

Perkin's analysis would also appear to over-simplify to the extent that it brings together under a single umbrella all those domestic occupations which in the course of the nineteenth century were made redundant by the advance of the machine and the factory system. The progress of technological and organizational change varied greatly from industry to industry, however. In the years between 1815 and 1850 textiles bore the brunt of such change, though even here the power-loom was more quickly in the ascendent in cotton than in wool. Domestic nail-making came under pressure from the 1830s, though its decline was most rapid after 1850. Other west midlands metal industries, domestically based, were longer spared and indeed still 'flourished exceedingly in mid-Victorian times',[1] and the boot and shoe industry did not begin to lose its domestic character until the last quarter of the century. By no means all domestic workers therefore were engaged simultaneously in the same hopeless and unrewarding struggle against the machine. Many indeed may have prospered in proportion as the demand for their products grew.

Agriculture, still in 1850 the largest single employer of labour, also calls for closer examination. There is abundant testimony to the poverty of the rural labourer in the southern and southwestern counties. Even in the depths of the industrial depression of 1842 W. Cooke Taylor observed that the Lancashire cotton operative and the south country farmworker were experiencing the 'same amount of destitution – greater there could not be', but that the position of the farm labourer was much the worse since he had long lived close to the margin of pauperism.[2] However, the experience of the south and west was

---

[1] W. H. B. Court, *Concise Economic History of Britain, 1750 to Recent Times* (Cambridge, 1954), p. 217.

[2] W. Cooke Taylor, *Notes of a Tour of the Manufacturing Districts of Lancashire* (2nd edn, London, 1842), p. 81.

not that of the north and of much of the midlands. In Lancashire, in particular, there is abundant evidence of improving living standards among farm workers in the twenty years after the French Wars, and Bowley's wage statistics not only confirm this but point to a continuance of the trend down to the middle of the century and indicate that it was common to all the northern counties and the industrial midlands.[1] What was true of farm labour was also the experience of manual labour in general throughout the industrial counties as the pace of wage movements was set by the demands of expanding industry.

These footnotes to Perkin's analysis are intended to do no more than suggest the usefulness of further exploration and to attach a reservation to his own cautious conclusion. Whether, however, it is finally possible to compare the numbers of gainers and losers over more than half a century of radical structural change in an economy must itself be open to serious question.

V

This introductory essay is intended less to point the way to conclusions than to look critically at the progress of the debate. Nevertheless certain broad generalizations may be made. It would seem probable that general working-class purchasing power improved over the period 1780/90 to 1840/50; that this improvement, though appreciable, was not as great as in the succeeding half-century; that the rise in working-class incomes was slower than that of the income of the nation at large; and that improvement was uneven in time and in respect of different sectors of the working population. Advance was more marked among industrial than agricultural workers and stronger in the north than the south of England. These occupational and regional differentiations, however, constitute only a general framework within which there were considerable detailed variations. While the fine-cotton spinner prospered, the handloom-weaver stagnated; the nearer he was to London, the less depressed was the condition of the southern farm labourer.

[1] J. D. Marshall, 'The Lancashire Rural Labourer in the Early Nineteenth Century', *Transactions of the Lancashire and Cheshire Antiquarian Society*, LXXI (1961) pp. 90–128; A. L. Bowley, *Wages in the United Kingdom in the Nineteenth Century*, (Cambridge, 1900) *passim*.

At the individual level experience could be even more diverse. Mrs C. S. Peel put the point clearly forty years ago:

> On the same wage, and at the same trade, one man might be comfortably housed and well-fed, and another wretchedly housed and half-starved. A street which was putting money by in 1830 might be existing on poor relief in 1840, bursting with prosperity in 1850 and kept alive by charity in the Cotton Famine.[1]

Short-term economic movements were obviously important determinants of an individual's prosperity; so, too, was his changing family situation. A young man, fully employed with an active working wife and no children, was in a very different position from his neighbour, also married but faced with the need to provide for a wife and three or four young children below working age, or a man and his wife past the prime of life and ill-supported by their sons and daughters.

These generalizations might seem platitudinous were it not that even they still fall within the realm of controversy. Development of them inevitably takes us further into the area of continuing dispute. The view that growth in purchasing power, though not as great as in the next fifty years, was nevertheless appreciable derives in part from the evidence on real wages and national income, in part from the limited evidence about consumption and in part from considerations of a more theoretical nature. Over the first half of the nineteenth century industrial production was expanding roughly twice as fast as population. Notwithstanding the growth in foreign trade, this rate of increase could not have been self-sustaining had it not been accompanied by a rising and widespread home demand for industrial products and this could only come from an equally broad-based increase in the power to consume. As Perkin puts it, 'if wages fell too low, demand, especially for the mass consumer goods in which the new industries specialized, would fall with them, and so too would the incentive for labour-saving investments and . . . growth would cease'.[2] Because the

[1] C. S. Peel, 'Homes and Habits', in G. M. Young (ed.), *Early Victorian England*, vol. I (London, 1934), p. 126.

[2] Perkin, op. cit., p. 139.

price of industrial products was falling significantly more quickly than that of agricultural commodities this increasing purchasing power expressed itself more in the purchase of manufactured goods – clothing, household requisites, etc. – than of food. One consequence of this was that the poor whose income was almost wholly expended on food fared worse both absolutely and relatively than their wealthier working-class brethren.

The differing experience of the south and the north also suggests an inference of a more far-reaching character. It has already been suggested that the most powerful short-term influence on economic prosperity in the eighteenth century was the pressure of a rapidly expanding population. Population continued to rise rapidly in the nineteenth century. Growth was more rapid to the north of the coal line; but even the southern counties showed an increase of over 80 per cent between 1801 and 1851. To the extent that population remained an exogenous element in this period, it and industrialization were the two major factors influencing the progress of living standards. The two were, of course, mutually interacting and while industry provided the means by which an increasing population was sustained, population in its turn strongly influenced the pattern of industrial growth. H. J. Habakkuk, John Hicks and François Crouzet[1] have all pointed to the relative abundance of labour in early nineteenth-century England. In the southern largely agricultural counties this produced conditions of underemployment and tended to depress both wages and earnings; and this situation was aggravated by the progress of northern industry which tended to destroy the ancillary domestic manufacture which the predominantly farming households of the south and west had used to supplement their incomes. Population pressure would have been no less severe in the north had not industrialization created both employment and income. To the extent, however, that even in the north labour was abundant the full forward movement of mechanization was frustrated. 'Abundance of labour favoured accumulation with existing tech-

---

[1] H. J. Habakkuk, *American and British Technology in the Nineteenth Century* (Cambridge, 1962), chapter, V; J. Hicks, *A Theory of Economic History* (Oxford, 1964), pp. 148–54; F. Crouzet, *Capital Formation in the Industrial Revolution* (London, 1972).

niques – widening rather than deepening of capital – even though the supply of capital might have permitted a technologically more advanced development.'[1] And as a consequence in the industrial north and still more in the agrarian south the return to labour in terms of purchasing power increased more slowly than it might otherwise have done. The implication of this is that if we seek a villain in this particular piece it may well be not to industry itself, whose function was ameliorative, but rather to population growth that we should look. In Crouzet's words, 'the decisive factor in the undoubtedly low standards of living and widespread poverty of the working classes in the eighteenth and early nineteenth centuries was the pressure of a rising population'.[2]

VI

For many the arguments that have been put under scrutiny in the preceding pages may seem unreal and perhaps even indecent when related to the wider issues of the quality of life. It was Clapham himself who emphasized 'that statistics of material well-being can never measure a people's happiness'.[3] This is certainly the view of Edward Thompson, and his work reflects and enhances a deep and noble tradition of impassioned protest which runs back through the writings of Hammond and Toynbee to the time of the Industrial Revolution itself. The view that the quality of life of the labouring classes deteriorated under the impact of industrialization is fully set out in the early chapters of *The Making of the English Working Class*, extracts from which are reprinted in this volume. Much of the argument and the evidence – on the urban environment, on morbidity and mortality and on conditions in workshops and factories – is directly relevant to the discussion of material living standards. It constitutes a formidable indictment of the new social order which accompanied the early development of industrialization.

[1] Habakkuk, op. cit., p. 141.

[2] F. Crouzet, op. cit., pp. 63–4.

[3] Clapham, op. cit. (2nd edn, 1939), p. x. Cf. also W. Cooke Taylor, op. cit., p. 161: 'The philanthropy which would measure its exertions purely by physical wants deserves to be stigmatized as the worst form of inhumanity.'

That this area of the debate has not developed further is no doubt due in part to the substantial evidence that can and has been marshalled on the deteriorationist side; but it is also attributable to two other factors. To talk of deterioration is to imply a comparison; but what relevant comparisons can be made between the condition of life in the predominantly rural–agrarian society of the seventeenth and eighteenth centuries and the urban–industrial society of the nineteenth? Evidence about the one is much less substantial than about the other but if like is compared with like – the London of the seventeenth and eighteenth centuries with the London of the nineteenth, for example – it is by no means clear that the balance of advantage lies with the earlier age. Likewise, though no one would wish to do other than condemn the miseries attendant on the employment of young children in mines and factories, such employment on farms and in domestic workshops was common practice before the coming of the factory. No less important in limiting the development of this particular debate has been the inability to establish criteria for comparison. How can an equation be established between the deficiencies of urban sanitation, on the one hand, and improvements in general literacy, on the other? How, still less, can a just comparison be made between the disturbance, felt particularly by the old, which removal from a rural to an urban environment entailed, and the social amenities which town and factory, however squalid, offered to the young when compared with the restricted life of an upland farm? Against 'the world that was lost' must be set the world which was already in process of being gained even in the darkest years of the second quarter of the nineteenth century.

To ask these questions is in no way to seek to minimize the disruption and distress which came with industrialization and urbanization, any more than to speak of the undoubted increase in living standards over the next half century is to diminish the poverty of Booth's London and Rowntree's York. We are here dealing with immeasurables but, because population growth and industrialization came rapidly and the reaction to the problems which they created was relatively slow, it is hard to see that in the short run the Industrial Revolution did other than increase the sum of human misery for large sections of the population. It is necessary, nonetheless, to examine critically such suggestions as that the effect of industrialization was to 'depersonalize' rather than to 'liberate' the individual. The psychological effects of any radical change in society are complex and their impact necessarily varies over time and from individual to individual. The first half of the nineteenth century was a time when an old society was in travail to bring forth a new. The pains of that labour were in part as inevitable as was the process of change itself, but they undoubtedly could have been limited. Greed, selfishness, ignorance and incapacity all contributed to the tensions and miseries of the age – in what proportions is a matter for individual judgment; but, in properly stressing these facts it is no less necessary to point to the goodwill, selflessness and intelligence by which the problems of the new order were met and in greater or less measure resolved, and the resilience of a society which, in Neil Smelser's words, came through 'the storm and confusion of the industrial revolution itself to emerge into the *relative* stability of the prosperous and optimistic Victorian period'.[1]

A NOTE ON THE ESTIMATES OF GROSS NATIONAL PRODUCT

After this essay was completed my attention was drawn to Phyllis Deane's 'New Estimates of Gross National Product for the United Kingdom 1830–1914', *Review of Income and Wealth*, XIV (1968) pp. 95–112. Whereas Miss Deane's earlier estimates were based on income data, the new – and more refined – series approaches the problem from the expenditure side. The newer estimates show a rate of growth between 1830 and 1850 appreciably lower than that indicated by the earlier estimates, and, with this, a slower increase in *per capita* income. Though they cover only twenty years of the pre-1850 period, the revised data suggest an interpretation less favourable to the meliorist position than do the earlier Deane and Cole estimates; but, more important, they emphasize the limited utility of early nineteenth-century national income data for the assessment of changing living standards.

[1] N. J. Smelser, *Social Change in the Industrial Revolution* (London, 1959), p. 408.

1 The Cost of Living and Real Wages in Eighteenth-Century England

E. W. GILBOY

[This article was first published in the *Review of Economic Statistics*, vol. XVIII, 1936.]

The course of the cost of living and that of real wages over time is a subject of never failing interest to the economist.[1] In studies of the business cycle, in explanations of the changing well-being of the labouring class, as in various other connections, trends of living costs and of real wages are important features. One does not need to cite examples, since the phenomenon is so common.

The movements of these indices during the eighteenth century are of special significance, not merely to the economic historian but also to the economic theorist. This century was one of particularly important changes on the technical side of industrial production. What effect did these changes have on the well-being of the working class? Were all parts of England similarly affected?

The author has worked previously on the English wage situation in the eighteenth century and has made some attempt to estimate real wages on the basis of wheat prices and con-

[1] The present article makes report upon the first of two studies on eighteenth-century prices conducted in common by Dr Elizabeth Boody and the writer. The research has been carried on jointly at all stages, but it was decided to divide the presentation of results. An article by Dr Boody, which will be published in a later issue of this *Review*, will deal with general business conditions and the price movements of producers' and consumers' goods from 1660 to 1815. She will also investigate cyclical movements in the various indices.

We are indebted to the Harvard University Committee on Research in the Trade Cycle for a grant of money which made possible this inquiry. We are also most grateful to Miss Dorothy Wescott and her staff for their efficiency in carrying out the statistical computations.

Dr Boody and Professor W. L. Crum have gone over the manuscript, and I am grateful to them for a number of valuable suggestions.

temporary comment.[1] At the time of this earlier research, there were no adequate data from which a cost of living index for this period might be derived.

Thanks to the generosity of Sir William Beveridge and the English section of the International Committee on Price History, some sixty price series covering the eighteenth century have been made available to Dr Boody. Some of these series go back to 1660; most of them to 1695. A number of them extend

CHART I   *Indices of the cost of living in London, annually*
(logarithmic vertical scale)

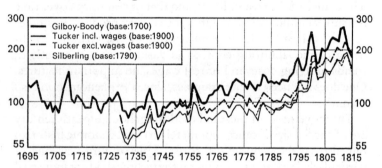

to 1815 or 1820. All were taken from original manuscript sources and have not as yet been published.[2] Thirty of them were sufficiently continuous to be utilized in our cost of living index. Even with these, a great amount of interpolation was necessary. The methods by which the latter was accomplished are explained in detail in the statistical appendix, but here it may be said that Tooke, Rogers, and the Parliamentary Reports provided the main bases for such expediencies.[3]

The final index (see Chart 1) is a weighted arithmetic average of price relatives, with 1700 as a base, extending over the decades from 1695 to 1815. It is composed of thirty-one price

---

[1] Elizabeth W. Gilboy, *Wages in Eighteenth Century England* (Cambridge, Mass. 1934).

[2] These series and many additional ones will be published shortly by the English Price History Committee. Sir William Beveridge has been kind enough to authorize our use of them in advance, for the purpose of this investigation.

[3] The exact references are given in the Appendix (p. 18ff).

series relating, as far as data permit, to goods which were consumed by the English labourer of that period. The commodities were divided into five groups: (1) cereals, (2) animal products (3) beverages and condiments, (4) candles and coal, and (5)

CHART 2 *Gilboy–Boody index of the cost of living in London by groups, annually*

(Base: 1700. Logarithmic vertical scale)

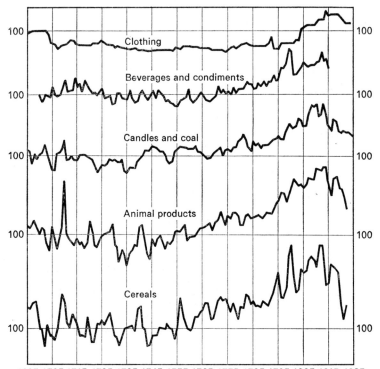

clothing. Unweighted arithmetic averages of price relatives were computed for each group (see Chart 2). The final index was based upon these group indices with the following weights: cereals 5; animal products 2; candles and coal 1; beverages and condiments 1; clothing 1. The weights were determined after a

careful study of sample budgets published by Eden and Davies.[1]
It was found that the average labourer spent 40 per cent of his
total expenditure on bread and flour, 20 per cent on animal
products, 9 per cent on sugar, tea, beer, etc., 4 per cent on
'groceries' (soap, candles, etc.), 15 per cent on rent and fuel,
and 8 per cent on clothing. In our index, no attempt was made
to allow for rent expenditure, and cereals were given a somewhat greater weight. This latter step has justification in that the
Eden and Davies budgets apply to the years 1790–6, when the
labourers' budget was more diversified and included a relatively smaller expenditure on cereals than in the first half of the
century.

STATISTICAL SOURCES

The actual series used in our index, with their sources, are as
follows:[2]

I. *Cereals*	*Source*
Biscuit, 1695–1814	Admiralty, Treasurers' and Contract Ledgers
Barley, 1695–1822	Kent Quarter Sessions Records to 1791; Tooke, 1792–1822
Beans, 1684–1822	Royal Household, Lord Stewards' Accounts to 1790; Tooke, 1791–1822
Flour, 1695–1826	Admiralty, Treasurers' and Contract Ledgers
Oats, 1695–1822	Winchester College Rents to 1806; Tooke, 1807–22
Peas, 1695–1826	Admiralty, Treasurers' and Contract Ledgers
Rye, 1695–1822	Kent Quarter Sessions Records to 1785; Tooke, 1791–1822 (Data interpolated from movement of barley series, 1786–90)
Wheat, 1695–1822	Admiralty, Treasurers' and Contract Ledgers to 1801; Tooke, 1802–22
Bread, 1728–1815	Westminster School and Abbey Accounts to 1784, Parliamentary Report (1814–15), 1785–1815

[1] Sir Frederick Eden, *State of the Poor*, vols. I–III (London, 1797), and David
Davies, *The Case of the Labourers in Husbandry* (Bath, 1795). Thirty-five budgets
were examined in detail; rough averages of expenditure for the several budgetary
items were secured; and the percentage of each to total expenditure was computed.

[2] The periods listed are those for which the series are available. In computing
the cost of living index, however, the earliest year used for any one series is
1695; the latest, 1815. Certain of the group indices were extended a few years
beyond 1815.

II. *Animal Products*

Beef for Salting, 1695–1824 — Admiralty, Treasurers' and Contract Ledgers to 1796; Tooke, 1797–1824

Butter, 1695–1826 — Admiralty, Treasurers' and Contract Ledgers

Cheese, 1695–1826 — Admiralty, Treasurers' and Contract Ledgers

Pork Hogs, 1695–1822 — Admiralty, Treasurers' and Contract Ledgers to 1813; Tooke, 1814–22

III. *Beverages and Condiments*

Tea (Bohea), 1740–1822 — British Document 390, Parliamentary Papers, 1845, Vol. 46, 191[1]

Ale, 1695–1812 — Royal Household, Lord Stewards' Accounts

Beer, 1715–1818 — Chelsea Hospital Accounts

Cider, 1695–1828 — Royal Household, Lord Stewards' Accounts

Hops, 1695–1826 — Admiralty, Treasurers' and Contract Ledgers

Sugar, 1700–1822 — Westminster School and Abbey Accounts to 1784; Tooke, 1785–1822

Malt, 1695–1826 — Admiralty, Treasurers' and Contract Ledgers

White Pepper, 1700–99 — Royal Household, Lord Stewards' Accounts

Raisins, 1701–99 — Westminster School and Abbey Accounts to 1776; Royal Household, Lord Stewards' Accounts, 1777–99

IV. *Candles and Coal*

Coal, 1683–1826 — Admiralty, Treasurers' and Contract Ledgers

Tallow Candles, 1660–1830 — Admiralty, Treasurers' and Contract Ledgers to 1799; Royal Household, Lord Stewards' Accounts, 1800–30

V. *Clothing*

Hair, 1695–1778 — Admiralty, Treasurers' Ledgers and Bill Books

Kersey, 1660–1795 — Admiralty, Treasurers' Ledgers and Bill Books

Leather Backs, 1660–1792 — Admiralty, Treasurers' Ledgers

Brussels Linen, 1700–35; Irish Linen, 1736–95 — Royal Household, Lord Stewards' Accounts

Stockings (blue yarn), 1712–1827 — Greenwich Hospital Accounts

Felt Hats, 1712–1827 — Greenwich Hospital Accounts

Broadcloth, 1660–1830 — Westminster School and Abbey Accounts

It will be noticed that in Group I, bread does not enter the index until 1728; in Group III – for which the first year of the index is 1700 rather than 1695 – tea enters in 1740 and beer in 1715; in Group V, linen enters in 1700, stockings and felt hats

---

[1] This was substituted for the tea series of the Price History Committee, which did not start until 1763 and showed almost no changes in level. The amount of the import duty was added to the East India Company's selling price.

in 1712. Groups III and V include several series which end before 1815: for example, ale in 1812; white pepper and raisins in 1799; hair in 1778; kersey and linen in 1795; and leather backs in 1792. The majority of the series cover the main part of the period, and this is particularly true of those in the most heavily weighted groups. Before 1700, however, and after 1790 the index is definitely less satisfactory than over the other decades. Although most of the prices refer to London or its vicinity, less inaccuracy than might be supposed is involved in using the index as representative of England. Prices, particularly for grains, showed little regional divergence. On the other hand, a similar statement cannot be made relative to wages; and our indices of money wages can be used to represent wage movements only in the regions to which they refer.

In a cost of living index, it is desirable to include only retail prices, for it is well known that wholesale and retail prices show differences in movement. Unfortunately the statistician who dares to deal with past periods cannot usually choose what he will use. He must take what is available and make the most of it. The prices here employed cannot clearly be marked as either retail or wholesale prices. The Admiralty prices (providing half of the series) are probably closely related to wholesale prices; on the other hand, the Greenwich Hospital, Chelsea, Westminster, Kent, and Royal Household prices are definitely akin to retail prices, in the opinion of the English Price History Committee. The index is, therefore, neither a wholesale nor a retail price average but something in between. All series represent contract prices. The contracts vary from a very short period of a few months to periods of several years. The only group which is markedly influenced by long-period contracts is the clothing group (see Chart 2). On the whole, the series within any one of the several groups showed a great similarity of movement, and all the commodities were selected either for their places in the labourers' budgets, or for their influences upon some article actually consumed. We are well aware of the defects of the index, but it is probably a better measure than has yet been found of the general course of the cost of living for the period.

COST OF LIVING MOVEMENT

According to the index presented in Chart 1 and Table 1, the broad tendency of living costs was slightly downward from the period 1708–11 until about 1755. A distinctly upward movement began in the late 'fifties, and was accelerated in the inflationary period after 1790, culminating in the peaks of 1800 and 1812. The index fluctuated around the level of the base year, 1700, until the 'fifties, rose to about 150 by 1793, and to 270 by 1812. The peaks are attributable, for the most part, to exceptionally bad harvests in particular years, notably 1698, 1710, 1740, 1756, 1766, 1782, 1795, 1800 and 1812. The rise in 1698 was influenced also by monetary difficulties; that of 1708–10 by the fact that Admiralty prices were unusually high as a result of a heavy discount on Navy bills. The whole period after 1790 was, of course, influenced by inflation. Pronounced cyclical movements are apparent, but they will not be dealt with here.

Among the group indices, the widest short-time fluctuations appear in cereals, with animal products not far behind. The two groups move together quite closely, except for a difference in timing of the upward trend. With cereals the rise begins in the 'fifties; with animal products, in the late 'thirties. The other three groups move less violently and are little affected by years of bad harvest. Beverages and condiments rise until 1714 and then decline slowly until the middle 'fifties. The upward movement then initiated is less marked than in the other two food groups. The rise in coal and candles begins in the 'thirties but is not pronounced until the end of the century. The clothing group shows great stability: after dropping sharply in the first decade of the eighteenth century to about 80 (1700 = 100), the index remained close to this figure until the 'nineties. Clothing prices do not rise noticeably until after 1800 and reach their peak in 1814.

The movement of the group indices is consistent with other information from contemporary sources. Textile prices, particularly cotton,[1] declined during the century. So did the prices

[1] We were not able to secure a series of cotton prices sufficiently continuous to include in the index. Mr A. P. Wadsworth – author with Miss Mann of *The Cotton Trade and Industrial Lancashire, 1600–1780* (Manchester, 1931) – wrote to Dr Boody recently that he has been unable to find a good series of cotton prices for this period.

TABLE I *Annual indices of the cost of living in London*
(Base: 1700)

Year	Index	Year	Index	Year	Index
1695	124	1735	88	1775	128
1696	122	1736	93	1776	120
1697	126	1737	94	1777	131
1698	131	1738	91	1778	123
1699	118	1739	109	1779	117
1700	100	1740	119	1780	125
1701	100	1741	103	1781	125
1702	91	1742	98	1782	144
1703	99	1743	82	1783	139
1704	88	1744	83	1784	129
1705	95	1745	94	1785	132
1706	86	1746	92	1786	128
1707	94	1747	95	1787	130
1708	116	1748	100	1788	127
1709	135	1749	98	1789	134
1710	147	1750	93	1790	133
1711	104	1751	98	1791	131
1712	98	1752	94	1792	140
1713	108	1753	95	1793	148
1714	105	1754	92	1794	168
1715	100	1755	98	1795	179
1716	92	1756	125	1796	153
1717	92	1757	118	1797	152
1718	92	1758	108	1798	165
1719	106	1759	99	1799	229
1720	102	1760	97	1800	252
1721	91	1761	99	1801	190
1722	86	1762	109	1802	166
1723	97	1763	110	1803	171
1724	99	1764	115	1804	204
1725	105	1765	117	1805	196
1726	100	1766	124	1806	201
1727	106	1767	123	1807	226
1728	112	1768	109	1808	236
1729	102	1769	108	1809	229
1730	89	1770	118	1810	225
1731	88	1771	130	1811	266
1732	81	1772	136	1812	270
1733	89	1773	131	1813	224
1734	91	1774	129	1814	198
....	...	....	...	1815	183

of certain imported luxuries such as tea, coffee, spices and the like. Contemporary comment is unanimous in stating that many of these commodities were included in the labourer's budget for the first time in the later eighteenth century. Grain and meat prices were known to increase in the last half of the century, with attendant misery on the part of the working classes, especially in years of bad harvest. The final index is largely influenced by the cereal and animal products groups, although the extreme violence of the short-time fluctuations and the severity of the rise in the late eighteenth and early nineteenth centuries is mitigated by the stability in prices of the other three groups.

WAGES

Chart 3 indicates the movement of money wages in London and Lancashire as compared with that of the cost of living. The

CHART 3   *Gilboy–Boody indices of the cost of living in London, money wages in London, and money wages in Lancashire, annually*

(Base: 1700. Logarithmic vertical scale)

indices of money wages (Table 2) were computed from data on daily wage rates of common labour, mostly in the building trades.[1] The London index is an arithmetic average of price

[1] See *Wages in Eighteenth Century England*, Appendix II, for the original series· Labourers' wages were used rather than those of craftsmen because the latter are less complete and more subject to quality differences. The long-time movements of the two are very similar, except that craftsmen's wages ordinarily rise first in periods of advance. They are also on a higher level throughout the century, as might be expected.

relatives of the daily wage rates of bricklayers', masons', paviours' and plasterers' labour at Westminster Abbey, with 1700 used as the base year. The Lancashire index is a simple series of price relatives, on a 1700 base, of the daily wages of labour on buildings and roads. These two series were found to represent wage rates in London and the north of England respectively, in the study mentioned above.

The stability of wages over long periods of years is evident, particularly in the London index.[1] Money wages in London

CHART 4   *Gilboy–Boody indices of real wages in London and Lancashire, and Tucker index of real wages in London, annually*

(logarithmic vertical scale)

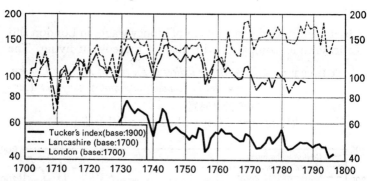

rose slightly until the 'forties, and the level again advanced in the 'sixties and 'eighties. The Lancashire series went up much more sharply. There was an irregular rise from 1700 to 1730, stability at the new level until the late 'fifties, and a steep rise in the 'sixties, until by 1768 the index was at 200 where it remained, with the exception of one year, until 1781. In the 'eighties and 'nineties, an upward movement to a still higher level took place. Over the century, money wages in the North moved upward in a far greater degree than in London.

Real wages are pictured in Chart 4. Real-wage indices (Table 2) were computed by dividing the money-wage indices by our

---

[1] Year-to-year fluctuations in wage rates cannot be relied upon, especially in the Lancashire series, since they may represent quality and place differences that could not be entirely eliminated.

TABLE 2 *Annual indices of wages in England*

(Base: 1700)

Year	London		Lancashire	
	Money wages	Real wages	Money wages	Real wages
1700	100	100	100	100
1701	99	99	95	95
1702	99	109	89	98
1703	109	110	89	90
1704	114	130	89	101
1705	109	115	105	111
1706	109	127	105	122
1707	109	116	105	112
1708	109	94	105	90
1709	111	82	89	66
1710	109	74	105	71
1711	110	106	105	101
1712	110	112	105	107
1713	110	102	100	93
1714	109	104	111	106
1715	109	109	111	111
1716	109	118	111	121
1717	109	118	89	97
1718	109	118	111	121
1719	109	103	111	105
1720	110	108	133	130
1721	110	121	123	135
1722	110	128	123	143
1723	110	113	123	127
1724	110	111	123	124
1725	110	105	111	106
1726	110	110	111	111
1727	110	104	133	126
1728	105	94	111	99
1729	110	108	133	130
1730	109	122	133	149
1731	114	130	123	140
1732	114	141	133	164
1733	114	128	133	149
1734	114	125	133	146
1735	118	134	133	151
1736	116	125	133	143

TABLE 2 (*continued*)

Year	London		Lancashire	
	Money wages	Real wages	Money wages	Real wages
1737	118	126	133	141
1738	116	127	133	146
1739	118	108	133	122
1740	116	97	133	112
1741	116	113	133	129
1742	118	120	133	136
1743	115	140	133	162
1744	118	142	133	160
1745	118	126	133	141
1746	118	128	128	139
1747	118	124	128	135
1748	118	118	133	133
1749	118	120	133	136
1750	120	129	133	143
1751	118	120	133	136
1752	118	126	133	141
1753	118	124	133	140
1754	118	128	133	145
1755	118	120	133	136
1756	118	94	133	106
1757	118	100	111	94
1758	118	109	111	103
1759	118	119	133	134
1760	118	122	123	123
1761	118	119	123	124
1762	118	108	123	113
1763	121	110	177	161
1764	121	105	156	136
1765	121	103	156	133
1766	121	98	156	126
1767	121	98	156	127
1768	121	111	200	183
1769	121	112	200	185
1770	121	103	200	169
1771	121	93	177	136
1772	121	89	200	147
1773	121	92	200	153
1774	121	94	200	155

TABLE 2 (*continued*)

Year	London		Lancashire	
	Money wages	Real wages	Money wages	Real wages
1775	118	92	200	156
1776	118	98	200	167
1777	118	90	200	153
1778	118	96	200	163
1779	123	105	200	171
1780	123	98	200	160
1781	123	98	200	160
1782	123	85	211	147
1783	123	88	200	144
1784	123	95	189	146
1785	123	93	205	155
1786	123	96	223	174
1787	123	95	211	162
1788	...	...	228	180
1789	...	...	228	170
1790	...	...	233	175
1791	...	...	223	170
1792	...	...	200	143
1793	...	...	267	180
1794	...	...	233	133
1795	...	...	233	130
1796	...	...	233	152

index of the cost of living.[1] London and Lancashire real wages
move almost in unison until 1719; thereafter the Lancashire
index is at a higher level than that for London. Real wages in
London begin to decline in the late 'forties; in Lancashire, they
rise until the late 'sixties, and then fluctuate about a level somewhat above 150 in terms of the 1700 base. The general picture is
that of slightly rising real wages for both London and the
North for the first half of the century, then declining real wages
for London, but another sharp upward movement for the North.

[1] There are those who will object to deflation of this sort. It may be said, however, that the index of cost of living makes as accurate a denominator as we could
devise, and that the numerator and denominator have no elements in common.
There seems to be no danger of spurious correlation.

Before any more general conclusions are attempted, it seems desirable to compare the indices above presented with others which have been published. The most extensive survey of the period is that recently made by Dr Rufus S. Tucker.[1] Dr Tucker's two indices of the cost of living appear on Chart 1; his index of real wages, on Chart 4. We are primarily interested in his indices for the period which is covered also by our own data, namely the years 1729–1815.

For the eighteenth century (or, more exactly, until 1805) Dr Tucker's cost of living index, excluding wages, is of the weighted geometric type, with 1900 taken as the base year. Essentially it is a five-year index of consumers'-goods prices, based on secondary, printed sources. His weights for the period before 1815 are approximately as follows: foods, 75 per cent; clothing, 14 per cent; fuel and light, 7 per cent; miscellaneous, 4 per cent. Dr Tucker's second cost of living index, the one which he himself uses to determine real wages, combines the consumers'-goods index just mentioned (which is given a weight of four) with the wage index (which is given a weight of one). The inclusion of wages in the cost of living index is founded on Mr Arthur Young's theory that rents and wages fluctuate together, and that wages may therefore be used to represent the movement of rent in the labourer's budget.[2] The two indices differ considerably in level, and the inclusion of wages seems to moderate the upward trends obvious in the

---

[1] 'Real Wages of Artisans in London, 1729–1935', *Journal of the American Statistical Association*, XXXI (1936), pp. 73–84.

[2] The evidence on this point is incomplete and confusing. Young found that rent tended to equal one-sixth of the annual wage, but his figures apply only to a few scattered years in the latter part of the century. There is no way of telling whether this relationship was the same for the whole period. My own research indicates that labourers' rents, especially in the country districts, were stationary over long periods and appear to have been fixed by custom. In many cases, cottages were given rent-free. There were complaints about the rise of rents in the London district at the end of the century. We know that in recent decades rents and wages lag behind other prices, but the relation between the lags is not clearly established for our early period. It is impossible to say, in the absence of continuous rent figures, what happened in the eighteenth century.

However, the deflation of a given wage series by means of a cost of living index in which the same wage series is a significant element appears to be a questionable statistical procedure.

former over the periods 1732–55 and 1792–1813. To be sure, short-time movements are very similar.

The most striking difference between Dr Tucker's indices of the cost of living and our index is that the upward movement in his indices becomes apparent in the 'thirties, whereas the advance in our index does not begin until the late 'fifties. At that time, Dr Tucker's index excluding wages – which really is more nearly comparable with our index than is his index including wages – overlaps our index at four points, despite the fact that its level is usually well below that of our series. The upward trend of Dr Tucker's index, which is especially marked from 1730 to the late 'fifties, becomes more gradual from the latter decade until the 'nineties, when it is again steeply inclined.

Dr Tucker's index of real wages reflects the difference in trend (see Chart 4), showing a continuous declining trend throughout the period, whereas our real-wage index for London does not decline until the 'fifties. The difference appears to be a result of the divergence in trend existing between Dr Tucker's cost of living index and ours. This divergence may be due to the fact that Dr Tucker interpolated from a few series[1] within the five-year periods of his original cost of living index; this would be true particularly if these series rose above his five-year points in the intervening years. At any rate, Dr Tucker's general conclusion that real wages in England declined throughout the eighteenth century[2] is not confirmed, even by our London index, and is strongly opposed by our index for Lancashire.

Chart 1 also contains Professor Silberling's cost of living index from 1779 to 1815.[3] His index is a weighted geometric average of price relatives, each series weighted individually, of fifteen commodities, on the base 1790. The nine series for food and drink are given a total weight of 75 per cent; the four series for clothing, approximately 14 per cent; and the coal and

[1] What these series are Dr Tucker does not say, except that wheat was used before 1735.

[2] Op. cit., p. 82.

[3] 'British Prices and Business Cycles, 1779–1850', *Review of Economic Statistics*, V (1923), pp. 223–61.

candles series together make up approximately 11 per cent of the total. Within the food group, animal products are weighted almost as heavily as cereals. Since Professor Silberling's weights are derived from nineteenth century budgets, it is not surprising that they should differ to some extent from ours.[1] The Silbering index follows the Tucker index (including wages) very closely, particularly at the end of the period. This is interesting inasmuch as the Tucker index is an average of retail prices,[2] whereas the Silberling index is a wholesale price index. Possibly the difference between retail and wholesale prices in this period is less than is generally supposed. More probably, the use of annual series and of contract prices (by Dr Tucker) has obscured any differences in movement that may exist. Both these indices differ in level and to some extent in trend from our index. The difference in level is undoubtedly due to the variant base years employed, while some divergence in trend may arise from the use of a geometric index by Tucker and Silberling as opposed to the arithmetic form that we utilized. However, the extent of the trend difference between Tucker's index and ours cannot be explained on this technical ground alone.

CONCLUSIONS

Crude as our index is, it is based on the most complete, continuous and homogeneous series now available. It affords a better basis for estimating the condition of the working classes in eighteenth-century England than the grain prices used earlier.[3] It is necessary to modify somewhat the conclusion there expressed concerning the trend of the standard of living of the London labourer. The present index shows a much more

[1] Weighting animal products equally with cereals is not justifiable, however, for any part of the eighteenth century, as far as labourers' budgets are concerned.

[2] The Greenwich Hospital prices which Dr Tucker uses are more related to retail than wholesale prices, but they are certainly affected by contracts and discounts, and cannot be called pure retail prices.

[3] Gilboy, op. cit. Detailed analysis of non-statistical evidence on real wages will be found here, as well as examination of the effects of hours of work, unemployment, etc., for which no continuous figures exist. It may be said that this non-statistical evidence tends to emphasize the rise in real wages in the north, and to mitigate the extent of the decline in London.

certain decline in real wages for London in the last half of the century. Real wages in the North, however, rose consistently during the entire hundred years, as indicated by the earlier investigation. An index of real wages in the west of England was not computed in connection with the present inquiry, but it would undoubtedly show a decline and, indeed, one that started much earlier than that of London. Regional differences in the course of real wages in eighteenth-century England are very evident. Sufficient data are not at present available to make any statements concerning the movement of real wages in England as a whole for this period.

It is of considerable interest to note that real wages as well as money wages in the North increased in the latter half of the century, when the cost of living was rising. It is Dr Tucker's opinion that gains in real wages are made almost entirely in periods of falling prices.[1] Mr Keynes states that money wages may be expected to rise in periods of rising prices but that real wages will ordinarily fall, except perhaps in the case of a single industry.[2] It is possible that the Lancashire wages fall into the category of Mr Keynes' exception. Although these wages are for common labour and labour in the building trades, not for industrial labour, they may reflect the increasing demand for labour set in motion by the expanding cotton and woollen industries. I am inclined to think, however, that the cause lies deeper than changes in a single industry. Increasing real wages may occur simultaneously with advancing prices in periods when extraordinary industrial and technical changes are under way. Such changes are in the nature of external economies and affect more than a single firm or a single industry. In the eighteenth century, the north of England was undergoing such changes and, although the cotton industry was in the van of this 'industrial revolution', it was only one element in the process. Under such circumstances, it might not be unreasonable to expect real wages and money wages to rise together. Even if money wages lag behind prices, as they frequently do, real wages need not fall except for a very short period at first. Once

[1] Op. cit., p. 84.
[2] J. M. Keynes, *The General Theory of Employment, Interest, and Money* (New York, 1936), p. 10.

wages begin to increase, they may rise relatively faster and in greater proportion than prices, thus making possible a real-wage increase despite the lag. In the north of England, money wages and prices rose almost simultaneously. From 1760 to 1775, prices went up about 40 per cent, while wages increased approximately 70 per cent. There appears to be no inherent reason why this situation should not be repeated, if similar economic conditions should occur.

STATISTICAL APPENDIX

Description of Series

It is not possible in a short paper of this type to print and describe the series in full. The relation of these prices to retail and wholesale prices and the main sources of the series are given in the article itself. It should be added here that most of the series are quoted in harvest years, from October to October, and that October 1700 to October 1701 is called 1700, so that the year 1700 is really made up in large part of 1701.

No correction for harvest years versus calendar years was made in the index as a whole, although in interpolating for certain of the grain series an adjustment was made. These series are listed below. On the whole, no clear and consistent difference in the timing of the movements of our index in comparison with the other indices was shown. Some differences in the timing of the peaks are noticeable in our index as compared with Tucker's and Silberling's, but these differences are not uniform throughout the period. They may, however, be attributable to the use of the harvest year. It is to be noted, however, that the peaks after 1790, particularly 1795, 1800 and 1812, coincide with the description of harvests and price movements given in *Business Annals*.[1]

Statistical Method

An arithmetic index was chosen because the authors felt the data too unsatisfactory to warrant the extra time and expense

[1] W. L. Thorp and W. C. Mitchell, *Business Annals* (National Bureau of Economic Research, New York, 1926), pp. 150–5.

necessary for the calculation of a geometric index. Miss Bezanson found that the geometric index was very little different from the arithmetic in her study of eighteenth-century Philadelphia prices.[1] The year 1700 was selected as a base year since we were particularly interested in comparing changes in the last part of the century with the beginning and since 1700 appeared to be a fairly 'normal' year at the beginning of the period for almost all the series. It is to be noted that the index fluctuates about the level of the year 1700 for the first half of the century.

Interpolation

Interpolations in the clothing and fuel groups were made by Dr Boody. I was responsible for interpolation in the cereal, animal products and beverages and condiments groups. There is not space to print the original series or an itemized list of interpolations. In general the procedure was as follows:

1. Where one or two years were missing, if no comparable series could be found from other sources an arithmetic average of the two adjoining years was taken. There were a few interpolations of this sort in almost every series.

2. When a number of years were missing, or it was desired to extend the series, the original series was charted with a comparable series derived from another source. In every case of this sort there were one or more overlapping years, and in most cases a number of overlapping years. If the series were similar during the overlapping years, with no difference in level or timing, the new series was substituted for the old without any change. This was done in the case of bread. Interpolation was based on the series quoted from *Wholesale and Retail Prices*.[2] If a constant difference in level was observed, but the movement was the same, a figure for 1700 was computed for the new series by the following simple method:

---

[1] Anne Bezanson, Robert D. Gray, and Miriam Hussey, *Prices in Colonial Pennsylvania* (Philadelphia, 1935).

[2] House of Commons Report (London, 1903).

Let x = the required estimate for 1700
  a = the 1700 value for the original series
  b = the value of any given year for the original series
  b_1 = the value of the same given year for the new series

$$\text{then } \frac{x}{a} = \frac{b_1}{b}$$

The new series was then corrected for the difference in level and added on to the original series. In the case of more than one overlapping year, an average of the estimated values for 1700 was taken as the base. This method assumes that a constant difference in level existed between the two series throughout the century, and although this assumption is doubtless not completely justified, it seemed more reasonable to make the adjustment than to add the interpolated series with no allowance for differences in level.

This method was used in the case of rye, beef, cheese, pork hogs and sugar. For these commodities, the interpolated series were taken from Tooke[1] in all cases except cheese. The original cheese series was composed of figures for Cheshire and Suffolk cheese which had to be adjusted in the same way.

3. In some series there was no figure for 1700. In the case of tea, this figure was determined by the above method of proportions from comparable figures listed in Rogers.[2] For the beer series, the 1700 figure was assumed to be the same as that for 1715. The 1701 value for raisins was used as that for 1700. Certain gaps in the raisins series were also filled in from Rogers.

4. Missing years in the flour series were interpolated from Greenwich Hospital figures by adding one shilling to the Greenwich values. The overlapping values indicated roughly a constant difference of this amount.

5. In some instances, the interpolated series showed clearly a constant lag in relation to the original series. This was adjusted by moving forward the interpolated figures. It is probably due to the difference between harvest years and calendar years. Barley, wheat, beans and oats, taken from Tooke, were adjusted in this way.

[1] *Thoughts and Details of the High and Low Prices . . . from 1793 to 1822* (London, 1824).
[2] *History of Agriculture and Prices*, vol. VII, part I (London, 1902).

2 Real Wages of Artisans in London, 1729–1935[1]

RUFUS S. TUCKER

[This article was first published in the *Journal of the American Statistical Association*, vol. XXXI, 1936.]

Probably no subject in the field of economic history is as important in its implications for present policy as the purchasing power of the working classes. It has been studied by many economists, who have accumulated a mass of statistical and non-statistical information, but very few attempts have been made to present the results in the form of an index number, except for the years since 1913. Index numbers, no matter how well constructed, do not furnish a complete picture of any economic problem, but they are desirable as a plane of reference, as a check of scattered quantitative expressions, and as a guide to points or epochs requiring further study. Non-quantitative opinions, even when buttressed by quotations from contemporaries, are inexact and frequently unreliable. People at any time compare conditions with earlier times within their own recollections, and human nature is such that for those who are out of office or out of luck the best that they can remember is the norm, and the present is always a time of depression or retrogression. For those in office or in funds, on the other hand, the present is usually a time of unprecedented progress and prosperity. Each side can present scattered bits of evidence to support its position, and base a social philosophy on the fate of hand-loom weavers or the price of wheat. Doubtless most economists would agree that an accurate knowledge of the purchasing power of the working classes during the industrial revolution is important enough to warrant the preparation of more quantitative checks, guides and sum-

[1] A paper presented at the ninety-seventh Annual Meeting of the American Statistical Association, New York City, 28 December 1935.

maries than have yet appeared. Since England was the home of the industrial revolution, and English statistical material more complete in the earlier years, this index has been prepared, referring to wages and prices in London.

As Dr Gilboy has pointed out, conditions in different parts of England were so diverse that a sound study of wages and prices must be restricted to one locality. It is perhaps not sufficiently realized that a study of the cost of living must also be restricted to commodities entering directly into the cost of living. Even in ordinary times raw materials and consumers' goods have very different movements. In an epoch when methods of production were being drastically changed the divergence between movements of raw material prices and those of finished goods must have been even greater. All the index numbers available for England before 1850 are based on raw materials and foods; most are weighted without reference to the relative importance of their components in the consumers' budget; most include imports without allowing for import duties that were added to the price the consumer had to pay. They cannot therefore be relied on as measures of the cost of living or the purchasing power of money, and the attempt to use them for that purpose has led to some very debatable conclusions. Mr Keynes has pointed out the theoretical reasons for suspecting that indices of wholesale commodity prices cannot portray accurately the purchasing power of money. The index that I am about to describe confirms his suspicions, for it differs widely from the existing wholesale indices.

In constructing an index number of commodity prices over a long period one is faced with two problems – one statistical, one economic – which require the same answer. The statistical fact is that there are practically no continuous series of price quotations referring to the same commodity, or the same quality of a commodity, that cover the whole period under review. The economic fact is that many commodities once important became unimportant, and that many once unknown came to occupy an important place in the typical consumer's budget. For example: the substitution of kerosene for candles and its subsequent replacement by gas and later by electricity;

or among foods the declining importance of beer and cheese and the increasing importance of tea, cocoa, sugar and fruits. Foods of all sorts took up a smaller part of the total consumption of workingmen as their condition improved, and manufactured articles and services became more important. The answer to both these problems is found in the construction of a series of indices, each covering a period of moderate length in which prices are comparable and consumers' habits nearly unchanged, and welding them on to one another to form a continuous chain.

The links in this chain are as follows: 1729–1800; 1790–1818; 1815–21; 1819–32; 1828–35; 1833–7; 1836–50; 1847–62; 1862–8; 1868–73; 1870–80; 1877–1900; and since 1900 the Ministry of Labour indices of the cost of living. In most cases the links overlapped two, three or four years. In 1862 overlapping was not necessary as the items dropped were unimportant and were replaced by similar ones. In 1868 the nature of the available material for adjoining years made overlapping inadvisable. A supplementary index including all the items continuously available was worked out for 1847, 1850, 1857 and 1873, and it was found to correspond very closely with the chain index. By using this device ordinary interpolation was almost entirely avoided after 1805. Before 1805 the complete index could only be constructed at five-year intervals, and figures for the intervening years are interpolations based on a smaller number of items.

Each link was a weighted logarithmic average of consumers' goods, i.e. goods that required no further processing than what was customarily performed in the consumers' households. Thus we have bread and flour but no wheat (except for interpolation before 1735); clothing, cloth, worsted and sewing thread but no wool, cotton or flax; shoes but no leather. The weights for the eighteenth century were based on budgets published by Dr Gilboy. For the first half of the nineteenth century they were based on studies by Wood, Chadwick, Neild and Lowe, and on the official ration of the Chelsea veterans' hospital. After 1870 the chief authority has been the Ministry of Labour, but the practice of American and Swedish authorities has also been considered, and the relative weight of food is slightly less than in the Ministry of Labour's index, in order to make room for sundry manufactured articles.

The weights of foods aggregated 75 per cent of the total index until 1815, 67 per cent until 1850, and 60 per cent thereafter. Clothing accounted for 14 per cent until 1815, 18 per cent from 1815 to 1850, and 20 per cent after 1850. Fuel and light accounted for 7 per cent before 1815 and 9 per cent after that year. The rest of the items, sundry manufactured articles, varied from 4 per cent to 11 per cent.

Although a complete list of articles quoted, the number of quotations for each, and their weights, cannot be given here in the space allowed, the list for 1729 will give an idea of the representative nature of the index in its least representative period – for in later periods the number and variety of items was much greater. In 1729 there were 18 quotations for food, 7 for clothing, 4 for fuel and light and 2 for sundries. There were 19 individual commodities: butcher's meat, bread, butter, cheese, peas, oatmeal, beer, malt, hops, salt, coats, shoes, stockings, hats, uniforms, coal, candles, mops and blankets. Tea, sugar and tobacco were soon added, then spirits and illuminating oil, and the number of sources for each commodity increased, especially after 1780. The number and variety of items increased so that from 1815 to 1835 there were usually over 100 quotations referring to over 50 distinct commodities, and directly covering probably over 90 per cent of the expenditure of a working-class family other than rent and medical attention. After 1835 the clothing items are less complete but foods are even better represented than before. The index after 1880 is merely a recalculation of the Ministry of Labour index with some manufactured sundries added; and after 1900 the Ministry of Labour indexes are used with no change except reduction to a common base.

All the prices used are taken either from official reports or from the data used by other compilers of index numbers, such as Silberling, Newmarch, Sauerbeck, Jevons and the Board of Trade. The chief source from 1729 to 1868 was the record of prices paid for supplies by Greenwich Hospital; from 1729 to 1832 the corresponding prices for Chelsea Hospital were also used; and from 1815 to 1853 similar prices for Bethlem Hospital. After 1853 most of the prices are taken from the Economist or Sauerbeck indexes, or from the Board of Trade's 1903 Report on Wholesale and Retail prices. From 1847 to 1880 sundry manufactures consisted largely of Soetbeer's average of fourteen manufactured British exports, which he used in compiling his index of the cost of living in Hamburg. From 1880 to 1900 Silverman's index[1] of British export prices was used to supplement the Ministry of Labour index, since it consists mainly of coal, textiles and sundry manufactures eligible for inclusion in a list of consumers' goods.

In this manner an index of prices of consumers' goods was attained. It is not a complete index of the cost of living for it omits services, including the services of retailers, and it omits rents. Rents are certainly important, but there is no way to ascertain directly what they amounted to from year to year. The scattered information compiled by Bowley and Wood and earlier writers seems to support the hypothesis that rents of artisans in London strongly tended to equal one-sixth of their weekly wage. It is reasonable to suppose that rents of workingmen's houses should fluctuate with wages, for wages constitute the chief element in demand, and also an important element in supply. Available figures for prices of building materials do not correlate well with the rents reported; neither do the statistics of interest rates or population density. Consequently in order to cover rents and services not included in the prices of commodities a hypothetical cost-of-living index has been calculated, consisting of the consumers' goods index with a weight of four and wages with a weight of one. A similar average of commodities and wages was used by Arthur Young for the same purpose over a century ago. This hypothetical cost of living index is the basis of discussion in the remainder of this paper. If anyone prefers he can use the consumers' goods index, and if he does so he will get more extreme fluctuations in real wages and a sharper upward trend from 1800 to 1900.

An index of real wages is of course constructed by dividing an index of money wages by an index of the cost of living. The index of money wages here used is based on compilations by

[1] A. G. Silverman, *Review of Economic Statistics*, XII (August 1930), vol. p. 139 ff.

Wood, Bowley, Hirst, and the Ministry of Labour, and Hardy's figures for artisans employed on public buildings. There are many trades included after 1780, although before 1850 most wage series are available only for selected years, except some series for artisans in the building trades. Here we have four kinds of labour at Greenwich for every year from 1729 to 1868 and at Chelsea from 1807 to 1818. Before 1780 the only available wages were in the building trades, and those used were largely taken from Dr Gilboy's book, or kindly supplied by her for this index. It is very likely that other wages were not so inflexible, and possibly they had more of a rising trend from 1750 to 1800; it is highly probable that wages of unskilled labourers rose more than wages of artisans, but conclusive evidence is lacking.

So here we have the index of real wages. Before describing its movements and drawing conclusions from it a warning is in order. An index of real wages is not a complete index of the income of the labouring class, still less of its welfare. For one thing, unemployment must be allowed for. However, Wood's study of this point, for the years between 1850 and 1900, shows that allowance for unemployment does not affect the picture very much, and especially does not alter the trend. Bagge's study of real wages in Sweden since 1860 leads to the same conclusion. Of course there are no reliable statistics of unemployment in earlier years. In view of a widespread impression it is worthwhile mentioning also that unemployment is not invariably greater in years of low prices, although there is a tendency for it to increase for a while when prices decline suddenly.

Another point to bear in mind is that working hours have been reduced from 72 or even 84 a week to 48 or less. Since these indexes are based on weekly wages they greatly underestimate the increase in the purchasing power of an hour's labour. A third point is that in the last hundred years the services rendered by the state have increased greatly in variety and importance. These fall mainly in the field of sanitation, education and amusement, and cannot be shown by price indexes. Finally the size and comfort of workingmen's dwellings have increased, partly on account of housing laws. On the whole the condition of the labouring class, if it could be represented by a curve, would rise more rapidly from 1832 to the present, with smaller fluctuations.

The index of real wages then measures the ability of a typical, regularly employed London artisan to purchase commodities of the sort artisans customarily purchased. It attempts to measure also his ability to purchase housing. It covers probably more than nine-tenths of his expenditures, which is as large a proportion as any published index number for recent years. But it is only one measure of the welfare of the working class and has to be supplemented by statistics of mortality, health, education, housing and employment and by non-statistical evidence.

Indices of prices of consumers' goods, money wages, cost of living, and real wages in London, 1729–1900

$(1900 = 100)$

Year	Food	Clothing	Fuel and light	Sundries	Total	Money wages	Cost of living	Real wages
1729	64·8	171·2	89·4	148·3	78·5	42·7	71·4	59·8
30	57·9	168·4	85·1	125·7	72·2	42·2	66·2	63·8
31					62·3	43·1	58·4	72·1
32					60·4	43·1	56·9	75·7
33					65·6	43·1	61·1	70·5
34					69·9	43·1	64·6	66·7
35	54·4	158·0	72·1	127·2	67·6	44·0	62·9	70·0
36					69·2	44·0	64·1	68·6
37					71·7	44·0	66·2	66·5
38					73·2	44·0	67·3	65·4
39					84·7	44·0	76·6	57·4
1740	83·8	157·7	90·1	137·3	95·1	44·0	84·y	51·8
41					77·8	44·0	71·0	60·2
42					76·4	42·4	69·6	60·9
43					71·6	42·7	61·0	70·0
44					71·9	43·6	66·2	65·9
45	68·0	156·0	91·2	140·6	81·3	39·8	73·0	54·6
46					88·2	43·6	78·1	55·8
47					86·7	44·0	77·9	56·5
48					88·8	44·0	79·7	55·2
49					91·3	44·0	81·6	53·9
1750	81·4	155·6	87·9	139·8	92·8	44·0	83·0	53·0
51					102·7	44·0	88·0	50·0
52					97·7	44·0	84·2	52·3

Indices of prices (continued)

Year	Food	Clothing	Fuel and light	Sundries	Total	Money wages	Cost of living	Real wages
1753					100·1	44·0	86·0	51·2
54					83·4	44·0	76·9	57·2
55	74·5	159·0	92·4	137·7	87·3	44·0	78·6	56·0
56					127·0	44·0	100·0	44·0
57					118·4	44·0	95·7	46·0
58					98·1	44·0	85·1	51·7
59					89·8	44·0	80·9	54·4
1760	79·0	158·0	98·1	140·9	91·6	44·0	82·0	53·7
61					86·6	44·0	78·1	56·3
62					90·8	44·0	81·4	54·1
63					88·2	42·2	79·0	53·4
64					91·1	44·0	81·7	53·8
65	82·8	160·3	94·5	141·4	95·4	44·0	85·1	51·7
66					97·1	44·0	86·5	50·9
67					100·8	44·0	89·4	49·2
68					99·7	44·0	88·6	49·1
69					91·8	44·0	82·2	53·5
1770	85·0	135·7	94·3	148·1	94·5	44·0	84·4	52·1
71					101·8	44·0	90·2	48·8
72					109·7	44·0	96·6	45·5
73					109·9	44·0	96·7	45·5
74					107·5	44·0	94·8	46·4
75	95·6	129·4	88·3	158·8	102·6	44·0	90·8	48·5
76					93·9	44·0	84·0	52·4
77					103·9	44·0	91·9	47·9
78					99·4	44·0	88·3	49·8
79					94·0	44·0	84·0	52·4
1780	88·1	131·3	107·5	164·2	98·1	44·0	79·3	55·5
81					106·6	44·0	94·1	46·7
82					111·4	44·0	98·0	44·9
83					110·4	44·0	97·1	45·3
84					107·5	44·0	94·8	46·4
85	96·4	130·4	107·5	164·2	105·0	44·0	92·0	47·4
86					101·8	44·0	90·2	48·8
87					102·4	44·0	90·7	48·5
88					102·0	44·0	90·4	48·7
89					105·1	44·0	92·9	47·4
1790	101·6	137·5	111·0	160·7	111·1	45·1	97·9	46·1
91					107·7	45·1	95·2	47·4
92					106·1	45·1	93·9	48·0
93					113·3	45·9	99·8	46·0
94					115·2	46·7	101·5	46·1
95	127·5	136·4	147·7	194·1	134·6	48·6	116·7	41·4
96					133·6	49·4	116·8	42·3
97					130·8	51·0	115·4	44·2
98					132·5	51·1	116·3	43·9

Year	Food	Clothing	Fuel and light	Sundries	Total	Money wages	Cost of living	Real wages
1799					144·0	51·1	125·5	40·9
1800	189·9	152·6	162·5	236·8	183·1	51·1	156·7	32·6
01					186·2	52·6	159·5	33·0
02					155·9	53·1	135·4	39·2
03					161·6	53·3	139·9	38·1
04					163·0	53·7	141·2	38·0
05	181·8	172·0	166·5	227·2	180·6	54·8	155·5	35·2
06	176·4	169·0	160·2	213·8	175·6	54·8	151·4	36·2
07	147·4	150·6	160·5	213·2	173·5	60·8	151·0	40·3
08	186·1	153·4	187·4	229·3	182·8	63·0	158·9	39·6
09	207·6	166·6	199·8	237·3	201·9	64·2	174·2	36·9
1810	207·6	166·8	192·6	236·7	201·9	66·5	174·4	38·2
11	205·1	164·4	189·8	233·6	198·9	69·5	173·0	40·2
12	231·7	168·6	191·2	229·3	219·1	69·5	189·2	36·7
13	234·7	165·5	201·1	244·1	225·4	70·0	194·4	36·0
14	198·4	184·8	207·2	356·9	201·8	70·6	175·5	40·2
15	174·0	188·8	178·4	315·1	180·6	70·6	158·6	44·5
16	171·3	185·6	148·4	303·2	176·2	67·3	154·4	43·6
17	188·6	163·2	158·6	266·4	181·4	66·4	158·4	41·9
18	184·8	166·0	162·3	293·7	183·3	66·4	160·0	41·5
19	178·3	176·5	155·9	259·2	180·2	65·1	157·2	41·4
1820	166·1	172·4	138·2	237·1	168·7	64·7	148·0	43·7
21	144·8	181·9	128·1	238·2	153·7	65·4	136·0	48·7
22	125·3	166·2	123·0	250·7	136·4	65·4	122·2	53·5
23	132·1	155·0	119·4	241·5	139·0	65·4	124·2	52·7
24	139·9	150·2	109·4	209·2	141·2	66·1	126·2	52·4
25	156·7	150·9	125·5	191·9	154·5	66·9	137·0	48·8
26	150·2	148·1	121·4	188·5	148·1	66·1	131·7	50·2
27	143·9	155·4	121·5	184·0	145·0	66·2	129·3	51·2
28	139·2	148·9	115·8	183·0	140·1	65·9	125·2	52·6
29	139·2	138·6	110·6	177·1	137·4	64·3	122·8	52·4
1830	128·1	137·5	106·3	167·4	128·9	65·3	116·2	56·2
31	137·9	147·8	99·5	156·1	137·9	63·3	122·9	51·5
32	133·6	156·2	99·6	162·1	135·5	63·2	121·0	52·2
33	129·3	137·7	83·0	166·3	128·1	63·4	115·2	55·0
34	118·8	145·3	82·0	177·7	122·6	63·5	110·8	57·3
35	113·2	150·2	84·9	181·2	120·6	62·3	108·9	57·2
36	124·3	149·1	87·6	182·1	127·8	61·3	114·5	53·5
37	135·2	147·5	100·4	172·5	136·5	61·2	121·4	50·4
38	135·5	144·8	100·1	162·4	135·7	61·2	121·6	50·3
39	153·7	145·4	104·7	162·5	148·3	61·2	130·9	46·7
1840	144·0	141·3	97·8	161·0	140·3	61·2	124·5	49·2
41	152·2	141·6	97·7	161·5	145·7	61·6	128·6	47·9
42	138·8	136·2	95·5	152·4	125·3	61·6	112·6	54·7
43	124·3	130·4	92·3	149·0	124·1	61·7	111·6	55·3
44	123·8	132·6	87·3	145·1	123·3	61·9	111·0	55·8

Indices of prices (continued)

Year	Food	Clothing	Fuel and light	Sundries	Total	Money wages	Cost of living	Real wages
1845	131·2	133·0	89·0	144·3	128·4	61·2	115·0	53·2
46	151·7	142·6	81·5	153·0	142·7	61·6	126·5	48·7
47	159·4	140·8	92·5	150·6	149·5	61·6	131·9	46·7
48	139·2	134·9	88·8	139·4	132·6	61·6	118·4	52·0
49	128·9	131·6	84·0	139·2	125·4	62·1	112·7	55·1
1850	118·5	135·0	78·5	141·1	119·2	62·6	107·9	58·0
51	115·8	140·5	73·3	130·5	117·0	63·0	106·2	59·3
52	115·9	125·6	73·6	131·1	114·5	64·0	104·4	61·3
53	136·1	131·3	83·4	135·1	129·2	66·0	116·5	56·7
54	148·4	129·4	103·2	130·1	137·8	66·6	123·5	53·9
55	151·7	128·3	97·7	127·8	138·4	67·3	124·2	54·2
56	153·6	128·7	96·0	128·4	140·6	67·4	126·0	53·5
57	150·9	132·9	93·2	132·2	138·8	67·3	124·5	54·1
58	127·9	135·9	96·5	130·6	126·5	67·3	114·6	58·7
59	135·8	139·1	90·0	135·6	131·4	68·0	118·7	57·3
1860	140·5	146·8	91·4	131·7	135·7	68·3	122·2	55·9
61	147·5	138·5	94·5	134·3	138·5	69·1	124·6	55·5
62	143·8	148·0	90·0	143·8	140·2	70·2	126·2	55·6
63	139·7	156·2	85·2	159·8	139·8	71·2	126·1	56·5
64	141·0	151·2	86·3	172·0	141·0	71·7	127·2	56·4
65	138·6	148·1	87·7	166·3	139·1	73·3	126·0	58·2
66	147·0	142·8	98·6	172·5	145·0	75·9	131·2	57·9
67	151·6	138·4	96·6	165·5	145·5	76·9	131·8	58·3
68	151·4	130·5	94·5	156·9	143·7	76·7	130·3	58·9
69	136·0	134·0	91·7	157·4	135·2	76·8	123·6	62·1
1870	135·1	128·4	92·4	151·7	131·0	79·0	120·6	65·5
71	141·9	126·3	90·7	151·8	134·6	81·0	123·9	65·4
72	144·9	134·0	105·7	159·2	140·0	84·1	128·7	65·3
73	141·8	135·1	121·2	157·7	139·7	86·8	129·1	67·2
74	136·0	132·2	104·4	123·1	130·5	88·2	122·0	72·3
75	129·9	133·3	97·5	120·8	126·5	88·1	118·8	74·2
76	132·7	124·3	96·3	114·6	124·3	87·7	117·0	75·0
77	133·2	119·9	92·5	109·9	123·4	86·7	116·1	74·7
78	128·2	114·1	83·6	106·5	117·7	82·8	110·7	74·8
79	123·1	107·0	81·6	100·9	112·4	83·2	106·6	78·0
1880	122·4	112·9	74·1	103·5	113·4	83·1	107·4	77·4
81	121·2	108·5	77·0	96·0	110·9	84·6	105·7	80·0
82	121·2	107·5	73·0	96·1	110·2	85·6	105·3	81·3
83	121·1	105·1	75·7	91·1	109·5	85·9	104·8	82·0
84	113·9	102·7	75·1	87·9	104·0	85·2	100·2	85·0
85	106·9	102·1	75·1	82·9	99·8	83·8	96·6	86·7
86	103·4	102·2	73·2	79·5	97·2	83·1	94·3	88·1
87	100·2	102·2	71·5	81·3	95·4	83·3	93·0	89·6
88	100·0	100·8	72·9	83·8	95·5	85·0	93·4	91·0
89	103·2	100·4	73·9	89·7	98·1	87·6	96·0	91·3
1890	101·6	101·8	79·6	95·6	98·8	90·8	97·2	93·4

Indices of prices (continued)

Year	Food	Clothing	Fuel and light	Sundries	Total	Money wages	Cost of living	Real wages
1891	103·7	101·9	78·2	88·1	99·0	91·1	95·8	95·1
92	103·9	101·0	77·7	80·5	97·9	90·5	96·4	93·9
93	99·3	100·3	84·5	80·5	96·2	90·5	95·1	95·2
94	94·9	99·1	73·4	75·8	91·3	90·5	91·1	99·3
95	92·1	97·8	71·3	72·5	88·7	90·5	89·1	101·6
96	91·7	98·6	72·1	73·9	88·8	91·1	89·3	102·0
97	95·5	98·2	72·6	72·4	88·8	93·1	89·7	103·8
98	99·5	97·0	73·3	75·3	93·4	93·3	93·4	100·2
99	95·4	96·2	79·5	84·3	92·7	96·0	93·4	102·2
1900	100·0	100·0	100·0	100·0	100·0	100·0	100·0	100·0
01	100·4	100·6	89·0		99·5	99·1	99·5	99·6
02	101·0	99·9	84·6		99·5	97·9	99·5	98·4
03	102·8	99·7	80·9		100	97·4	100	97·4
04	102·4	102·3	79·4		100	96·9	100	96·9
05	102·8	103·0	78·4		101	97·3	101	96·3
06	102·0	104·5	79·5		100·5	98·7	100·5	98·2
07	105·0	106·2	88·9		103	102·2	103	99·2
08	107·5	107·1	85·6		105	101·6	105	97·3
09	107·6	108·4	84·1		105	100·4	105	95·6
1910	109·4	110·7	83·8		106	100·8	106	95·1
11	109·4	112·4	85·1		106·5	101·1	106·5	94·9
12	114·5	115·5	87·0		110	103·7	110	94·3
13	114·8	115·9	90·7		111	106·8	111	96·2
14	116·8	117·4	92·5		115·5	107·8	115·5	93·1
15	147·4	142·3	115·9		135	119·7	135	88·5
16	180·0	183·7	127·7		161	130·2	161	81·1
17	223·3	241·5	137·8		194	167·0	194	86·3
18	241·9	362·8	165·3		223	209·0	223	93·6
19	246·4	422·6	183·4		236	233·0	236	98·5
1920	288·0	485·3	201·4		274	271·7	274	99·2
21	258·2	353·5	230·4		249	260·6	249	104·8
22	198·0	275·3	221·1		201	203·3	201	101·0
23	190·1	259·6	211·4		191	181·9	191	95·0
24	191·2	262·5	213·8		192	184·8	192	96·0
25	192·4	267·2	217·6		194	188·4	194	97·3
26	184·5	257·8	194·8		189	186·8	189	98·7
27	180·0	249·7	173·9		184	186·4	184	101·2
28	176·6	255·5	160·6		183	183·1	183	100·3
29	173·2	254·3	162·5		180	182·8	180	101·3
1930	163·1	246·2	163·9		174	182·0	174	104·7
31	147·4	228·7	165·3		162	178·2	162	109·9
32	141·7	220·5	163·4		158	174·6	158	110·2
33	135·0	214·7	161·5		154	173·7	154	112·8
34	137·2	217·6	161·5		155	173·9	155	111·9
35	144·0	215·8	161·5		156	174·5	156	112·2

Subject to these qualifications what does the index show? From 1732 to 1756 a downtrend in real wages, caused not by declining money wages but by increased costs of food and fuel. Clothing fell in price with the extension of the factory system, even before the introduction of steam- or water-driven machinery.

From 1756 to 1793 the trend was horizontal, but after 1793 real wages fell rapidly, as war and fiat money made commodity prices rise. Peace and restoration of the gold standard raised real wages to the level that had prevailed from 1750 to 1780. Food went up much more than clothing during the war, as machinery reduced factory costs while agriculture continued to struggle against the law of diminishing returns as the population increased and the area of cultivation was extended to include inferior soils.

Money wages fell after 1815 but more slowly than the cost of living, with the result that real wages rose. By 1836 the downtrend of money wages was halted, but crop failures in 1839, 1841 and 1846 so raised the cost of living that real wages turned down again until 1847. Then began an uptrend in money wages that continued until 1873 without a setback and resumed its progress in 1887. Real wages, though interrupted by the Crimean War, rose rapidly after 1847, and unlike money wages did not react in the 'seventies and 'eighties. They reached a peak in 1897 that was not again attained until after the war. That peak was over twice the level of 1847 and over three times the level of 1800. But after 1897 money wages did not keep pace with the cost of living, and only caught up in the post-war deflation. Since 1929, on the other hand, money wages have not fallen as fast as the cost of living, and the index of real wages is now about 8 per cent above its 1897 peak. This difference is probably not enough to offset the higher rate of unemployment. On the other hand, the working man, whether employed or not, gets much more from the public funds now than then and working hours are shorter.

It is interesting to compare this index with the indices of real wages in Sweden since 1860 and in this country since 1790 – the only similar indices of which I am aware.[1]

[1] G. Bagge, *Wages in Sweden, 1860–1930*; and an article by the present writer in The *Review of Economic Statistics*, (January and February 1934 XVI), pp. 8–16, 25–7.

The long trend of real wages in England from 1791 to 1900 was not greatly different from the trend in this country. But the rise was more rapid in the United States before 1860 and in England after 1860. Also there is a strong resemblance between the trend of real wages in Sweden and in England from 1860 to 1900. The lack of improvement since 1900 in England is, however, in striking contrast to the great increase in real wages here and in Sweden from 1918 to 1929.

Many conclusions may be suggested by a study of these indices, and many explanations offered. One striking fact stands out and may be more than a coincidence. During the eighteenth century real wages in England declined. England like all of western Europe was ruled by a government that thought it its duty to control economic activities. The fashionable philosophy was in favour of economic planning. China was the model and inspiration for amateur social scientists because economic planning was supposed to have reached there its highest degree. Mercantilism was the creed of the business man, and the balance of trade was a constant source of anxiety. Nearly all branches of industry were closely regulated by law, except cotton manufacture. Under those circumstances the population increased, but the purchasing power of labourers fell to such a degree that it was probably no higher in 1800 than in the days of Diocletian 1500 years before. But cotton manufacture expanded and progressed.

After 1776 the up-to-the-minute publicists all came out for laissez-faire and by 1815 the new attitude had even come to pervade governmental and trade circles. Restrictions on industry and trade were gradually abolished and the tariff was reduced, especially in 1846 although free trade was not finally introduced until 1860. A glance at the chart (p. 34) shows how rapidly real wages rose after that date.

Aside from the general trend of real wages shown by this index the most interesting feature is the timing of important recessions. Every recession was plainly more a result of rising costs of living than of falling money wages. In fact money wages rarely fell before 1921, and almost never as fast as the cost of living. On the other hand when the cost of living rose money wages almost always lagged behind, and real wages

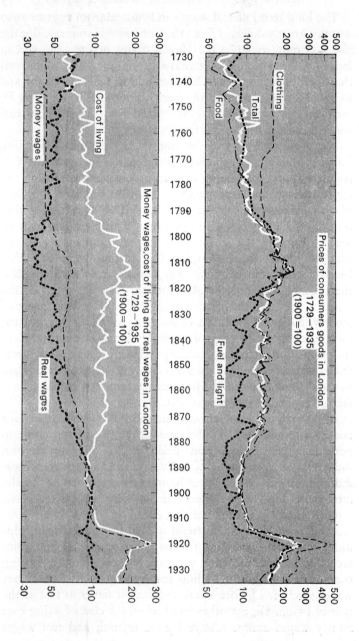

Prices of consumers goods in London
1729–1935
(1900 = 100)

Clothing

Food

Total

Fuel and light

Money wages, cost of living and real wages in London
1729–1935
(1900 = 100)

Money wages

Cost of living

Real wages

therefore fell. This was conspicuously the case during the early part of the Napoleonic and World Wars. Other periods of distress were caused by high prices of agricultural products occasioned by crop failures, especially in the nineteenth century. The last example of a real famine or an approach to one in time of peace was in 1847 when the index of consumers' goods was at its highest point between 1825 and 1916. After 1847 consumers' goods fell rapidly in price until 1852 and never regained their loss until the World War, although in 1866 and 1867 they came close to doing so. Prices of consumers' goods were apparently not affected by the gold discoveries. They were regularly much less affected by cyclical credit expansions than were the prices of raw materials. In fact the movements of raw materials and those of finished goods differed greatly both in their fluctuations and in the slope of their trends. In 1782, for example, the first year for which comparisons are possible, the usual combination of Jevons' and Sauerbeck's indices gives 162 as the level if 1900 equals 100. This index of consumers' goods gives 111 for that year. At the peak of the Napoleonic period the Jevons–Sauerbeck index is 262, while this index is only 225. In 1849 the Jevons–Sauerbeck index is 107, while this index is 125. In 1873 the Sauerbeck index is 148 while this is 140. During the World War consumers' goods rose only two-thirds as far as raw materials, and since 1920 have fallen only two-thirds as far.

In conclusion I wish to state what seems to me to be the most important fact shown by the index. It is that while the purchasing power of labourers has been increased threefold or more since 1800, this increase has taken place almost entirely in periods when commodity prices were falling. All that increases in money wages have accomplished is to maintain those gains in part when prices rose again. This is statistical support for the thesis recently propounded by Dr Moulton, that the aim of society should be to reduce prices, not to raise them. The essential soundness of this conclusion does not depend on the absolute accuracy of these statistics. It is supported by every index of real wages that has ever come to my attention. That being the case, I end with a prayer that the politicians who control our destinies may see the light and cease attempting to bring back prosperity by raising prices.

3 The Standard of Life of the Workers in England, 1790–1830

T. S. ASHTON

[This article was first published in the *Journal of Economic History*, Supplement IX, 1949.]

I

What happened to the standard of life of the British working classes in the late decades of the eighteenth and the early decades of the nineteenth centuries? Was the introduction of the factory system beneficial or harmful in its effect on the workers? These, though related, are distinct questions. For it is possible that employment in factories conduced to an increase of real wages but that the tendency was more than offset by other influences, such as the rapid increase of population, the immigration of Irishmen, the destruction of wealth by long years of warfare, ill-devised tariffs, and misconceived measures for the relief of distress. Both questions have a bearing on some political and economic disputes of our own day, and this makes it difficult to consider them with complete objectivity. An American scholar (so it is said) once produced a book entitled *An Impartial History of the Civil War: From the Southern Point of View*.[1] If I seek to emulate his impartiality, I ought also to strive to equal his candour. Let me confess, therefore, at the start that I am of those who believe that, all in all, conditions of labour were becoming better, at least after 1820, and that the spread of the factory played a not inconsiderable part in the improvement.

There is, it must be admitted, weighty opinion to the contrary. Most of the economists who lived through the period of rapid economic changes took a somewhat gloomy view of the

[1] Referred to in Thomas Jones, *Rhymney Memories* (n.p.: Welsh Outlook, 1939), p. 142.

effect of these changes on the workers. 'The increasing wealth of the nation,' wrote Thomas Malthus in 1798, 'has had little or no tendency to better the conditions of the labouring poor. They have not, I believe, a greater command of the necessaries and conveniences of life; and a much greater proportion of them, than at the period of the Revolution, is employed in manufactories and crowded together in close and unwhole-some rooms.'[1] A couple of generations later J. R. McCulloch declared that 'there seems, on the whole, little room for doubt-ing that the factory system operates unfavourably on the bulk of those engaged in it'.[2] And, in 1848, John Stuart Mill wrote words that, if they gave some glimmer of hope, were never-theless highly critical of the society from which the tech-nological changes had sprung. 'Hitherto,' he said, 'it is ques-tionable if all the mechanical inventions yet made have lightened the day's toil of any human being. They have enabled a greater proportion to live the same life of drudgery and imprisonment and an increased number of manufacturers and others to make fortunes. They have increased the comforts of the middle classes. But they have not yet begun to effect those great changes in human destiny, which it is in their nature and in their futurity to accomplish.'[3] Alongside the economists was a miscellany of poets, philosophers and demagogues; parsons, deists and infidels; conservatives, radicals and revolutionaries – men differing widely one from another in fundamentals but united in their hatred of factories and in their belief that economic change had led to the degradation of labour.

In the opposing camp there were publicists whose opinions are no less worthy of respect and whose disinterestedness and zeal for reform can hardly be called in question – men like Sir Frederic Eden, John Wesley, George Chalmers, Patrick Col-quhoun, John Rickman and Edwin Chadwick. To offset the passage from Mill, let me quote two sentences from Chadwick,

[1] Thomas Malthus, *First Essay on Population, 1798* (London, Macmillan, 1926), pp. 312–13.

[2] J. R. McCulloch, *Treatises and Essays on Money, Exchange, Interest, the Letting of Land, Absenteeism, the History of Commerce, Manufactures, etc.* (Edinburgh, 1859), pp. 454–5.

[3] John Stuart Mill, *Principles of Political Economy*, ed. W. J. Ashley (London and New York, Longmans, Green & Co., 1909), p. 751.

who surely knew as much as anyone else of the squalor and poverty of large numbers of town dwellers in the 'forties: 'The fact is, that hitherto, in England, wages, or the means of obtaining the necessaries of life for the whole mass of the labouring community, have advanced, and the comforts within the reach of the labouring classes have increased with the late increase of population. . . . We have evidence of this advance even in many of the manufacturing districts now in a state of severe depression.'[1] (He wrote in 1842.)

If a public opinion poll could have been taken, it is probable that the adherents of the first group would have been found to outnumber those of the second. But this is not a matter to be settled by a show of hands. It has been said of the people of Herbert Heaton's native county that they like to speak the truth – especially when it is unpleasant; and there is some evidence that this engaging trait is not found exclusively in Yorkshiremen. Writing to Southey in 1816, Rickman observed, 'If one listens to common assertion, everything in grumbling England grows worse and worse';[2] and in a later letter, to a Frenchman, in which he pointed to the way in which the poor had benefited from public relief and cheap food, Rickman was careful to add, 'But these arguments would encounter contradiction in England.'[3] The romantic revival in literature, which coincided in time with the Industrial Revolution, tended to strengthen the despondency. Popular writers, like William Cobbett, pictured an earlier England peopled with merry peasants or sturdy beef-eating, beer-drinking yeomen, just as their predecessors of the age of Dryden had conjured up the vision of a Patagonia peopled with noble savages. But neither native pessimism nor unhistorical romanticism is sufficient in itself to explain the prevalence of the view that the condition of the workers had deteriorated. It is part of my thesis that those who held this view had their eyes on one section of the working classes only.

[1] Edwin Chadwick, *Report on the Sanitary Condition of the Labouring Population of Great Britain* (London, 1843), p. 188.
[2] Quoted by M. Dorothy George, *England in Transition* (London, Routledge, 1931), p. 104.
[3] Ibid., p. 137.

II

It may be as well to begin by making a rapid survey of the economic and demographic landscape. In these early decades of the nineteenth century population was increasing rapidly. Whether it is good or ill that more human beings should experience the happiness and misery, the hopes and anxieties, the ambitions and frustrations of life, may be left for the philosopher or the theologian to determine. But the increase in numbers was the result not of a rise of the birth rate but of a fall of the death rate, and it might be thought that this was indicative of an improved quality of life. 'Human comfort,' said Rickman in his letter to Southey, 'is to be estimated by human health, and that by the length of human life. . . . Since 1780 life has been prolonged by 5 to 4 – and the poor form too large a portion of society to be excluded from this general effect; rather they are the main cause of it; for the upper classes had food and cleanliness abundant before.'[1] Such an argument was not easy to refute; but Gaskell tried to meet it by declaring roundly that there was no direct connection between morality and wellbeing. The noble savage was invoked. In his case, it was asserted, life was 'physical enjoyment' and disease 'hasty death'. For the worker in the manufacturing town, on the other hand, life was 'one long disease' and death 'the result of physical exhaustion'.

If only he had known it, Gaskell might have answered Rickman with a flat denial. For it is now held by statisticians that the fall in the crude death rate was the result of a change in the age distribution of the population and that there was, in fact, no prolongation of the average life. (The deaths per thousand fell simply because population changes in the later eighteenth century had produced a society in which the number of young adults was abnormally high.) But, even if the expectation of life was not raised, it may be urged that the fall of the death rate conduced in some measure to a higher standard of life. For the pomp and circumstances of death and burial swallowed up no small part of the annual income of the workers.[2] When the

[1] Ibid., pp. 104–5.

[2] David Davies, *The Case of Labourers in Husbandry* (Bath, 1795), pp. 23–7.

percentage of deaths to population fell, the proportion of income devoted to the dead probably diminished and resources were thus freed to add to the comforts of the living.

The growth of population, and, in particular, the increase in the number of people of working age, might well have resulted in a fall of wages. But there took place simultaneously an increase in the supply of other factors of production. Estimates of the national income for this period are few and unreliable. But the statistics of output, expenditure and consumption all suggest that over the period as a whole it was growing somewhat more rapidly than population. Is there any reason to believe that the proportion of this increased income that went to the workers diminished and that other classes obtained a larger share? This is a question to which no sure answer can be given; all that is possible is to estimate probabilities. In attempting this, it is important to distinguish between the period of the war, the period of deflation and readjustment, and the succeeding period of economic expansion.

During the war heavy government expenditure of an unproductive nature produced a high level of employment but a low standard of comfort. Difficulties of obtaining foodstuffs from abroad led to an extension of the margin of cultivation, and the profit of the farmer and the rent of the landowner increased.[1] Wartime shortages of timber, bricks, glass and other materials limited the construction of houses; high rates of interest and a burdensome property tax reduced the incentives to build. With a growing population and an increased proportion of people of marriageable age the demand for homes increased; urban rents, like agricultural rents, rose. The growth of the national debt led to an expansion of the number of bondholders. The high rates at which loans were floated swelled the income of the passive investor, and since the tax system was highly regressive the gain to the rentier was largely at the expense of the poor. Prices in general rose, and though rates of wages also moved up they did so more slowly. This, as Earl

[1] Between 1809 and 1815 rents in the eastern counties and north Wales increased by 40 per cent (R. J. Thompson, 'An Inquiry into the Rents of Agricultural Land in England and Wales during the Nineteenth Century', *Journal of the Royal Statistical Society*, LXX [1907], 587-616).

Hamilton has argued, put additional resources at the disposal of the entrepreneur, and the tendency was reinforced by other, institutional factors.[1] The trader's or manufacturer's token, the 'long pay', and the truck system had existed at earlier times. But it is probable that the shortage of coin, which became acute during the period of inflation, led to an extension of these and other devices, the effect of which was to shift purchasing power from the workers to their employers. During the war, then, there took place a whole series of transfers of income – to landlords, farmers, houseowners, bondholders, and entrepreneurs – and these almost certainly worsened the economic status of labour.

The five or six years that followed the peace brought little alleviation. The landlords obtained legislation that enabled them to perpetuate their windfall gains. House rents remained high. Rates of interest fell but slightly.[2] And, though wage rates were less affected than profits, the reduction of government expenditure, the contraction of the currency, banking failures, and a general reluctance to embark on long-term investment reduced the level of activity. Any gains that may have come from the lag of wage rates behind falling prices were probably offset by high unemployment. It is difficult to believe that these years of deflation and civil tumult saw any marked improvement in the condition of the wage-earners.

After 1821, however, economic forces bore less harshly on labour. The gold standard had been restored. A larger quantity of silver and copper was available for the payment of wages. Reforms of the fiscal system were in train. A series of conversions reduced the burden of the national debt, and by 1824 the gilt-edge rate was down to its pre-war level of 3·3. Wartime scarcities had disappeared. A more ample supply of bricks and timber combined with cheap money to stimulate the building of factories and dwellings. By the early 'thirties rents (in the north at least) had fallen about 10 per cent, and in spite of a number of

[1] Earl Hamilton, 'Prices, Wages and the Industrial Revolution', in Wesley C. Mitchell and Others, *Studies in Economics and Industrial Relations* (Philadelphia, University of Pennsylvania Press, 1941).

[2] The yield on Consols was 4·9 per cent in 1814 and 4·5 in 1815. In 1820 it still stood as high as 4·4.

disturbing reports on conditions in the towns it is fairly clear that the standard of housing was improving. The fall of prices – less marked than in the years immediately after the war – now represented not depression but a reduction of real costs. All in all, the economic climate had become more genial; it was possible for the workers to look forward to better conditions of life and work.

III

So far attention has been directed only to forces internal to the economy. What of those that operated from outside? It has been suggested that over the greater part of this period the power of British exports to exchange for goods from abroad was diminishing and that the unfavourable movement of the net barter terms of trade must have resulted either in lower money incomes for those engaged in the export trades or in higher costs of imported goods. Hence, other things being equal, it must have led to a fall in the standard of life of the workers.

The defects of early British commercial statistics are well known. Since both imports and exports were officially measured by a scale of prices that had become stereotyped in the first half of the eighteenth century, the movements of the figures from year to year represent changes in the volume, and not in the value, of overseas trade. From 1798, it is true, there are annual figures of the values of exports, derived from the declarations of merchants; but until recently there have been no corresponding estimates of the values of imports for the years before 1854. Mr Schlote and Mr Imlah have now filled the gap.[1] I am glad to have this opportunity of paying tribute to the industry and scholarship of Mr Imlah; every student of the history of international trade must be grateful to him. I have ventured to use his figures to construct crude index numbers of, first, values of British exports; second, the prices of exports and retained im-

[1] Werner Schlote, 'Entwicklung und Strukturwandlungen des englischen Aussenhandels von 1700 bis zur Gegenwart', *Probleme der Weltwirtschaft* (Jena: n.p., 1938), esp. Appendix Table 17. See also Albert H. Imlah, 'Real Values in British Foreign Trade', *Journal of Economic History*, VIII (November 1948), 133–52.

ports; and, third, the terms of trade from 1798 to 1836 (see Table 1 (p. 44)).[1]

From 1803 to 1834 the course of export prices was almost continuously downward. That of import prices was less consistent. From 1802 to 1812 there were wide fluctuations with no marked trend, but from 1814 there was a descent – steep to 1821, less steep thereafter. The terms of trade moved strongly against Britain during the second phase of the war and less strongly, though markedly, against her in 1816 to the middle 'thirties. Before jumping, however, to the conclusion that here was a factor pressing heavily on British labour, it may be well to look at the composition of the price index for exports. Table 2 (p. 45) gives the price relatives for some important export commodities for the years 1814–29.[2] It will be observed that the prices of cotton yarn and fabrics fell much more steeply than those of the products of the linen, woollen and iron industries. During the war manufactured cotton had taken the place of manufactured wool as the British staple export, and during the whole of the first half of the nineteenth century its lead over other commodities lengthened. It was the fall in the price of cotton yarn and cotton cloth that was responsible for the adverse trend of the terms of trade; the prices of exports exclusive of cotton goods actually declined less steeply than those of imports.

The reason for this extraordinary fall is twofold. Instead of producing muslins, cambrics and other goods of high quality for sale in Europe and the United States, the factories of Lan-

[1] The index numbers of prices have been obtained by dividing the index of declared or computed values by that of official values in the case of both exports and imports. The method is open to criticism, for the weighting is curious. The degree of importance assigned to each commodity depends on the rate at which a unit of it was assessed by the inspector-general at a time long before that to which the index relates. It depends also on the amount of the commodity imported or exported, and this means that the weighting changes from year to year. My non-mathematical mind is encouraged, however, to believe that this peculiarity does not completely destroy the value of the figures. For Mr Schlote's index of the terms of trade from 1814 (obtained by dividing a price index of *manufactured* exports by a price index of imports as a whole) is constructed by similar, but more refined, methods, and when adjusted to the same base year it shows, at least until 1832, movements in striking conformity with those of the series offered here.

[2] The prices have been obtained by dividing the value of the export of each commodity by the quantity exported as recorded by Porter.

cashire were increasingly concerned with cheap calicoes for Indian and Far Eastern markets; a large part of the fall in price is to be accounted for by a change in the nature of the product

TABLE I   *Export and import prices and the terms of trade*
(1829 = 100)

Year	Export index of values	Export price index	Import terms of trade	Net barter terms of trade	Income terms of trade
1798	90	264	176	150	51
1799	103	252	183	138	56
1800	105	253	183	138	57
1801	113	255	189	135	60
1802	128	280	150	187	85
1803	103	281	164	171	63
1804	107	262·5	172	153	62
1805	106	255	178	143	60
1806	114	247	164	151	70
1807	104	248	167	148	62
1808	104	237·5	159	149	65
1809	132	220	193	114	68
1810	135	221	188	118	72
1811	92	227	155	146	59
1812	116	220	173	127	67
1813	—	—	—	—	—
1814	127	208	194	107	64
1815	144	187·5	172	109	84
1816	116	183	148	124	78
1817	117	162·5	160	102	73
1818	130	170	178	96	73
1819	98	164	148	111	66
1820	102	148	136	109	75
1821	103	141	120	117·5	86
1822	103	131	119	110	87
1823	99	127	118	108	84
1824	107	123	112	110	96
1825	109	128	137	93	80
1826	88	120	108	111	81
1827	104	111	107	104	97
1828	103	109	103	106	100
1829	100	100	100	100	100
1830	107	98	98	100	109
1831	104	95	102	93	102
1832	102	87·5	96	91	106
1833	111	89	104	85	107
1834	116	87·5	107	82	118
1835	132	94	114	82	116
1836	149	98	120	82	124

TABLE 2   *Price relatives of exports of home-produced manufactures*

$(1814 = 100)$

Year	Cotton yarn	Cotton manu-factured	Linen manu-factured	Woollen manu-factured	Iron	Total exports	Total excluding cotton goods
1814	100	100	100	100	100	100	100
1815	83	80	86	101	106	90·6	99
1816	77	77	85	107	98	87·8	95
1817	71	67	79	97	93	78·5	90
1818	74	63	82	99	94	81·9	91
1819	64	70	81	101	92	79·6	88
1820	56	64	77	99	89	71·4	83
1821	49	62	77	87	80	67·6	79
1822	47	57	76	81	71	62·9	76
1823	44	55	71	76	70	60·7	73
1824	42	54	67	73	72	59·3	71
1825	45	54	71	77	90	62·0	78
1826	38	47	65	73	79	57·9	72
1827	36	46	60	65	72	53·6	69

of the industry. The other reason was the cost-reducing effect of technical and economic progress. The new mills of the post-war years were driven by steam instead of by water; improvements were being made year after year in the mule and the spinning frame; the power loom was steadily taking the place of the less efficient hand loom; with falling rates of interest capital charges were reduced; and with innovations in transport and trade the expenses of moving and merchanting the goods were diminished. The fall of the prices of cotton yarn and fabrics was not then the result of any decline of foreign demand; it reflected a reduction of real costs. And, though the labour cost of a pound of yarn or a yard of calico fell in a spectacular manner, there was no corresponding drop in the earnings of labour. The downward trend of the terms of trade did not represent any worsening of the economic situation either for the nation as a whole or for that part of it that depended on wages.

Figures purporting to show changes in the terms of trade are of dubious value for long-period studies; it is only over short series of years, when the nature of the commodities entering

into trade and the state of technique do not change very much,
that any safe conclusion can be drawn from them. Even in the
short run, indeed, it is far from clear that a downward movement of the index should be taken as a sign of adversity.
According to Table 1, the terms of trade moved sharply downwards in 1809–10, 1812–15, 1817–18 and 1825 – all periods
when the volume of trade rose to a peak. They moved sharply
upwards in 1811, 1816, 1819 and 1826 – all years of diminished
or stagnant trade. The explanation is, of course, that the prices
of British exports rose in times of prosperity and fell in times
of depression less violently than those of imports, for the raw
materials and foodstuffs Britain imported were inelastic in
demand and supply. It would be absurd, however, to suppose
that the welfare of the workers diminished when trade was
active and increased when trade declined.

An apparatus that is concerned only with prices is clearly
inadequate as a measure of changes in the benefits derived from
international trade. Not only the cost of living but also the
opportunities of earning determine the degree of well-being.
Incomes earned by exports provide employment and generate
other incomes. How far these incomes will go in the purchase
of goods from abroad depends on the prices of imports. In the
light of such reasoning a colleague of mine, Mr Dorrance,
recently suggested that a better instrument for measuring the
social effects of international trade may be obtained by dividing
the indexes of the *values* of exports by those of the *prices* of
imports.[1] I have applied his formula to the trade statistics of the
period, again making use of Mr Imlah's figures. The results
are shown in the final column of Table 1 under the not altogether satisfactory heading 'Income terms of trade'. Here
we have a set of figures free from the paradoxes of those in the
preceding column. Both the trend and the year-to-year changes
are what our knowledge derived from other sources would lead
us to expect. The index shows little change during the war. It
rises sharply in 1815 but falls from 1816 to 1819. In these four
years of low investment and unemployment forces operating
from overseas trade added, it would seem, to the distress. But

[1] G. S. Dorrance, 'The Income Terms of Trade', *Review of Economic Studies*,
XVI (1948–9), pp. 50–6.

from 1820 there is a marked upward movement broken only by the slumps of 1825–26 and 1831. In the 'twenties and 'thirties incomes derived from overseas trade were increasing, and these incomes purchased more of the goods that came in from abroad. Commerce was exerting an increasingly beneficial influence on the economic life of Britain; and in view of the fact that the imports consisted largely of such things as tea, coffee, sugar and the raw materials of industry it is difficult to believe that the workers had no share in the gain.

IV

It is time to pass from speculation and to say something about such figures as we have relating to wages and the cost of living. The outstanding contribution to our knowledge of the first of these was made forty years ago or more by A. L. Bowley and G. H. Wood. It is based mainly on printed sources, but it is unlikely that further research will invalidate it in any serious way. Nevertheless, it is greatly to be hoped that it may be supplemented by data derived from the wages books which, in spite of bombing and paper salvage, still exist in many scattered factories up and down England. In the hands of careful students these records may be made to yield much information not only about rates of payment but also about actual earnings and sometimes about hours of work and the rents of working-class houses. Until the task is performed, it will continue to be impossible to speak with assurance on the topic on which, greatly daring, I have ventured in this paper.

For information about the cost of living we are dependent almost entirely on the work of American scholars. If some of the remarks that follow are critical, I would add that I am filled with shame that English economic historians have done so little in this field and with admiration for the tenacity and skill which American statisticians have brought to the task.

No single contribution to the study of the industrial revolution in England exceeds in importance that made by Norman J. Silberling, whose untimely death has deprived both economic history and statistics of an outstanding exponent. His index number of wholesale prices must remain an indispensable tool for as long ahead as we need look. It is unfortunate that, in my opinion, the same cannot be said of that by-product of his labours, the annual cost of living index from 1799 to 1850. This, I need not remind you, is based on the prices of fifteen commodities selected because of their supposed significance to consumers. The prices, however, are chiefly those of the wholesale not of the retail market; the index is valid only on the assumption that retail prices moved in the same direction and at approximately the same time as wholesale prices and that the spread between the two remained fairly constant. Now it is true that the structure of retail prices seems to have been far less rigid than it is today. The shopkeeper had not yet fully assumed his function as a shock absorber between merchant and consumer, and the price of a loaf of bread or a pound of beef might double or halve within the course of a few months or even weeks. Several of the commodities used in the index are, however, not consumer's goods at all but merely the raw materials of these. My ancestors of the period did not nourish themselves by munching wheat and oats; they did not cover their nakedness with raw wool and cotton and flax; they were not, literally, shod with leather. According to Silberling, this elementary fact is of small account. 'It is well known,' he wrote, 'in the case of cotton goods that prices adjusted themselves with fair alacrity to the price of raw cotton.' When, however, the price relatives of the two are set side by side we find, as most of us would expect, a considerably greater amplitude of fluctuation in the figures for raw cotton than in those for cotton fabrics. It is surely unrealistic to assume that the prices of food and clothing and footwear are faithfully reflected in those of the substances of which they were made. Also, the prices used by Silberling have been refined by the elimination of customs duties. In actual fact duties constituted a large proportion of the cost of nearly everything brought into the country – a proportion that, moreover (as Mr Imlah has shown), increased steadily down to the 1840s.

Nor is this all. The man whose scheme of expenditure conformed to that drawn up by Silberling had many idiosyncrasies. He did not occupy a house, or at least he was not called upon to pay rent. He allowed himself only a moderate amount of bread and very little porridge, and he never touched potatoes or strong drink. On the other hand, he got through quite considerable quantities of beef and mutton and showed a fondness for butter. Perhaps he was a diabetic. The ordinary Englishman of the eighteenth century would have been puzzled by him. For this ordinary Englishman (like his descendant of 1949) was a granivorous and not a carnivorous animal. His staple of diet was bread or, in the north of England, oatmeal; meat was for him a luxury to be taken once, or at most twice, in the week. Silberling's creature who quenched his thirst only with tea and coffee (with sugar but without milk) would have seemed to him a poor sort of fish. For however abstemious the ordinary Englishman may have been in respect to meat and many other things, he took small beer with each main meal of the working day and ale, in no small measure, whenever he had occasion to celebrate.

The portrait that appears in the scholarly pages of Elizabeth Gilboy has somewhat different features.[1] In her index, cereals have a weight of 50 per cent of the total, as against 32 per cent assigned to them by Silberling, and animal products are rightly given a lower status. But her prices are those that were paid by hospitals, schools and government departments and not by individual workmen; they are contract and not truly retail prices. Moreover, they are mainly London prices. One of the outstanding features of English life was (and still is) its regional variety. The prices of foodstuffs varied greatly between one part of the country and another, and it was not uncommon for something approaching a local famine to coincide with conditions of relative abundance at places only a hundred miles or so away. As improvements were made in transport by river, road and canal, prices in the provinces tended to come into line with those of the metropolis. 'All the sensible people,' wrote Arthur Young in 1769, 'attributed the dearness of their country to the turnpike roads; and reason speaks the truth of their opinion . . . make but a turnpike road through their country and all the cheapness vanishes at once.' But even fifty or more years later there were many areas of England without turnpikes. In these areas the prices of foodstuffs might be either

[1] Elizabeth W. Gilboy, 'The Cost of Living and Real Wages in Eighteenth Century England', *Review of Economic Statistics*, XVIII (1936), pp. 134–43.

lower or higher than in London; they were certainly subject to wider fluctuations.

No one has done more than Mrs Gilboy to make us aware of local variations in the price of labour. But she has not taken full account of the possibility of a similar variation of retail prices or of local peculiarities of diet. Oatmeal remained the staple food of the poor in the north, and rye bread the staple in the Midlands, long after wheaten bread had come into common use in London and the south. To apply contract prices derived from the metropolitan area, and a system of weights based on metropolitan habits, to the earnings of workers in the provinces is indeed a hazardous procedure. What someone has unkindly called Mrs Gilboy's bricklayers dressed up as bluecoat boys would hardly have been recognized as brothers by the pitmen of Northumberland or the weavers of Lancashire or Somerset.

But, if the scheme of expenditure varied from place to place, it varied also from time to time. Rufus T. Tucker, whose gallant attempt to trace the course of real wages of London artisans over two centuries must excite admiration, shows himself alive to this difficulty. His solution is to abandon the use of a fixed yardstick. When some new commodity seems to become significant in the workers' budget, a place is found for it, and the weights attached to other things are adjusted. Mr Tucker divided the figures in his index of wages (for our period the wages of four kinds of building labour at Greenwich and Chelsea) by his chain index of prices in order to determine 'the ability of a typical, regularly employed London artisan to purchase commodities of the sort artisans customarily purchased'.

This typical London artisan was no static figure. At first his consumption was limited to a few commodities, including some inferior grain stuffs. Later he spread his expenditure over a wider range of goods, some of which were relatively expensive ('the commodities of the sort artisans customarily purchased' had changed). One might have supposed that the wider choice now open to him was one element in a rising standard of living. But no. Mr Colin Clark has used Tucker's figures to support his thesis that average real income fell 'from a fairly high level in the seventeenth century to an Asiatic standard at the beginning

of the nineteenth'. That Asiatic standard, I may remark in
passing, included tea and sugar and some other minor products
of Asia hardly known to the London artisan of the seventeenth
century. Would the man of the early nineteenth century really
have welcomed a return to the diet of his great-great-grand-
father? The reception he gave to some well-intentioned efforts
to induce him to use rye instead of wheat in his bread hardly
leaves one in doubt regarding the answer. Like the labourers of
Nottinghamshire, he replied that he had lost his 'rye teeth'.[1]

Mr Tucker's artisan was peculiar in another respect. Whatever his income, he always spent one-sixth of it on rent or one-
fifth on rent and services combined. This is a proportion far
higher than any I have been able to discover in other areas, but
no doubt dwellings were dear in London. It is the fixity of habit
that is peculiar. Mr Tucker says that his index 'attempts to
measure the workman's ability to purchase housing'. But, if it
is true that the workman always spent a fixed proportion of his
income on housing, would not the figures of wages alone serve
as a measure of that ability? In fact, rents are perhaps the most
difficult of all prices to draw into an index number. Few consumer goods are completely standardized. A loaf of bread at a
given time and place may be a very different commodity from a
loaf at another time and place. 'The veal that is sold so cheap in
some distant counties at present,' wrote Malthus, 'bears little
other resemblance than the name, to that which is bought in
London.'[2] But this variation of quality is especially marked in
the case of houses. A cottage with a living room and a single
bedroom is a different commodity from one with four rooms
and an attached wash-house or loom shed. A cottage near a
factory would usually produce a higher rent than one far distant; for the tenant of the first not only avoided a long walk to
and from work but was also able, if he wished, to increase his
income by working overtime without trenching unduly on the
hours of sleep.[3]

---

[1] See C. R. Fay, *The Corn Laws and Social England* (Cambridge University
Press, 1932), p. 4.

[2] Op. cit., p. 317.

[3] A point made in an unpublished thesis by Walter Lazenby, 'The Social and
Industrial History of Styal, 1750–1850' (University of Manchester, 1949).

The truth is that it is not possible to compare the welfare of two groups of people separated widely in time and space. We cannot compare the satisfaction derived from a diet that includes bread, potatoes, tea, sugar and meat with that derived from a diet consisting mainly of oatmeal, milk, cheese and beer. In the early and middle decades of the eighteenth century only a narrow range of commodities competed for the surplus income of the workers. That is why (to the distress of the well-to-do observer) any easement of the position of the poor was taken out in the form of more drink and more leisure – or in 'debauchery and idleness', as the sedate and leisured observer usually put it. Later in the century the range of commodities available widened, and after the French wars new opportunities of travel and education were opened up. No index number can possibly take full account of such matters.

I have made these criticisms and asked these questions in no carping spirit. My object is simply to point to the difficulties of measuring arithmetically changes in the standard of living. The pioneers, as so often happens, have attempted too much. We must restrict our ambitions, realize the limitations of our bag of tricks and refrain from generalizations. We cannot measure changes in real wages by means of an index of wholesale or institutional prices. We cannot apply the price data of one area to the wage data of another. We cannot safely draw up a table to cover a long series of years during the course of which changes may have occurred not only in the nature and variety of the goods consumed but also in human needs and human wants. We require not a single index but many, each derived from retail prices, each confined to a short run of years, each relating to a single area, perhaps even to a single social or occupational group within an area.[1]

I cannot hope at this stage to meet these requirements. All I have to offer are three short tables exhibiting the changes in the

[1] This is a view taken by a distinguished statistician. 'I do not believe that index numbers can serve over very long periods. If the same form is used throughout the difficulty of shifts in the "preference map" cannot be overcome. If the index is obtained by drawing together different forms, then a bias is to be expected, a bias which tends to be amplified over time. In general, index numbers are to be limited to short-run comparisons' (R. G. D. Allen, 'The Economic Theory of Index Numbers', *Economica*, XVI [N.S.], no. 63 [August 1949], 197–203).

cost of staple articles of diet in the area that is often spoken of as the cradle of the factory system. Such virtue as they possess derives from the fact that they are based on retail prices recorded by contemporaries. The first relates to Oldham, a textile town five or six miles from Manchester. The figures are drawn

TABLE 3 *Index of cost of diet in Oldham*
(1791 = 100)

Year	Oatmeal	Flour	Potatoes	Beef	Mutton	Bacon	Butter	Cheese	Total cost of diet
1791 Spring	100	100	100	100	100	100	100	100	100
1792 Spring	105	90	85	100	100	100	100	60	94
1793 Fall	126	102	154	80	100	100	106	90	113
1794	—	—	—	—	—	—	—	—	—
1795 January	121	110	154	110	110	94	112	100	117
1795 May–June	132	151	185	120	120	106	112	110	138
1796	—	—	—	—	—	—	—	—	—
1797	84	82	100	130	130	106	112	130	98
1798	—	—	—	—	—	—	—	—	—
1799 Spring	103	73	85	100	100	88	112	110	92
1800 May	316	245	309	180	180	131	175	200	249
1801 January	290	270	309	160	160	150	188	180	253
1801 October	112	122	92	160	170	150	125	140	124
1802 January	126	135	92	176	180	138	115	132	133
1803 January	100	116	123	160	160	138	138	132	123
1804 January	142	114	154	160	160	124	162	154	139
1805	—	—	—	—	—	—	—	—	—
1806 January	153	141	115	140	140	100	144	154	139
1807 January	—	—	—	—	—	—	—	—	—
1808 January	153	133	185	140	140	112	175	140	148
1809 January	163	176	123	154	154	112	175	170	158

from an unpublished manuscript entitled 'The Chronology or Annals of Oldham' by William Rowbottom,[1] and I am greatly indebted to a former colleague, Miss Frances Collier of the University of Manchester, for the toil involved in extracting them. Like other annalists of the period, Rowbottom began by describing the more sensational events, such as murders and thefts, which occurred in the locality. For 1787 and the succeeding three years there is little of economic interest in his manuscript. But in 1791 he began to make jottings about the prices charged by shopkeepers in Oldham, and as time went on the range of his observations widened and the record became more systematic. There are many months and some years for which little or no information about prices is given; and there

[1] Transcript by Giles Shaw now in the Manchester Public Reference Library.

are several commodities, such as sugar, treacle, malt, coal and candles, the prices of which are given so infrequently as to make it impossible to include them in the index.

When Rowbottom began to keep his record, most of his fellow-townsmen were still domestic workers employed in weaving fustians, calicoes and checks or making hats. Their staple diet consisted of bread, oatmeal porridge, potatoes and a little beef and mutton. In compiling the index, I have accordingly given a weight of 4 each to oatmeal and flour, 2 to potatoes and 1 each to beef, mutton, bacon, butter and cheese. It

TABLE 4   *Index of cost of diet in Manchester and other textile towns*

(1810 = 100)

Year	Oatmeal	Flour	Potatoes	Beef best	Beef coarse	Bacon	Cheese	Butter	Index of cost of diet
1810	100	100	100	100	100	100	100	100	100
1811	100	91	100	100	100	82	112	100	97
1812	150	127	165	100	100	91	108	100	129
1813	130	111	120	106	108	100	119	106	116
1814	93	76	110	112	117	100	119	100	96
1815	87	69	110	100	108	95	112	100	91
1816	83	80	110	94	92	73	85	79	86
1817	127	120	130	94	92	64	85	79	111
1818	107	91	135	100	100	91	108	94	97
1819	90	73	130	100	100	91	92	94	86

will be noticed that the prices of the first three of these fluctuated more violently than those of the others. The very poor, who lived chiefly on meal and potatoes, suffered much in 1795 and were reduced to extremities in 1800–1. In these two years of famine, Rowbottom records, new kinds of cereals, such as barley flour and 'American flour' (presumably of corn), were on sale. The poor gathered docks, 'green sauce', and water cresses to serve as a substitute for potatoes, and nettles were on sale in Oldham at twopence a pound.

The same picture of wide fluctuations in the cost of a standard diet is shown in the figures for the years 1810–19 (see Table 4). These are drawn from a table giving details of wages, the price of provisions and expenditure on poor relief published in the *Manchester Mercury* of 18 January 1820. They relate to 'Manchester and the other principal seats of the Cotton Manufacture' and, although the source is not disclosed, the prices are said to be 'the average retail prices of each year, according to the best information that could be procured'. Again it is clear that the prices of grain foods and potatoes were more volatile than those of meat, bacon, butter and cheese. The table suggests that the cost of the standard diet fell little, if at all, in the four years of depression and distress that followed the end of the war.

The figures in Table 5 relate to Manchester. They are taken

TABLE 5   *Index of cost of diet in Manchester*
(1821 = 100)

Year	Oatmeal	Flour	Potatoes	Beef best	Beef coarse	Pork	Bacon	Cheese	Index of cost of diet
1821	100	100	100	100	100	100	100	100	100
1822	94	117	79	100	117	96	115	95	102
1823	100	92	88	100	108	135	112	121	101
1824	116	115	141	115	117	139	127	126	122
1825	116	119	106	125	158	135	138	137	120
1826	122	112	172	125	158	130	115	137	130
1827	128	112	84	120	133	139	115	147	119
1828	119	119	100	130	133	130	123	132	120
1829	106	127	115	120	125	130	100	132	118
1830	112	119	106	110	100	113	115	105	112
1831	112	115	110	120	117	122	123	116	115

from an estimate of the retail cost of provisions made by the Manchester Chamber of Commerce and published in an appendix to *Manchester Merchants and Foreign Trade* by Arthur Redford.[1] They indicate that throughout the 'twenties the cost of the staple diet moved to a higher rather than to a lower level.

I have resisted the temptation to throw these three figures together so as to offer a single index of the cost of provisions from 1791 to 1831, partly because of slight differences of area and of the range of commodities but mainly because the data are not derived from a common source. The outlines are, however, clear. Following a fall after the famine of 1800–1, the upward movement of prices continued, to a peak in 1812. Thereafter food prices fell to about 1820 but rose again during

[1] Manchester University Press, 1934.

the following decade. In 1831 the standard diet of the poor can hardly have cost much less than in 1791.[1] If this was so, it would seem that any improvement in the standard of living must have come either from a rise in money wages or from a fall in the prices of things not included in this index. One of the striking features of domestic production was the wide variations in the prices offered for labour. In December 1793, according to Rowbottom, the weavers of ginghams at Oldham received 10s. per end; in April 1794 they were paid 19s. and in August of the same year 24s. 4d. During the same period the price of weaving nankeens rose from 16s. to 26s. a piece. Generally, for reasons set forth by Adam Smith, the price of labour rose when the cost of provisions fell and years of dearth were usually years of low wages. In these circumstances the standard of life of the worker was subject to violent fluctuation. One of the merits of the factory system was that it offered, and required, regularity of employment and hence greater stability of consumption. During the period 1790–1830 factory production increased rapidly. A greater proportion of the people came to benefit from it both as producers and as consumers. The fall in the price of textiles reduced the price of clothing. Government contracts for uniforms and army boots called into being new industries, and after the war the products of these found a market among the better-paid artisans. Boots began to take the place of clogs, and hats replaced shawls, at least for wear on Sundays. Miscellaneous commodities, ranging from clocks to pocket handkerchiefs, began to enter into the scheme of expenditure, and after 1820 such things as tea and coffee and sugar fell in price substantially. The growth of trade unions,

---

[1] The first of each of the following figures is the price at Oldham in 1791, the second that at Manchester in 1831: meal (per peck) 19d., 18d.; flour (per peck) 24d., 30d.; potatoes (per load) 6s. 6d., 6s. 3d.; beef (per pound) 5d., 6d.; pork (per pound) 5d., 5½d.; bacon (per pound) 8d., 7d.; cheese (per pound) 5d., 8d. The cost of diet in 1810 was apparently about 5 per cent higher than in 1809 and 60 per cent higher than in 1791. For purposes of comparison with the figures in Table 3 the figures in Table 4 should be increased by 60 per cent.

Between 1819 and 1821 there was a marked drop in the prices of most of the commodities in the index. Roughly the cost of diet in 1821 was the same as in 1791, and the figures in Table 5 are broadly on the same base as those in Table 3. The sample basket of commodities cost about 15 per cent more in 1831 than in 1791.

friendly societies, savings banks, popular newspapers and pamphlets, schools and nonconformist chapels – all give evidence of the existence of a large class raised well above the level of mere subsistence.[1]

There were, however, masses of unskilled or poorly skilled workers – seasonally employed agricultural workers and hand-loom weavers in particular – whose incomes were almost wholly absorbed in paying for the bare necessaries of life, the prices of which, as we have seen, remained high. My guess would be that the number of those who were able to share in the benefits of economic progress was larger than the number of those who were shut out from these benefits and that it was steadily growing. But the existence of two groups within the working class needs to be recognized. Perhaps the explanation of the division of opinion, to which I called attention at the beginning of this paper, rests on this. John Stuart Mill and his fellow economists were thinking of the one group; Rickman and Chadwick had their eyes fixed on the other.

[1] In 1837 or 1838 Thomas Holmes, an old man of eighty-seven, born in 1760, gave to a member of the Liverpool Statistical Society his impressions of the changes that had taken place since his youth at Aldbrough (Holderness): 'There has been a very great increase in the consumption of meat, wheaten bread, poultry, tea and sugar. But it has not reached the poorest, except tea, sugar, and wheaten bread. The poorest are not so well fed. But they are better clothed, lodged and provided with furniture, better taken care of in sickness and mis-fortune. So they are gainers. This, I think, is a plain statement of the whole case.'

Referring to mechanics and artificers, he says, 'The wages of almost all have increased in a proportion faster than the rise in the expenses of living.' When asked, 'Are the poorer classes more intelligent?' he replied, 'Beyond all com-parison.'

4 The British Standard of Living, 1790–1850[1]

E. J. HOBSBAWM

[This article was first published in the *Economic History Review*, second series, vol. X, no. 1, 1957.]

The debate about the standard of living under early industrialism has now continued for some thirty years. Among academic historians, in Britain at any rate, the pendulum has swung away from the classical view, held by inquirers and historians of all political views[2] until the appearance of Clapham's *Economic History of Modern Britain*. It is today heterodox to believe that early industrialization was a catastrophe for the labouring poor of this or other countries, let alone that their standard of living declined. This article proposes to show that the currently accepted view is based on insufficient evidence, and that there is some weighty evidence in favour of the old view. So far as possible, I propose to refrain from using the type of evidence (Royal Commissions, observers' accounts) which has been criticized as biased and unrepresentative. I do not in fact believe it to be unreliable. It is dangerous to reject the consensus of informed and intelligent contemporaries, a majority of whom, as even critics admit,[3] took the dark view. It is illegitimate to assume that even reformers who mobilize public support by drawing attention to dramatic examples of a general evil, are not in fact attacking a general evil. But the classical case can be based, to some extent, on quantitative evidence, and, in order to avoid irrelevant argument, I shall

[1] I am obliged to the staff of the Customs House, Goldsmith's and School of Hygiene and Tropical Medicine libraries for help, and to Prof. T. S. Ashton and Mr John Saville for comments and criticisms.

[2] Cf. J. L. Hammond's list in 'The Industrial Revolution and Discontent', *Economic History Review*, II (1930), pp. 215–28.

[3] T. S. Ashton, 'The standard of life of the workers in England, 1790–1850', *Journal of Economic History*, Supplement IX (1949), pp. 19–38.

rely mainly on it. For the sake of convenience the classical (Ricardo–Malthus–Marx–Toynbee–Hammond) view will be called the *pessimistic*, the modern (Clapham–Ashton–Hayek) view the *optimistic* school.

I

An initial observation is perhaps worth making. There is no *a priori* reason why the standard of living should rise markedly under early industrialism. An initial rise must almost certainly take place, on demographic grounds,[1] but it may be very slight indeed and need not be lasting once the new rhythm of population increase has been set up. It should be remembered that the decrease in mortality which is probably primarily responsible for the sharp rise in population need be due not to an *increase* in *per capita* consumption per year, but to a *greater regularity of supply*; i.e. to the abolition of the periodic shortages and famines which plagued pre-industrial economies and decimated their populations. It is quite possible for the industrial citizen to be worse fed in a normal year than his predecessor, so long as he is more regularly fed.

This is not to deny that the increase in production, which greatly exceeded that of population, in the long run brought about an absolute improvement in material living standards. Whatever we may think of the relative position of labourers compared to other classes, and whatever our theory, no serious student denies that the bulk of people in Northwestern Europe were materially better off in 1900 than in 1800. But there is no reason why living standards should improve at all times. Whether they do, depends on the distribution of the additional resources produced among the population. But we know that under early industrialism (*a*) there was no effective mechanism for making the distribution of the national income more equal and several for making it less so, and (*b*) that industrialization under then prevailing conditions almost certainly required a more burdensome diversion of resources from consumption

---

[1] T. McKeown and R. G. Brown, 'Medical Evidence relating to English population changes', *Population Studies*, IX (1955), p. 119. I find it difficult to escape from the conclusion on p. 141.

than is theoretically necessary, because the investment mechanism was inefficient. A large proportion of accumulated savings were not directly invested in industrialization at all, thus throwing a much greater burden of savings on the rest of the community. In countries with an acute shortage of capital a depression of popular living standards was almost inevitable. In countries such as Britain, where plenty of capital was theoretically available, it was likely, simply because much of what was available was not in fact pressed into the most useful investment. At best, therefore, we should expect improvements in the standard of living to be much slower than they might have been, at worst we should not be surprised to find deterioration.

There is no reason to assume that in countries with a rapidly rising population and a large reserve of rural or immigrant labour, shortage as such is likely to push up real wages for more than limited groups of workers.

It may be argued that industrialization and urbanization automatically improve living-standards in any case, because industrial wages normally tend to be higher than non-industrial or rural ones, and urban consumption standards than village ones. But (*a*) we are not merely concerned with the incomes of one section of the labouring poor, but of all. We must not isolate any group of the labouring poor, whether better or worse off, unless it forms a majority of the population. Moreover (*b*) the argument is not always correct. Thus while in many continental countries social indices, like mortality and literacy, improve faster in town than country, in Britain this was not always so. Lastly (*c*) we must beware of interpreting the qualitative differences between urban and rural, industrial and pre-industrial life *automatically* as differences between 'better' and 'worse'. Unless we bring imponderables into the argument, townsmen are not necessarily better off than countrymen; and as the Hammonds showed, imponderables can also be thrown on the pessimistic side of the scale.

One final point must be made. Optimists often tend to exonerate capitalism from blame for such bad conditions as they admit to have existed. They argue that these were due to insufficient private enterprise, to hangovers from the pre-industrial past or to similar factors. I do not propose to enter into such metaphysical arguments. This paper is concerned primarily with fact, and not with accusation, exculpation or justification. What would have happened if all citizens in Europe in 1800 had behaved as text-books of economics told them to, and if there had been no obstacles or frictions, is not a question for historians. They are, in the first instance, concerned with what did happen. Whether it might have happened differently, is a question which belongs to another argument.

II

We may now consider the views of the 'optimistic' school. Its founder, Clapham, relied primarily on calculations of real wages which showed them to rise in the period 1790 to 1850 at times when contemporaries, and the historians who followed them, assumed that the poor were getting poorer. On the money side these calculations depended mainly on the well-known collections of wage-data by Bowley and Wood. On the cost of living side they depended almost wholly on Silberling's index.[1] It is not too much to say that Clapham's version of the optimistic view stood or fell by Silberling.[2]

It is now generally realized that the statistical basis of Clapham's conclusions is too weak to bear its weight; especially as the argument for the period 1815–40 odd turns largely on the question whether the curve of the cost of living sloped downwards more steeply than that of money-wages, it being admitted that both tended to fall. Clearly in extreme cases, e.g. when prices fall and wages rise or the other way round, even a thin index may be reliable. In this case, however, the possibilities of error are much greater.

[1] Clapham, *Economic History of Modern Britain*, I, p. 601.
[2] To a slight extent it also depended on the choice of period. Today, when most economic historians would place the turning-point between the post-napoleonic period of difficulties and the 'golden age' of the Victorians rather earlier than was once fashionable – in 1842–3 rather than in 1848 or thereabouts – few would deny that things improved rapidly in Britain (though not in Ireland) from the earlier 'forties on, the crisis of 1847 interrupting a period of progress rather than initiating it. But the admission that the middle and later 'forties were a time of improvement does not imply that the whole of the period 1790–1842 or 1815–1842 was, though this is sometimes assumed in careless discussion, as by Chaloner and Henderson, *History Today*, July 1956.

Now our figures for money-wages are chiefly time-rates for skilled artisans (Tucker, Bowley). About piece-workers we know very little. Since we also know little about the incidence of unemployment, short-time etc., our figures cannot be regarded as a reliable reflection of actual earnings. (Clapham, by the way, makes no attempt to discover the extent of unemployment, though mentioning the absence of data about it. His index to vol. I does not even contain the word.) For large sections of the 'labouring poor' – the unskilled, those whose income cannot be clearly expressed in terms of regular money-wages – we are almost completely in the dark. We therefore possess nothing which would be regarded as an adequate index of money-wages today. The weakness of the cost of living figures is equally great. Silberling has been criticized by Cole, by Judges and most recently by Ashton, the most eminent of the 'optimists'.[1] For practical purposes it is no longer safe to generalize about the working-class cost of living on this basis. Indeed, practical, as distinct from methodological, doubt has been thrown on such attempts to construct real wage indices for the first half of the nineteenth century. Thus Ashton's figures for retail prices in some Lancashire towns 1790–1830 show nothing like the post-war fall which Silberling would lead one to expect.[2] Tucker's index of London artisan real wages shows the major improvement in their position in the period 1810–43 to have occurred in 1813–22.[3] But, as we shall see, these were years of stagnant or falling *per capita* consumption of meat in London, and of sugar and tobacco nationally; facts which hardly support the assumption of rising real wages.

In defence of Clapham it ought to be said that he was more cautious in his conclusion than some of the optimistic vulgarizers have been. Thus Silberling's index itself shows living costs to have remained fairly steady for about twenty years after 1822, rising and falling about a level trend. Not until after 1843 did they drop below the 1822 level. Tucker's, a later index,

---

[1] Cole and Postgate, *The Common People*; G. D. H. Cole, *Short History of the British Working Class Movement* (1947 edn); A. V. Judges in *Riv. Stor. Italiana*, 1951, pp. 162–79; T. S. Ashton, loc. cit.

[2] T. S. Ashton, loc. cit.

[3] R. S. Tucker, 'Real Wages of Artisans in London 1729–1935', *Journal of the American Statistical Association*, XXXI (1936, no. 193).

shows that between 1822 and 1842 the real wages of London artisans rose above the 1822 level in only four years, the average improvement for the whole period, even for them, being only about 5 or 6 per cent. The two decades of, at best, relative stagnation of real wages – which R. C. O. Matthews confirms for the 1830s[1] are significant, though often omitted from the argument. In fact, one is bound to conclude that Clapham has had a surprisingly easy passage, thanks largely to the extreme feebleness of the reply of his chief opponent, J. L. Hammond,[2] who virtually accepted Clapham's statistics and shifted the argument entirely onto moral and other non-material territories.

However, today, the deficiencies of Clapham's argument have been admitted and the most serious of the optimists, Professor Ashton, has in fact abandoned it, though this fact has not always been realized.[3] Instead, he relies on arguments or assumption of three types. First, on various theoretical arguments designed to prove that a rise in real wages must have taken place. Second, on factual evidence of rising material prosperity – such as improvements in housing, food, clothing, etc. Third, on the – so far as one can judge – unsupported assumption that the part of the labouring population whose real wages improved must have been larger than the part whose real wages did not. It is admitted that conditions for part of the working population did not improve. I do not propose to discuss the first lot of arguments, since, if there is evidence that the standard of living did not improve significantly or at all at the relevant periods, they automatically fall to the ground.

It is perhaps worth observing how scanty the hard evidence for the optimistic view is today, when it can no longer rely on Clapham's type of support. It rests essentially on the sort of evidence adduced by McCulloch, an early optimist, in 1839, though today it is often less detailed.[4] Now McCulloch's case[5]

[1] R. C. O. Matthews, *A Study in Trade Cycle History: Economic Fluctuations in Great Britain, 1833–42* (Cambridge, 1954).

[2] J. L. Hammond, loc. cit. and J. H. Clapham, I, pp. ix–x.

[3] T. S. Ashton, loc. cit. and *Economic History of England: The Eighteenth Century* (1955), pp. 233–5.

[4] T. S. Ashton in *Journal of Economic History*, and *The Industrial Revolution* (1948).

[5] *Statistical Account of the British Empire* (1839), II, p. 494 ff.

is built on the following foundations. The substitution of white bread for brown is known by the known, but not measured, decline in the consumption of brown cereals since 1760, in Cornwall of barley-eating since 1800. But McCulloch's estimate that only 20,000 rye-eaters were left by 1839 is patently wild. (Incidentally, his source for Cornwall[1] seems to talk only of the St Austell area, not the whole county.) The increase in meat consumption rests on the assumed increase in the weight of livestock sold at Smithfield, the actual numbers of animals having only kept pace with the growth of London population since 1740–50. But (*a*), as we shall see, the number of beasts sold at Smithfield had *not* kept pace with London population growth, as McCulloch must have known quite well, and at least one contemporary did know.[2] Moreover, (*b*) the view that weight increased dramatically has been virtually put out of court by Fussell.[3] Lastly, (*c*) McCulloch's estimate of 800 lb. as the contemporary carcass weight of beef was grossly inflated. Other estimates give it as 668 lb. (1821), 630 lb. (1836), 640 lb. (Smithfield 1842),[4] while both Braithwaite Poole (1852) and the Smithfield butchers consulted on McCulloch's estimate in 1856 were also less sanguine.[5] For clothing, McCulloch relied on the fall of prices of cotton goods and not on direct evidence. For Scotland he gave a confident, but statistically undocumented, comparison between past and present. He did not mention potatoes, dairy produce, groceries, etc.

His statistical basis was thus slight, and his bias verged on the disingenuous. (The critics of industrialism were not the only ones to choose evidence to suit themselves.) Subsequent

[1] *Select Committee on Agriculture*, Parl. Papers, 1833, V, Q. 3431 ff.

[2] *London*, ed. C. Knight (1842), II, 318 (chapter: 'Smithfield') estimates the rise in population from 1740/50 to 1831 at 218 per cent, in beef at 110, in sheep at 117 per cent. As the author is also aware that Davenant's estimate of 370 lb. for the carcass weight of beef in the early eighteenth century is probably much too low, it is difficult to see how he arrives at his optimistic conclusions about the *per capita* rise in London meat consumption.

[3] G. E. Fussell, 'The size of English cattle in the 18th century', *Agricultural History*, III (1929), p. 160 ff; also *Agric. Hist.* IV (1930). McCulloch accepts Sinclair's estimate of Smithfield weights in 1785 uncritically.

[4] *Select Committee on the Depressed State of Agriculture*, Parl. Papers, 1821, IX, 267; *General Statistics of the British Empire* (1836); Knight, op. cit., p. II, 325.

[5] Braithwaite Poole, *Statistics of British Commerce* (1852); G. Dodd, *The Food of London* (1856), p. 213.

optimistic scholars have not investigated the evidence much further. Thus the data on meat-consumption appear to have been almost totally neglected. Even Professor Ashton's paper on the standard of living, 1790–1830, perhaps the fullest recent discussion, and vastly more scholarly than McCulloch, rests on few and scattered data.[1]

The evidence is certainly too sketchy to sustain the assumption, which today appears to be fundamental to the optimistic view, that the proportion of the labouring population whose conditions improved must have been larger than the rest. There is, as we have seen, no theoretical reason for making this assumption about the period 1790–1840 odd. It is, of course, impossible to verify owing to the absence of adequate data on the British income structure at the time, but what we know about this structure in later periods (and in admittedly better-off periods at that) does not support it. As I have attempted to show at greater length elsewhere,[2] about 40 per cent of the industrial working class in later periods lived at or below the poverty-line, i.e. at or below subsistence level on the prevailing definitions of this concept. Perhaps 15 per cent belonged to a favoured stratum which was in a clear position to improve its real wages at almost all times. That is, the first group lived in what amounted to a permanently glutted labour market, the second in one of the permanent relative labour scarcity, except during bad slumps. The rest of the labouring population was distributed between the two groups. Only if we assume *either* that in 1790–1850 the favoured stratum was markedly larger, the poor stratum markedly smaller than later *or* that at least five-sevenths of the intermediate stratum were more like than unlike the labour aristocracy, does the optimistic view, in so far as it is based on assumptions about income structure, hold good. This is not very plausible, and until there is more

---

[1] In addition to the usual wage-sources (Bowley and Wood, Gilboy, Tucker) this paper, in fact, contains only factual material about Lancashire prices drawn from Rowbottom, the *Manchester Mercury* and A. Redford's *Manchester Merchants and Foreign Trade 1794–1858* (1934), and an opinion of Thomas Holmes. This last is the only new source definitely supporting the optimistic view. Of course, Prof. Ashton's purpose in the paper was to provide new arguments rather than new evidence.

[2] 'The Labour Aristocracy in 19th century Britain', in J. Saville (ed.), *Democracy and the Labour Movement* (1954).

evidence for the optimistic assumption, there is no reason for making it. For the sake of brevity, I do not propose to enter further into the complex discussion of social stratification among the 'labouring poor' here.

It thus seems clear that the optimistic view is not based on as strong evidence as is often thought. Nor are there overwhelming theoretical reasons in its favour. It may, of course, turn out to be correct, but until it has been much more adequately supported or argued, there seems to be no major reason for abandoning the traditional view. In view of the fact that there is also statistical evidence tending to support that view, the case for its retention becomes stronger.

III

We may consider three types of evidence in favour of the pessimistic view: those bearing on (*a*) mortality and health, (*b*) unemployment and (*c*) consumption. In view of the weaknesses of wage and price-data, discussed above, it is best not to consider them here; in any case actual consumption figures shed a more reliable light on real wages. However, we know too little about the actual structure of the population to isolate the movements of working-class indices from the rest of the 'labouring poor' and of other classes. But this would be troublesome only if the indices showed a fairly marked rise, which they do not. Since the 'labouring poor' clearly formed the majority of the population, a general index showing stability or deterioration is hardly compatible with a significant improvement of their situation, though it does not exclude improvement among a minority of them.

A.   SOCIAL INDICES

Our best indices are mortality rates (average expectation of life, infantile, TB mortality etc.), morbidity rates and anthropometric data. Unfortunately in Britain we lack any reliable anthropometric data such as the French, and any index of health such as the percentage of rejected recruits.[1] Nor have we

[1] We cannot assume that British servicemen in this period, or prisoners, are a representative sample of the population.

any useful morbidity figures. The Friendly Societies, whose actuarial advisers made some useful calculations about sickness rates,[1] cannot be regarded as representative samples, since it is agreed that they included mainly the more prosperous or stably employed workers; and in any case, as Farr (1839) demonstrates,[2] there is little enough evidence from them before that date. It is possible that work on hospital records may allow us to find out more about sickness trends, but too little is available at present for judgment.[3]

We must therefore rely on mortality rates. These have their limitations, though it has been plausibly argued that even the crudest of them – general mortality below the age of 50[4] – is a sensitive indicator of living standards. Still, a high or rising mortality rate, a low expectation of life, are not to be neglected. We need not be too much troubled by the known imperfections of the figures, at any rate where trends emerge over periods of time. In any case, the worst imperfection, the fact that births are less completely registered than deaths – thus swelling earlier figures for infant mortality – helps to correct a pessimistic bias. For as registration improves, recorded mortality rates also drop automatically on paper, though in fact they may change much less in reality.

The general movement of mortality rates is fairly well known. On theoretical grounds, such as those discussed by McKeown and Brown,[5] it is almost inconceivable that there was not a real fall in mortality rates due to improvements in living standards at the beginning of industrialization, at least for a while. General mortality rates fell markedly from the 1780s to the 1810s and thereafter rose until the 1840s. This 'coincided with a change in the age-distribution favourable to a

[1] E.g. F. G. P. Neison, 'Contributions to Vital Statistics', *J. Stat. Soc.*, VIII (1845), p. 290 ff; IX (1846), 50 ff.

[2] In J. McCulloch, *Statistical Account*, II.

[3] However, two long series for Doncaster and Carlisle (1850) in the *Reports to the General Board of Health* point in the same direction.

[4] S. Swaroop and K. Uemura, 'An attempt to evolve a comprehensive indicator to quantify the component "health, including demographic conditions" ', *World Health Working Paper No 8*, WHO/PHA/25 (22 November 1955), duplicated. I owe this reference to Mrs M. Jefferys, School of Hygiene and Tropical Medicine, London.

[5] Ibid.

low death-rate, namely an increase in the proportion of those in healthy middle life'.[1] The figures therefore understate the real rise in mortality rates, assuming the same age-composition throughout the period. The rise is said to have been due chiefly to higher infantile and youth mortality, especially in the towns, but figures for Glasgow 1821–35 suggest that there it was due primarily to a marked increase in the mortality of men of working age, greatest in the age-groups from 30 to 60.[2] Social conditions are the accepted explanation for this. Edmonds, who discusses the Glasgow figures, observed (1835) that 'this is just what might be expected to occur, on the supposition of the rising adult population possessing a lower degree of vitality than their immediate predecessors'.[3] On the other hand we must not forget that mortality rates did not improve drastically until very much later – say, until the 1870s or 1880s – and may therefore be less relevant to the movement of living standards than is sometimes supposed; (alternatively, that living standards improved much more slowly after the 1840s than is often supposed). Nevertheless, the rise in mortality rates in the period 1811–41 is clearly of *some* weight for the pessimistic case, all the more as modern work, especially the studies of Holland during the Second World War, tend to link such rates much more directly to the amount of income and food consumption than to other social conditions.[4]

B. UNEMPLOYMENT

There is room for much further work on this subject, whose neglect is rather inexplicable. Here I merely wish to draw attention to some scattered pieces of information which support a pessimistic rather than a rosy view.

[1] T. H. Marshall, 'The Population Problem during the Industrial Revolution' *Economic History* (1929), p. 453.

[2] T. R. Edmonds, 'On the Mortality of Glasgow and on the increasing Mortality in England', *Lancet*, II (1835–6), p. 353. Summarized by Farr in McCulloch, op. cit., II.

[3] T. R. Edmonds, 'On the law of mortality', *Lancet*, I (1835–6), p. 416.

[4] Prof. McKeown of Birmingham has drawn my attention to these. The rise of Dutch death and sickness rates during and their fall after the war must have been due exclusively to variations in food consumption, since other social conditions – e.g. housing – did not improve seriously during the period when the rates declined.

Little as we know about the period before the middle 1840s, most students would agree that the real sense of improvement among the labouring classes thereafter was due less to a rise in wage-rates, which often remained surprisingly stable for years, or to an improvement in social conditions, but to the up-grading of labourers from very poorly to less poorly paid jobs, and above all to a decline in unemployment or a greater regularity of employment. In fact, unemployment in the earlier period had been heavy. Let us consider certain components and aspects of it.

We may first consider *pauperism*, the permanent core of poverty, fluctuating relatively little with cyclical changes – even in 1840–2.[1] The trends of pauperism are difficult to determine, owing to the fundamental changes brought about by the New Poor Law, but its extent is sufficiently indicated by the fact that in the early 1840s something like 10 per cent of the total population were probably paupers. They were not necessarily worse off than the rest, for Tufnell, in the Second Annual Report of the Poor Law Commissioners, estimated that farm labourers ate less than paupers; perhaps 30 per cent less in crude weight of foodstuffs. This was also the case in depressed towns.[2]

As to the impact of *cyclical slumps*, we have evidence for the worst of these, that of 1841–2. Ashworth's survey of Bolton may be summarized as shown in Table I. It will be seen that unemployment of ironworkers in this industrial centre was higher than the national average for the Ironfounders' Union, which was then about 15 per cent.

We are, as it happens, quite well informed about unemployment in this depression. In the Vauxhall Ward of Liverpool[3] a little over 25 per cent of smiths and engineers were unemployed,

---

[1] Thus in 581 Unions the number of able-bodied paupers only rose by one-eighth from the Lady Day quarter of 1841 to that of 1842. *J. Stat. Soc.*, VI (1843), p. 256.

[2] *Devizes and Wiltshire Gazette*, 13 January 1842.

[3] J. Finch, *Statistics of the Vauxhall Ward, Liverpool* (Liverpool, 1842); a first-rate piece of work, which gives unemployment figures for each working-class stratum, and part-time figures broken down into 5, 4, 3, 2, 1 day's work. The last two groups he reckons among the unemployed, the first two among the employed.

TABLE I   *Unemployment in Bolton, 1842*[1]

Trade	Total employed in 1836	Total employed whole or part-time in 1842	Percentage unemployed
Mills	8,124	3,063 (full time)	60
Ironworkers	2,110	1,325 (short time)	36
Carpenters	150	24	84
Bricklayers	120	16	87
Stonemasons	150	50	66
Tailors	500	250	50
Shoemakers	80	40	50

Source: H. Ashworth, 'Statistics of the present depression of trade in Bolton', *Journ. Stat. Soc.*, V (1842), p. 74.

in Dundee[2] somewhat over 50 per cent of the mechanics and the shipbuilders. Slightly under 50 per cent of the Liverpool shoemakers, over half the Liverpool tailors, two-thirds of the London tailors[3] were unemployed, only 5 out of 160 Dundee tailors were in full work. Three-quarters of the plasterers, well over half the bricklayers in Liverpool, almost five-sixths of the masons, three-quarters of the carpenters, slaters, plumbers, etc. in Dundee had no work. Neither had half the 'labourers' and almost three-quarters of the women workers in the Liverpool ward. Table II summarizes various contemporary inquiries.

The list could be prolonged. (I have myself suggested some indices of skilled unemployment at this period elsewhere.)[4]

Such figures mean little, unless we remember what they implied for the standard of living. Clitheroe (normal population 6,700, normal employment in the five main factories 2,500) had 2,300 paupers in 1842; the Brontës' Haworth (population 2,400), 308.[5] Twenty per cent of the population of Nottingham

---

[1] The percentages do not allow for the possible increases in the labour force since 1836, and thus overstate unemployment. But they may serve as an order of magnitude.

[2] *Report of the Statistical Committee appointed by the Anti-Corn Law Conference held in London 8–12th March 1842* (London, n.d.). All data in this paragraph, except where otherwise stated, are from this valuable compendium.

[3] *Facts and Figures. A periodical record of statistics applied to current questions* (London, October 1841), p. 29.

[4] E. J. Hobsbawm, 'The Tramping Artisan', *Economic History Review*, 2nd series, III (1951).

[5] *Report to the General Board of Health: Clitheroe* (1850); ibid. *Haworth* (1853).

was on the Poor Law, 33 per cent of that of Paisley on charity.[1]
15–20 per cent of the population of Leeds had an income of
less than *one shilling* per head per week;[2] over one-third of the
families in the Vauxhall Ward of Liverpool had an income of

TABLE II   *Unemployment in some towns, 1841–2*

Town	Fit for work	Fully	Partly	Unemployed
		Employed		
Liverpool, Vauxhall	4,814	1,841	595	2,378
Stockport	8,215	1,204	2,866	4,145
Colne	4,923	964	1,604	2,355
Bury	3,982	1,107	—	—
Oldham	19,500	9,500	5,000 (half-time)	5,000
Accrington (textiles)	3,738	1,389	1,622	727
Wigan	4,109	981	2,572	1,563

less than five shillings a week, indeed most of them had no
visible income at all.[3] In this ward total earnings had halved
since 1835, meat consumption had halved, bread consumption
had remained stable, oatmeal consumption had doubled, potato
consumption risen by more than a third, and similarly dramatic
declines in purchases – 40 per cent in Manchester – are reported
in all the towns investigated by the Anti-Corn Law League. No
discussion which overlooks the massive waves of destitution
which swamped large sections of the labouring poor in every
depression, can claim to be realistic.

Vagrancy provides another little-used index of unemployment, since out-of-work labourers tended to tramp in search of
jobs. The actual amount was large enough to have appalled the
Tudor administrators who were troubled with sturdy beggars.
The only full 'census' of vagrants, that undertaken in 1847–51
by the police of the Derwent division of Cumberland, recorded
42,386 in 1847 (*excluding* Poor Law vagrants), 42,000 in 1848
(*including* them) and – as proof of the cyclical nature of this
aspect of unemployment – rapidly declining numbers in subsequent years: 33,500, 24,000, 18,000.[4] Allowing for those who

---

[1] *Statistical Committee of Anti-Corn-Law League*, p. 45.
[2] *Facts and Figures*, loc. cit.   [3] Finch, op. cit., p. 34.
[4] *Report to the General Board of Health: Keswick* (1852), p. 45. Part of the
diminution was due to a Poor Law ruling to bar long-distance vagrants.

used neither common lodging houses nor the Poor Law, but probably not allowing for the 'tramping artisans' who were catered for by their unions, we may well have had something like 1,000 tramps a week passing up and down this highway during a slump. Whether the estimate that 13,000 vagrants of all kinds passed through Preston in 1832[1] indicates incomplete information or a rise in unemployment between 1832 and 1847–51, is an open question.

It is, however, clear that vagrancy tended to increase from the Napoleonic wars until the early 1830s, largely because of 'commercial fluctuation',[2] partly because of the increase in Irish vagrants – that is to say, Irish-born unemployed rather than seasonal harvesters.[3] The following Table III illustrates this trend:

TABLE III   *Vagrancy trends, 1803–34*

	Great North Road Vagrants with passes			Irish vagrants passed out of		
	all*		Irish***		Middlesex***	Berks**	Wilts***
1803	569 (Royston)						
1807–28	540						
1811–12	1,014	1811	7	1811	1,464	301	80
1815–16	2,894	1816	58	1816	1,974	690	121
1820	7,000			1821	4,583	1,850	1,148
		1826	331	1826	3,307	2,044	1,811
		1831	1,751	1831	9,281	5,428	4,510

* V.C.H. Cambridgeshire, II, 103–4.
** *Report of R.C. on Poor Law*, App. E, Parl. Papers 1834, XXXVIII, pp. 249–50.
*** Same source. Includes Scots paupers.

Unemployment indices such as these may bear directly on the argument between optimists and pessimists, as in the case of the building trade, where the optimistic view (Clapham) based on 'real wages' clashes particularly sharply with the pessimistic

[1] *Report of Royal Commission on the Poor Law*, Appendix E, Parl. Papers, XXXVIII (1834), p. 318.

[2] Ibid., pp. 305–6: 'It cannot be denied that our annual reports tend to prove that the gross number of pauper travellers has been doubled between the years ending 1 January 1822 and 1 January 1833. It has been a period of great commercial fluctuation and much political excitement.' (S. S. Duncan of Bristol.)

[3] *Select Committee on Irish Vagrants*, Parl. Papers, XVI (1833), 362 (40) specifically points out that they were not seasonal harvesters.

view (Postgate), based also on literary evidence.[1] There is no debate about the relatively good wages of building artisans. However, Shannon's brick index[2] shows that output, and hence also employment, in the industry fluctuated in the following manner. Periods of rapid expansion (e.g. 1800–4) are followed by periods of slower expansion (e.g. 1805–14) and these in turn by slumps (e.g. 1815–19). Both of the latter phases create unemployment, for in an industry geared to expansion – and which, haphazardly recruited under private enterprise, tends to produce an excess labour force anyway – even a slowing of expansion will throw marginal workers out of jobs. In an era of pioneer industrialization under private enterprise this effect will be all the greater, because workers are not yet accustomed to a fluctuating and blind economy. Thus builders in pre-industrial places are accustomed to a labour force whose size is fairly well adjusted to the 'normal' amount of repair and replacement, and perhaps to a gradual expansion of demand by known consumers.[3]

Now we know for a fact that builders, including artisans, tended to become exceptionally militant in the early 1830s. There is also some literary evidence about poverty and destitution among them. Clapham's arguments cannot explain the first or admit the second, but Shannon's index explains both, for it suggests a short, sharp, building boom in 1820–4, followed by a slowing expansion in 1825–9 and a marked slump in 1830–4. Nothing is more plausible than that, by the early 'thirties, there should be both poverty and discontent. This example shows very clearly how dangerous it is to rely on what purports to be statistical evidence, while neglecting equally relevant quantitative factors, which happen not always to be as easily traced as the building trade.

Nor is the force of such arguments confined to builders. They apply to all manner of other crafts (including their attached labourers and dependents) which made the transition from the pre-industrial to the industrial rhythm of economic movement. The London furniture-makers whose plight Mayhew describes,

[1] Clapham, *Economic History of Modern Britain*, I, p. 548, esp. the superior-sounding footnote, R. W. Postage, *The Builders' History* (1923), p. 33.

[2] H. A. Shannon, 'Bricks, a trade index', *Economica*, 1934.

[3] The case of large capital cities and public works is somewhat different.

and whose decline is shown by the collapse of their unions and collective agreements in our period, are a case in point.[1] Local studies would no doubt reveal similar cases elsewhere, perhaps among the Sheffield metal operatives, after the collapse of their 'golden age' in the 1810s and 1820s. It is too often forgotten that something like 'technological' unemployment was not confined purely to those workers who were actually replaced by new machines. It could affect almost all pre-industrial industries and trades surviving into the industrial age; that is, as Clapham has shown, a great many. Doubtless the general expansion of the early industrial period (say 1780–1811) tended to diminish unemployment except during crises; doubtless the decades of difficulty and adjustment after the wars tended to make the problem more acute. From the later 1840s, as I have tried to show elsewhere,[2] the working classes began to adjust themselves to life under a new set of economic rules, recognized and – in so far as 'political economy' and union policy could do so – counteracted. But it is highly probable that the period 1811–42 saw abnormal problems and abnormal unemployment, such as is not revealed by the general 'real wage' indices.

Whether further study can give us more adequate figures about unemployment in the first half of the century is a matter for debate. It will certainly be unable to measure adequately the occasional, seasonal or intermittent unemployment and the permanent bulk of underemployment, though no estimate of real wages is worth much which neglects this. An estimate for Leeds may be quoted. It almost certainly underestimates the case, even if we assume that Leeds builders worked a much longer season than the 6–7 months of eighteenth-century London builders,[3] but at any rate it indicates the deductions from theoretical wage-rates which might have to be made (Table IV). The mass of unskilled and, by definition, casual trades are not comprised in this or any other practicable list.

These notes on unemployment are sufficient to throw doubt

---

[1] H. Mayhew, *London Labour and the London Poor*, III, p. 232 ff. For a similar crisis among tailors 1825–34, *The Red Republican*, I, 23 (1850), pp. 177–9.

[2] 'The Tramping Artisan', loc. cit.

[3] R. Campbell, *The London Tradesmen* (1747).

TABLE IV   *Average unemployment per year, and weekly wages corrected for this. Leeds, 1838.*[1]

Trades working 12 months	Weekly wages	Corrected weekly wages	Trades working 11 months	Weekly wages	Corrected weekly wages
Clothdrawers	24/6	24/6	Tailors	16/–	14/8
Smiths	19/–	19/–	Joiners	19/6	17/11
Millwrights	26/–	26/–	Saddlers	21/–	19/3
Plane Makers	21/–	21/–	Curriers	20/–	19/1
Gunsmiths	25/–	25/–	Brassfounders	25/–	24/1
Mechanics	24/–	24/–	Coopers	20/–	19/1
Ironmoulders	25/–	25/–	Printers	21/–	19/3
Turners	22/–	22/–			
Worsted Piecers	4/6	4/6			
Preparers	6/6	6/6			

Trades working 10 months			Trades working 9 months		
Shoemakers	14/–	11/8	Painters	20/–	15/–
Plumbers	23/–	19/2	Clothpressers	20/–	15/–
Woolsorters	21/–	17/6	Slubbers	24/–	18/–
Woodturners	17/–	14/2	Plasterers	18/–	13/6
Masons	22/–	18/4	Bricklayers	23/–	17/3
Weavers	13/–	10/10	Woollen Piecers	5/–	3/9
Hatters	24/–	20/–	Woollen Fillers	6/–	4/6
Woolcombers	14/–	11/8	Dyers	22/–	16/6
Wheelwrights	18/–	15/–	Woodsawyers	20/–	15/–

upon the less critical statements of the optimistic view, but not to establish any alternative view. They may perhaps serve to remind us how much work there is still to be done in this field.

IV

C. CONSUMPTION FIGURES

The discussion of these neglected sources is necessarily rather long, and the technical aspects of it have been relegated to a special Appendix. As Britain was not a bureaucratic state, we lack official national data, except for wholly imported articles. Nevertheless, we can get a good deal more information than has hitherto been brought into the discussion. This shows that,

[1] 'Conditions of the Town of Leeds and Its Inhabitants', *J. Stat. Soc.*, II, (1839), p. 422.

from the later 1790s until the early 1840s, there is no evidence of any major rise in the *per capita* consumption of several food-stuffs, and in some instances evidence of a temporary fall which had not yet been completely made good by the middle 1840s. If the case for deterioration in this period can be established firmly, I suggest that it will be done on the basis of consumption data.

Tea, sugar and tobacco, being wholly imported, furnish national consumption figures which may be divided by the estimated population to give a crude index of *per capita* consumption.[1] However, we note that Clapham, though an optimist and aware of the figures, wisely refused to use them as an argument in his favour since absolute *per capita* consumption in this period was low, and such increases as occurred were disappointingly small. Indeed, the contrast between the curve before and after the middle 1840s when it begins to rise sharply, is one of the strongest arguments on the pessimistic side.[2] All three series show a slowly rising trend and after the 1840s a much sharper rise, though tobacco consumption fell (probably owing to increased duties) in the 1810s. The tobacco series includes Irish consumption after the middle 1820s and is thus difficult to use. The tea series is also hard to interpret, since it reflects not merely the capacity to buy, but also the secular trend to abandon older beverages for a new one. The significance of tea-drinking was much debated by contemporaries, who were far from considering it as an automatic sign of improving living standards. At all events it only shows four periods of decline – 1815–16, 1818–19, a dramatically sharp fall in 1836–7 after a sharp rise, and a slighter fall in 1839–40. Tea seems to have been immune to the slumps of 1826 and, more surprisingly, 1841–2, which makes it suspect as an index of living standards. Tobacco does not reflect the slump of 1836–7, but does reflect the others, though not much. Anyway, this article shows virtually stable consumption. Sugar is the most sensitive indicator though – owing to various outside factors – it does not always reflect trade-cycle movements. It shows the slumps of 1839–40 and

[1] The most accessible source for them is Gayer, Rostow and Schwartz, *Growth and Fluctuations of the British Economy 1790–1850.*

[2] Henderson and Chaloner, loc. cit., blur this distinction by using the sugar consumption figures for 1844–7 to indicate an improvement which, e.g., the consumption figures for 1837–43 do not show.

1841–2 well. Broadly speaking there is no tendency for sugar consumption to rise above the Napoleonic peak until well into the 1840s. There is a sharp post-war decline, a sharp rise to rather lower levels after 1818, a slow rise – almost a plateau – until 1831, and then an equally slow decline or stagnation until 1843 or 1844. Tea, sugar and tobacco indicate no marked rise in the standards of living, but beyond this little can be deduced from the crude series.

The case of *meat* is different. Here we possess at least two indices, the Smithfield figures for London for the entire period, and the yield of the excise on hides and skins for the period up to 1825. The Smithfield figures[1] show that, while London's population index rose from 100 in 1801 to 202 in 1841, the number of beef cattle slaughtered rose only to 146, or sheep to 176 in the same period. The following Table V gives the figures by decades:

TABLE V   *Decennial percentage increase in London population,*
beef and sheep at Smithfield, 1801–51

Date population	Animals ave. of	Index figure			Decennial increase		
		Population	Beef	Sheep	Population	Beef	Sheep
1801	1800–4	100	100	100			
1811	1810–12	119	105	119	+19	+ 5	+19
1821	1819–22	144	113	135	+25	+ 8	+16
1831	1830–34	173	127	152	+29	+14	+17
1841	1840–43	203	146	176	+30	+19	+24
1851	1850–52*	246	198	193	+43	+42	+17**

* The choice of base-dates for the animals cannot be rigid. Thus 1800–4 is chosen, because say 1800–2 would give abnormally high figures, thus under-stating the rise in the following decade. For sheep 1840–2 has been taken as a base-date, because the exceptional high figure for 1843 would overstate the decennial rise. The choice of different dates would change the results slightly, but not substantially.

** A possible explanation for this low figure is found in the Appendix.

[1] There are numerous printed sources for these. For the eighteenth century, Ashton, *Economic History of England, The Eighteenth Century.* Thereafter, *House of Lords Sessional Papers 56 of 1822:* 'Meat cattle and sheep sold in Smithfield 1790–1821', *Parl. Papers,* 1837–8, XLVII, 164, *Statistical Illustrations of the British Empire* (1827), p. 105; J. Fletcher, 'Statistical Account of the markets of London', *J. Stat. Soc.,* X (1847), p. 345; Dodd, op. cit., p. 241. The sources give weekly figures. For the population figures see R. Price-Williams, 'The Population of London 1801–81', *J. R. Stat. S.,* XLVIII (1885), p. 349.

It will be seen that the increase in beef lagged behind that in population in all decades until the 1840s. Mutton also lagged – though less – except in the first decade. On the whole a *per capita* decline in London meat consumption up to the 1840s is thus almost certain.

The Excise on hides and leather yields somewhat cruder figures. (The sources are discussed in the Appendix.) The following table summarizes what little we can get from them (Table VI):

TABLE VI   *Yield of Excise on hides and skins in London and rest of country 1801*
(1800–1 for Excise) = 100

Date	Population	Country yield	London yield
1801	100	100	100
1811	114·5	122	107
1821	136	106*	113*
1825	150	135	150

* For reasons discussed below, this is probably understated.

Without going further into the somewhat complex discussion of the sources, it seems clear that the figures do not indicate a major rise in *per capita* meat consumption.

About *cereals and potatoes*, the staple of the poor man's diet, we can also find out some things. The fundamental fact is that, as contemporaries already knew,[1] wheat production and imports did not keep pace with the growth of population so that the amount of wheat available *per capita* fell steadily from the late eighteenth century until the 1850s, the amount of potatoes available rising at about the same rate.[2] It follows that, whatever the literary evidence, somebody *must* during this period have shifted away from wheat; presumably to potatoes. The simplest view would be that the major change from brown to white bread had already taken place by, say, the 1790s, and that the drift from wheat took place thereafter; but this would not explain the almost certain later drift from brown to white

[1] W. Jacob in *Select Committee on the State of Agriculture*, Parl. Papers, VIII, (1836), i, Q. 26–32.
[2] I have followed the calculations of R. N. Salaman, *History and Social influence of the Potato* (Cambridge, 1949), App. IV, which discusses sources.

bread in the North and West. But this may have been 'paid for' by a decline of *per capita* consumption elsewhere. This is technically possible. The mean consumption of breadstuffs among farm labourers in 1862 was about $14\frac{1}{2}$ lb. per week. Twelve counties[1] consumed less than this – from $10\frac{1}{4}$ to $11\frac{3}{4}$ lb., six more than 13 lb., fourteen about the average.[2] Where *per capita* consumption varied so widely – between $10\frac{1}{4}$ and $15\frac{1}{4}$, not to mention the $18\frac{3}{4}$ of Anglesey, there is scope for both an earlier decline in *per capita* consumption in some places and for considerable 'compensation' between counties. However it is not my purpose to suggest explanations. All we can say is, that a rise in the *per capita* consumption of white bread in this period *at nobody's expense* is out of the question. Wheat consumption may have fallen with or without additional potato consumption, or some areas may have seen it rise at the expense of others (with or without a rise in potatoes).

We have no general statistics about the consumption of other common foodstuffs. It is difficult to see anything but a decline of *milk*, because cow-keeping must have declined with urbanization (though it probably continued in towns on a larger scale than is sometimes admitted) and because of the decline of the traditional rural diet which relied heavily on 'white meats'. It survived longer in the North and West. Even in 1862 some fortunate groups of poor workers stuck to it, doubtless much to their benefit: the Macclesfield silk weavers consumed 41·5 fluid oz. per head per week, as against the 11 oz. of the Coventry weavers, the 7·6 oz. of the Spitalfields weavers and the 1·6 oz. of Bethnal Green.[3] But all the evidence points to a decline in milk consumption. Not so with *butter*, which was evidently – and naturally, since bread formed so large a part of the labourer's diet – considered a greater necessity than meat.[4] In Dukinfield and Manchester (1836) outlays on it were

---

[1] Six in the south-east and south, the rest industrial ones. No figures are given for six other southern and south-western counties.

[2] *6th Report of the Medical Officer to the Privy Council* (1863), pp. 216–330: 'The Food of the Poorer Labouring Classes. A pioneer investigation.'

[3] Ibid.

[4] The (non-quantitative) survey of town workers' diets in *Royal Commission on the Poor Laws*, App. B., Parl. Papers, 1834, XXXVI, Q. 40 of town questionnaires, seems to mention butter mainly as part of rather poor diets.

comparable to those on meat, and comparison with 1841 shows that they were rather inelastic.[1] The few comparable budgets from Eden[2] show a similar pattern of expenditure, though perhaps a rather smaller outlay on butter than on meat. The poor man thus ate butter; only the destitute man might be unable to. It is not impossible that butter consumption rose during urbanization, for other things to spread on bread – e.g. lard or dripping – must have been harder to come by when people kept fewer pigs and meat consumption was low and erratic. *Cheese* consumption seems to have declined, for many urban workers seem not to have had or to have developed the fashion of substituting it for meat. In Dukinfield and Manchester they spent much less on cheese than butter, and the 1862 farm labourers ate much more of it, even allowing for their slightly better position, than the 'urban poor'. *Eggs* seem to have been of small importance. *Per capita* consumption can hardly have risen.

The evidence is thus not at all favourable to the 'optimistic' view. Though it does not necessarily or firmly establish the 'pessimistic' one, it rather points towards it. The growth of *adulteration* slightly strengthens the pessimistic case. Even if we assume that late eighteenth-century urban shopkeepers were no less dishonest than nineteenth-century ones, it must have affected more people, since a greater number and proportion had to rely on them. The *Lancet* inquiry in the 1850s[3] brings the following points out very clearly: (i) *all* bread tested in two separate samples was adulterated; (ii) over half of the oatmeal was adulterated; (iii) *all* but the highest quality teas were invariably adulterated; (iv) a little under half the milk and (v) *all* butter was watered. Over half the jam and preserves included deleterious matter, but this may have been due simply to bad production. The only commodity of common use not largely adulterated was sugar, almost 90 per cent of which seems to have been straight, though often filthy.

The discussion of food consumption thus throws considerable doubt on the optimistic view. However, it should be

[1] W. Neild, 'Expenditure of the Working Classes in Dukinfield and Manchester in 1836 and 1841', *J. Stat. Soc.*, IV (1841), p. 320.

[2] *The State of the Poor*: 6 cases. In three the quantities are given: $\frac{1}{6}$ lb., $\frac{2}{7}$ lb., $\frac{1}{2}$ lb. (woolcomber).

[3] A. H. Hassall, *Food and its adulteration* (1855).

pointed out that this does *not* mean that early nineteenth-century Britons had an 'Asiatic' standard of living. This is nonsense, and such loose statements have caused much confusion. Britain was almost certainly better fed than all but the most prosperous peasant areas, or the more comfortable classes, in continental countries; but then it had been so, as Drummond and Wilbraham pointed out[1] long before the Industrial Revolution. The point at issue is not whether we fell as low as other countries, but whether, by our own standards, we improved or deteriorated, and in either case, how much.

V

There is thus no strong basis for the optimistic view, at any rate for the period from *c.* 1790 or 1800 on until the middle 1840s. The plausibility of, and the evidence for, deterioration are not to be lightly dismissed. It is not the purpose of this paper to discuss the evolution of living standards in the eighteenth century, since the major discussion on living standards has been about the period between the end of the Napoleonic Wars and 'some unspecified date between the end of Chartism and the Great Exhibition'. It is altogether likely that living standards improved over much of the eighteenth century. It is not improbable that, sometime soon after the onset of the Industrial Revolution – which is perhaps better placed in the 1780s than in the 1760s[2] – they ceased to improve and declined. Perhaps the middle 1790s, the period of Speenhamland and shortage, mark the turning-point. At the other end, the middle 1840s certainly mark a turning-point.

We may therefore sum up as follows. The classical view has been put in Sidney Webb's words:[3] 'If the Chartists in 1837 had called for a comparison of their time with 1787, and had obtained a fair account of the actual social life of the working-man at the two periods, it is almost certain that they would have recorded a positive decline in the standard of life of large classes

---

[1] J. Drummond and A. Wilbraham, *The Englishman's Food* (1939).

[2] J. U. Nef, 'The Industrial Revolution Reconsidered', *Journal of Economic History*, III (1943).

[3] S. Webb, *Labour in the Longest Reign*, Fabian Tract 75 (1897), p. 2.

of the population.' This view has not been so far made un-
tenable. It may be that further evidence will discredit it; but it
will have to be vastly stronger evidence than has so far been
adduced.

APPENDIX

Problems of food consumption

Four problems must be considered: (i) the theoretical problem
of the change from old to new types of diet, (ii) the technical
problem of measurement and the use of sources, (iii) the
problem of trends and (iv) the problem of the actual quantities
consumed. The last three will be discussed in terms of *meat-
consumption*.

I. The adoption of a new type of diet does not *a priori* mark
either an improvement or a deterioration in living standards.
The first view seems to be held by some optimists about white
bread, tea, etc., the second by pessimists like J. Kuczynski
(*History of Labour Conditions*), whose extremism has done some
harm to the cause he wishes to propound. A new food can be
regarded as evidence of a rising standard of living only if it is
adopted because believed to be superior (nutritionally or
socially) to the old, and if bought without sacrificing what
people believe to be necessities. Thus the mere fact that a new
diet is nutritionally inferior to an old one is irrelevant, except
to the nutritionist. If white bread is adopted because it is
believed to be a sign of a higher standard, then its adoption must
be regarded as a sign of improvement. Conversely, if – as was
widely held in the early nineteenth century [Hammond, *Village
Labourer*, pp. 124–5 for opinions] – labourers take to tea in
order to make an increasingly grim diet tolerable, an increase
in tea-drinking cannot prove a rising standard of living.
Nobody would claim that the labourers of Sunbury who in
1834 lived on 'bread, potatoes, a little tea and sugar' [R. *C. on
Poor Laws*, Parl. Papers, 1834, XXXVI] were better off just
because sixty years earlier – I am assuming they ate white
bread – they had probably consumed less of all these new foodstuffs.

The general problem has long since been well formulated by

Grotjahn [*Ueber Wandlungen in der Volksernaehrung* (Leipzig, 1902)]. Industrialization leads to a change in the traditional and – except in famines – nutritionally adequate if dull diet. If enough is spent on the new diet, it can be equally good and more varied. However, often only the well-paid worker can spend enough on it, and few workers know enough initially to choose an adequate new diet. [See the complaints of bad domestic management in R. *C. on Poor Laws*, 1834, XXXVI, passim.] Hence, for equal incomes, the old diet is normally nutritionally better than the new. Until either the workers earn enough, or governments take adequate action, industrialization tends to produce a worse-fed population for a time. However, if we blame the diet of the early nineteenth century, it is not only because the dietician prefers the magnificent dietaries of the old North Country [see e.g. Marshall, *Review of the Reports to the Board of Agriculture for the Northern Department* (York, 1808)], to white bread, potatoes, tea and sugar, but because the new diet contained less of the foods which Englishmen regarded as desirable, than did earlier ones.

II. It is reasonable, especially in England with its mystique of meat-eating, to take meat consumption as a criterion of the standard of living. However, all our sources have considerable weaknesses.

There are the general estimates of which Gregory King's [quoted in Trevelyan's *English Social History* (1946 edn.), p. 276] is the first to interest us. It claims that half the poor households at the end of the seventeenth century ate meat daily, most of the rest ate it twice weekly, and only paupers once weekly. How much we rely on this depends on our estimate of the accuracy and judgment of that able man. Later general estimates, such as Mulhall's guess (*Dictionary of Statistics*) of 80 lb. per year in 1811–30, 87 in 1831–50 are based on no known facts, since there were no censuses of livestock during this period. As we shall see, they are almost certainly too high.

Our largest single body of information about meat consumption comes from descriptions, budgets and a few investigations which may perhaps just deserve the name of social surveys. For the *eighteenth* century the most impressive evidence comes from the seventy-odd workhouse dietaries recorded in

Eden's *State of the Poor*, since pauper diets are obviously constructed for the least prosperous and exigent type of labourer. Sixty of these dietaries served meat three times a week or more, fifteen from five to seven times a week. Where quantities are given, they are sometimes surprisingly high – $\frac{1}{2}$ lb. per meal per person. What men thought desirable for full-grown hard-working labourers can be seen from the harvest diets (Batchelor, *Agriculture of Bedfordshire* (1813), p. 584, *Agriculture of Hertfordshire* (1813), p. 219): meat three times a day including one-quarter or one-third butcher's meat, beef or mutton daily. We do not know where the average consumption lay between these two conventional extremes. It is not unreasonable to assume that it rose during the eighteenth century, and was quite high by the 1790s, when the food situation turned worse: 'Now they dine off butcher's meat, potatoes and pudding' (Westmorland, 1793, in Marshall, *Review of the Reports to the Board of Agriculture for the Northern Department* (York, 1808), p. 214). It is also reasonable to assume that in England, unlike the continent, the worker who ate 'John Bull's food: bread, beef, beer' (R. C. on Poor Law, 1834, XXXVI, answers from Warsop) would not regard himself as wildly rich, but as decently paid, while one who could not afford meat regularly would regard himself as near-destitute. (One recalls the phrase of 'A Lady' – *Domestic Cookery* (1819), p. 290 – advising on cooking for the poor: 'Cut a very thick upper crust of bread, and put it into the pot where salt beef is boiling and near ready; it will attract some of the fat, and when swelled out, will not be an unpalatable dish for those who rarely taste meat.')

It seems clear that after the 1790s the meat consumption of farm labourers declined, as probably did cottage pig-keeping. For Shropshire both declines seem established (J. P. Todd, 'The State of Agriculture in Shropshire, 1775–1825', *Trans. Shropshire Archaeological Society*, LV (1954), 2; Marshall, *Review of Reports . . . for the Western District* (1810), p. 242). In the 1830s local parsons and similar people believed that, out of 899 parishes, labourers in 491 could live on existing wage-rates with meat; but the detailed returns show (*a*) that meat rarely meant butcher's meat and (*b*) that it was not normally eaten regularly or in quantity. (These returns are discussed in R.

Giffen, 'Further Notes on the Progress of the Working Classes', *J. R. Stat. Soc.* XLIX (1886), 55–61, 81–9.) In fact, the picture of the Hampshire labourers in 1813 eating bacon and pickled pork only, the Berkshire ones bacon, seems to be fairly typical. (Vancouver, *Agriculture of Hampshire*, p. 338; Mavor, *Agriculture of Berkshire*, p. 419; R. C. on Poor Laws, 1834, XXXI, question 14, *passim*.) The first estimate of quantities, made in 1862, shows farm labourers to have eaten on average 16 oz. per week per adult. (*6th Report of Medical Officer to Privy Council*, 1863.) It is difficult to believe that this diet, even though probably an improvement on the earlier nineteenth century, was more plentiful in meat than that of the later eighteenth century, or that men fed on it would have developed the myth of the bluff, beef-fed John Bull.

As to the towns, we must forget the optimistic estimates of middle-class observers who saw labourers eating 6 lb. of meat or thereabouts per week (W. Lethaby, *Lectures on the Economy of Food*, 1857; *The Family Oracle of Health*, 1824). Even Le Play's Sheffield cutler in 1855 seems to have had an annual adult consumption of only 81 lb., which is considerably less. (Le Play, *Les Ouvriers Européens* (1855), p. 197.) An estimate for a London artisan family in 1841, earning the good wage of 30 shillings, allows for a weekly *per capita* consumption of 2·8 lb., say an adult ration of 4 lb. At the 20 shilling level this declines to 1·4 lb., at the 15 shilling level to 1 lb., estimates which incidentally show the high income elasticity of demand and the wide range of consumption. (S. R. Bosanquet, *The Rights of the Poor* (1841), pp. 97–8.) The town questionnaires of 1834 (Parl. Papers, 1834, XXXVI) give results not unlike the rural ones. Out of something like 57 towns about whose working-class diets adequate details are given, meat is not mentioned in 10, consumption is described as 'ample', 'decent' or 'four or more times a week' in 6, in some such terms as 'occasionally', 'a little', 'once a month' in 24, and no quantities are mentioned for the rest, except for 7 cases where consumption is described as 'fair' or 'one or two days a week'. The meat eaten was normally pork rather than butcher's meat (i.e. bacon, pickled pork), though pork at ordinary times, butcher's meat on high and holidays is sometimes mentioned. The answer from Limehouse (London) may provide a link with the cost of living: 'A family might subsist upon £100 with meat twice a week; the general fare consisting of soup, gruel, bread, potatoes, herrings and other fish when cheap.' But an income of almost £2 a week was high.

Neild's figures for Manchester and Dukinfield, 1836 and 1841 (*J. Stat. Soc.* IV, 320) are the most detailed for the industrial areas. In 1836 the average *per capita* expenditure there ranged from $2\frac{1}{2}d$. to $11\frac{1}{2}d$. per week, the mode being nearer $3d$. than $4d$. At prevailing prices this would hardly have bought 1 lb. Some other estimates: the best of the depressed class of Keighley woolcombers (1855) ate $1\frac{1}{4}$ lb. (one family), two families ate about $\frac{1}{2}$ lb. a head, 15 not more than 5 oz. but generally much less, while half did not buy meat or calculate meat consumption by the week at all (*Report to the General Board of Health: Keighley*, 1855). Of the urban poor investigated by the Privy Council in 1862 (loc. cit.) 96 per cent ate meat, the average consumption being 13·6 oz. per adult, ranging from the $18\frac{1}{4}$ oz. of the glove-stitchers to the 3·25 oz. of the Macclesfield silk-weavers.

For comparison we may note that in 1936–7 the poorest class, those earning less than £2 10s. 0d. a week, ate on average 30·4 oz. of meat a week (W. Crawford and H. Broadley, *The People's Food* (1938), pp. 177–88), while the poor law dietaries recommended by Chadwick in the 1830s ranged from 8 to 16 oz. (W. Guy, 'Sufficient and insufficient dietaries', *J. R. Stat. Soc.* XXVI (1863), 253.) It is thus not unreasonable to assume that the average urban meat consumption per head in the first part of the nineteenth century was at least one-third below that of the poorest class in 1936–7, and probably not much more than 1 lb., if that. That of butcher's meat was obviously much less.

There remain the statistical sources. These consist primarily of the Smithfield and Excise series, but also of a few other scattered data. Further research would doubtless add to them.

The chief weakness of the Smithfield series is that it does not comprise all meat sold in London, since it neglects all pork, and both home- and country-killed meat, which was sold mainly at Newgate. About pork we know little, except that urban pig-keeping was almost certainly negligible: in the Birmingham urban area in 1843 only 3,375 pigs were kept

(Appendix to *2nd Report of the Inquiry into the State of Large Towns*, Parl. Papers, 1845, XVIII, 134). Home killing of other kinds of meat almost certainly declined. Indeed some of the meat-consumption indicated by market figures may be due to a transfer from home- to butcher-killed meat, such as, Dr Pollard tells me, took place in Sheffield. Our ignorance about home-killing gives our figures, if anything, an upward bias.

We have no quantitative estimates of country-killed meat before the late 1840s (*Report of the Commissioners . . . relating to Smithfield Market*, Parl. Papers, 1850, XXXI; G. Dodd, *The Food of London* (1856), p. 273). But, for the following reasons, I do not think that it invalidates the Smithfield figures. (1) The major increase in country-killing resulted from the railways, but in 1842 these had not yet affected the supply much (C. Knight, ed., *London* (1842), II, 322; see also the evidence of R. Moseley for the Eastern Counties Railway in *Smithfield Commission*, Q. 1871). (2) The railways also increased the supply of live meat to Smithfield, especially from the home counties, which had previously sent carcass meat to town, the main increase in dead meat now coming from further afield (*Smithfield Commission*, Q. 795, 892–3). (3) At certain earlier periods there had been a marked *decline* in dead meat: it had almost halved from 1818 to 1830 (ibid. Q. 892). (4) In spite of considerable pressing, witnesses at the Smithfield Commission – from the rival market – were unwilling to say that Smithfield had lost much ground (Q. 250 ff, 1105). At most it may be held that the Smithfield figures for sheep increasingly understate the facts, as the sale of dead mutton passed to Newgate (*Report*, p. 17), a view which is supported by the tendency of Smithfield sheep sales to lag in the three months in which dead meat sales were briskest – December to February (Q. 1866). They were practically dead in summer anyway. It thus seems clear (*a*) that the beef series is not really affected, (*b*) that the sheep series may be affected somewhat, (*c*) that conversely the neglect of dead killing introduces an optimistic bias between 1818 and 1830 and (*d*) that the distorting effect is not likely to be very great until the early 'forties, when *per capita* consumption was beginning to rise in any case. It may be observed that much of the dead meat, mostly sold at Newgate, was not additional to Smithfield meat, but had originally been sold live at Smithfield. On the whole we can therefore use the Smithfield series without too much hesitation.

The chief question about the Excise series – which stops short in 1825 – is how far they can be used as indices of meat consumption at all. All one can say is that they were so used as far back as 1821 (*Select Committee on the Depressed State of Agriculture*, Parl. Papers, 1821, IX). Unfortunately only national series are available for longer periods, except for a single one which distinguished between the yield of London and the Country Collections (*Customs House Library*). Some of the national series are also available in *S. C. on Agriculture*, Parl. Papers, 1833, V, 628; Parl. Papers, 1830, XXV, 61; 1851–2, XXXIV, 503 and in *Statistical Illustrations of the British Empire* (1825), pp. 68–9. For the problems of these series, see Gayer, Rostow and Schwartz, *Growth and Fluctuations of the British Economy*, II, 720. Figures for the individual Country Collections must have once existed, for they are used in the *S. C. on the Depressed State of Agriculture*, 1821, but the only ones which appear to survive in the Customs Library are one Abstract of Country Collectors Accounts for Consolidated Duties of Excise 5 January 1826 to 5 January 1827, which provides only a static comparison of orders of magnitude. These excises have the advantage that the rate for all but vellum and parchment and a few rare skins (elk, buck, deer) remained quite unchanged for the whole period, except for the period 1812–22 when they were doubled. They were normally charged by the lb., so that they – at least to some extent – allow for changes in the size of animals. Hence the actual yields can be used as an index of production, though if we divide the yield in 1812–22 by two, the result is rather lower than the rest of the curve justifies, presumably due to a greater amount of evasion. In order to avoid the complications which arise when one seeks to put together series representing, say, sheep or beef-cattle from among the skins tanned, tawed or dressed in oil, in their various sub-varieties, I have relied on the gross produce of collections, though this also includes skins of other animals and is thus rather cruder than is desirable.[1]

---

[1] Gross produce is what the collectors actually collected. The accounts are made up in the old-fashioned way, the 'Charge' facing the 'Discharge'.

The annual gross produce figures for London and the
Country are printed in the following table as percentages of
1801, the accounting year running from 5 July to 5 July:

TABLE A   *Gross produce of excise on skins and hides 1796–1826*

Year	London	Country	Year	London	Country
1796–7	87	96	1811–12	126	128
1797–8	89	96	1812–13*	97	117
1798–9	94	92	1813–14	106	119
1799–1800	103	96	1814–15	110	120
1800–1	100	100	1815–16	100	106
1801–2	94	100	1816–17	97	106
1802–3	89	99	1817–18	108	111
1803–4	87	100	1818–19	116	111
1804–5	90	106	1819–20	110	106
1805–6	87	111	1820–1	113	106
1806–7	84	113	1821–2	108	101
1807–8	84	114	1822–3**	142	123
1808–9	94	119	1823–4	142	129
1809–10	90	122	1824–5	150	135
1810–11	107	122	1825–6***	137	133

* New duties: figures represent half their yield. Allow for greater evasion!
** Return to old duties.
*** Annual figures represent yield on half-year multiplied by two.

It will be seen that the London yield showed no sign of absolute
increase until 1810. It seems improbable that meat consumption
as measured on this basis had recovered to anything like the
1800 level by 1820, even allowing for the underestimate of the
series, but the boom of the early 1820s was marked. The series
is not incompatible with the Smithfield figures. The provinces
were clearly better off – or at least they lagged less – except for
the rather bad years of 1815–21.

The actual local figures, as given in the 1821 Committee,
demonstrate, above all, the remarkable income elasticity of
demand for meat. Thus, between 1818 and 1820, Birmingham slaughterings fell by 29 per cent, Walsall ones by 38
per cent, Dudley ones by 29 per cent, Leeds ones by 19 per
cent, Liverpool ones by 18 per cent, but Manchester only by
13 per cent and Sheffield by 12 per cent. Conversely the
slaughter of calves in Liverpool rose by about 25 per cent in

1803–5, that of beef by 37 per cent (1814–17), by 26 per cent in Manchester in the same period. Comparisons by decades are only possible for Liverpool and Manchester, and show a decline in *per capita* consumption in Liverpool, a probable rise in Manchester (Table B):

TABLE B

	Liverpool	Manchester
% rise in population		
1811–20 over 1801–11	22	25
% rise in annual average		
slaughter of *beef*, same periods	18	29
% rise for *veal*	0	20
% rise for *mutton*	12	25

All the data given in the *S. C. on the Depressed State of Agriculture*, 1828 (pp. 243–4, 265–7) are tabulated on p. 91. For Birmingham the figures for 1818 are 127, 91 and 582; for 1819, 104, 93 and 470; for 1820, 91, 90 and 388. It will be observed that the depression 1815–16 appears not to affect beef slaughtering in any of the four towns, and veal only in one. Only mutton is consistently affected. This is surprising, since we should normally expect the cheapest meat to be less sensitive to such fluctuations.

A few individual estimates are also available for Dundee and Glasgow, 1833 (in M'Queen, op. cit.), Wolverhampton, Liverpool, Manchester, Glasgow, Newcastle for 1848–50 (in Braithwaite Poole, op. cit.). For Glasgow, these show an increase of 25 per cent in beef, a decrease of 60 per cent in veal and of 10 per cent in mutton. There are also figures for comparative weekly slaughter in Leeds, 1835/6 – 2,450 animals and in 1841 – 1,800 animals, and in Rochdale – 180 oxen a week in 1836, 65–70 in 1841 (C. Knight, op. cit. p. 325). I do not know what are the sources for these figures.

The question of changes in the size of animals has not yet been discussed. All one can say is, that in London beef consumption must have declined unless the average carcass weight of beef cattle increased by at least 40 per cent between 1801 and 1841, that of sheep by at least 15 per cent. Even if the

TABLE C *Number of hides inspected (in '00s) in various centres 1801–20*

Date	Liverpool			Manchester			Sheffield			Leeds		
	Beasts	Calves	Sheep	Beasts	Calves	Sheep	Beasts	Calves	Sheep	Beasts	Calves	Sheep
1801	105	133	681	105	124	569						
1802	95	158	670	114	145	571						
1803	85	128	593	100	132	481						
1804	86	150	584	93	127	589						
1805	94	169	606	124	98	576						
1806	95	170	670	109	120	696						
1807	96	188	582	102	130	770						
1808	103	187	598	116	107	503						
1809	112	192	687	117	109	512						
1810	109	180	679	121	132	602						
1811	100	180	633	111	130	604						
1812	100	168	588	106	122	414	35	45	310			
1813	104	168	614	126	128	717	35	40	390			
1814	105	147	698	132	124	760	39	40	300			
1815	118	170	788	151	143	827	45	50	324	39	56	526
1816	120	148	736	163	164	730	53	58	320	45	68	421
1817	144	179	817	166	167	822	50	51	311	45	62	550
1818	133	171	766	165	162	845	54	39	301	50	54	560
1819	122	170	706	161	160	837	55	43	318	50	50	530
1820	110	166	700	145	170	835	44	43	274	44	56	490

average weight of both had gone up by 25 per cent or so, a decline is still likely.

All these figures are global; that is, they do not distinguish working-class consumption from the rest, or the consumption of different strata of the labouring poor. This means they are subject to misinterpretation on the optimistic side, for the changes in meat consumption by the relatively small section of the population which ate a good deal of meat, carry a disproportionately heavy weight. The possibilities of error inherent in such figures may be gauged by the following example. The *Report of the Statistical Committee appointed by the Anti-Corn Law Conference*, held in London 8–12 March 1842 (London, n.d.), p. 18, estimates that in Leeds consumption had declined by 25 per cent since 1835–6; but since the consumption of the better-off classes had not declined, it estimated the reduction in working-class consumption at 50 per cent.

5 The Rising Standard of Living in England, 1800–50[1]

R. M. HARTWELL

[This article was first published in the *Economic History Review*, 2nd series, vol. XIII, no. 3, 1961.]

I

The most interesting and most inconclusive debate on the industrial revolution in England has been concerned with the standard of living of the workers, particularly the industrial and urban poor, during the first half of the nineteenth century. In the past, those who have argued for deterioration have outnumbered those who believed that conditions of life improved, and the intransigency of both has resulted inevitably in extreme points of view.[2] To a large extent the argument has been, not an objective debate on the interpretation of the facts as known, but a controversy about values, about the desirability of social and economic change.[3] Disagreement has stemmed also from the conflicting character of the evidence, which has allowed plausible allegiance to opposed theories; from the facts that there was, for much of the period, no *marked* trend in living

[1] This article has benefited from the criticisms of T. S. Ashton, A. J. Taylor, E. Russell, C. P. Kindleberger.

[2] Thus, for example, J. Kuczinski (*A Short History of Labour Conditions in Great Britain from 1750 to the Present Day*, London, F. Muller, 1947 edn, p. 16) declared that the period 'brought about a rapid deterioration of the condition of the working class', whereas J. H. Clapham (*An Economic History of Modern Britain. The Early Railway Age 1820–1850*, Cambridge University Press, 1925, p. 561) argued, for the same period, that 'for every class of urban or industrial labour about which information is available . . . wages had risen markedly'. Herbert Heaton, however, claims that Clapham can be excused for his 'extremism', for he entered 'a field occupied largely by neoliberal or socialist intellectuals . . . It took courage, skepticism, caution, and patient industry to breast that tide, to put popular and often legendary generalizations to the test of measurement and proportion.' (*Journal of Economic History*, September 1957, p. 489.)

[3] See R. M. Hartwell, 'Interpretations of the Industrial Revolution in England: A Methodological Inquiry', *Journal of Economic History*, June 1959.

standards, and that the increase in *per capita* real income still left the majority of workers at a low standard of living, aware more of their unfulfilled wants than of their increasing prosperity. And so historians have argued – often exaggerating trends and over-dramatizing events – without feeling that they have done violence to the facts. The *exact* measurement of the standard of living in the years 1800 to 1850 may be impossible, but, eschewing prejudice and preconceived theories, a firm statement about the trend of living standards can be derived from the mass of evidence that has survived, and from an analysis of the likely changes in income distribution during a long period of economic growth. This article argues for an upward trend in living standards during the industrial revolution; in section II, from an examination of national income and other aggregate statistics that have survived (or can be calculated or guessed with some certainty), from wage-price data, and from analogy; in section III, from an analysis of consumption figures; and in section IV, from the evidence of vital statistics, from a comparison with eighteenth-century living standards, and from details of the expansion after 1800 of social and economic opportunities. Briefly the argument is that, since average *per capita* income increased, since there was no trend in distribution against the workers, since (after 1815) prices fell while money wages remained constant, since *per capita* consumption of food and other consumer goods increased, and since government increasingly intervened in economic life to protect or raise living standards, then the real wages of the majority of English workers were rising in the years 1800 to 1850.[1]

[1] See E. J. Hobsbawm, 'The British Standard of Living, 1790–1850' *Economic History Review*, August 1957), for a vigorous plea for deterioration. This article is marred, however, by carelessness in the use of evidence, argument and language: for example, the statement that the controversy is only thirty years old, and that 'the consensus of informed and intelligent contemporaries . . . took the dark view', ignoring Tooke, Porter, Macaulay, etc.; or the unqualified claim that 'there is no *a priori* reason why the standard of living should rise markedly under early industrialism', prejudicing the argument by inserting 'markedly', and ignoring *a priori* reasons (and historical evidence) why the standard of living might well rise under early industrialism; or the consistent use of trough years of the cycle to indicate 'normal' vagrancy figures; or the insertion of adjectives to make otherwise reasonable statements unreasonable – 'there is no evidence of any

II

Economic growth implies an increase in *per capita* national income, and, if distribution leaves labour with at least the same relative share of the increasing product, an increase in the average standard of living. Generally, as the historical analyses of economic development have shown, an increase in *per capita* income has been accompanied by a more equal income distribution.[1] In Britain, contemporary estimates of the national income between 1800 and 1850 indicate that average real income doubled in this period, and although the upward trend was uneven with stagnation during the war and a possible small decline in the 'thirties, average *per capita* income had already increased 50 per cent by 1830.[2] No juggling of the figures could suggest deterioration, but the estimates are inadequate both in their methods of compilation and in their statistical bases, so that they can be used only as an indication of trend, and not as a measure of change. This probable increase, of uncertain size, in *per capita* income becomes more plausible, however, when three other phenomena are taken into account: the increase in the output of manufacturing industry relative to the increase in population; the increasing and substantial proportion of manufacturing income in the national income; and the

---

major rise in the *per capita* consumption'; or the assumption, without any proof, of deterioration – 'Eggs seem to have been of small importance. *Per capita* consumption can hardly have risen.'

[1] See S. Kuznets, 'Economic Growth and Income Inequality', *American Economic Review*, March 1955. Theoretically there may be an increase in inequality in the early stages of growth to allow for larger savings and more investment. This possibility is discussed below.

[2] P. Deane, 'Contemporary Estimates of National Income in the first half of the Nineteenth Century', *Economic History Review*, April 1956; and 'The Industrial Revolution and Economic Growth: The Evidence of Early British National Income Estimates', *Economic Development and Cultural Change*, January 1957. Miss Deane uses the contemporary estimates of H. Beeke (1800), B. Bell (1802), P. Colquhoun (1806 and 1815), J. Lowe (1822), P. Pebrer (1833), W. F. Spackman (1843 and 1847), W. R. Smee (1846) and G. R. Porter (1847), supporting them with the later estimates of M. Mulhall, R. D. Baxter, L. Levi and R. Giffen. Her consequent index of 'average real incomes' is as follows: 1800—100, 1812—94, 1822—114, 1831—174, 1836—168, 1841—145, 1846—160, 1851—193. See also the figures (*not* the conflicting text) of C. Clarke, 'The Trend of Real Income in Great Britain', *Review of Economic Progress*, July 1952; and Paul Studenski, *The Income of Nations* (New York University Press, 1958), chapter. 7.

increasing and substantial proportion of the total working population employed in manufacturing industry. According to W. Hoffmann, the rate of growth of industrial output between 1782 and 1855 was 3 to 4 per cent per annum (except during the war years when the rate was about 2 per cent);[1] over the same period the annual rate of growth of population varied from 1·2 to 1·5 per cent, with the highest rate between 1811 and 1831, and a declining rate thereafter. This, however, would have been of little significance if industrial output was so small a part of national income that changes in it could not have affected the average standard of life. But the contribution of manufacturing industry to the national income increased from about one-fifth in 1770, to one-quarter in 1812, to one-third in 1831. Census figures for 1841 and 1851 show that about one-third of the occupied population of England and Wales was engaged in manufacturing industry and that the 1851 proportion 'was not exceeded until 1951'.[2] In 1850, M. Mulhall estimated, manufacturing industry provided £269 millions (about 40 per cent) of a British national income of £690 millions.[3] It is probable, therefore, that by 1830 manufacturing had a similar rôle as income producer as it has had since 1850, and that the growth of manufacturing output substantially affected living standards.

Of the factors that raised *per capita* output the most important were capital formation, technical progress and improved labour and managerial skills. It is necessary, from a combination of those, to explain the shift between 1760 and 1840 from a situation where population and incomes were rising very slowly to one where population was increasing at the annual rate of *c*. 1·5 per cent, and incomes at *c*. 3 per cent. This could be explained by assuming that the capital income ratio increased from 1 or 2 to 1, to 3 to 1 (something like the modern ratio), and the savings ratio from 3 to 5 per cent to over 12 per cent, from 1 or 2 per cent to 4·5 per cent to keep capital stock intact

[1] W. Hoffmann, *British Industry, 1700–1950* (Oxford, Blackwell, 1955), and C. Snyder, 'Measures of the Growth of British Industry', *Economica*, November 1934.

[2] E. A. G. Robinson, 'The Changing Structure of the British Economy', *Economic Journal*, September 1954, pp. 447, 459.

[3] P. Deane, 'Contemporary Estimates of National Income in the second half of the Nineteenth Century', *Economic History Review*, April 1957, p. 458.

in a growing population, and a further 9 per cent to increase incomes 3 per cent annually. Contemporary and subsequent analyses of the industrial revolution have assumed such ratios, without quantifying them. The rate of capital formation certainly increased over the period, but to determine accurately its effect on real income it would be necessary to know both the savings ratio and the capital output ratio, neither of which can be determined. Of the various possibilities (a high savings ratio, S/Y, and a high capital output ratio, C/O; high S/Y and low C/O; low S/Y and high C/O; low C/O and low S/Y), however, the most likely up to about 1840, when railway investment was becoming important, was a modest rate of savings and a low capital output ratio. Modern analyses of under-developed economies in process of growth often assume low savings and low capital income ratios. In the England of the industrial revolution, likewise, the rate of saving was necessarily relatively low in a society where average incomes were still not much above subsistence, and where the capital market was imperfect; and the replacement of men by machines, of wind and water by steam power, and of the home by the factory, marked an increase in productivity that was often spectacular. But whereas the productivity of much new industrial equipment was high, its cost was often low. Thus the comparatively low capital output ratio was not incompatible with rising real incomes. By 1800 improvements in techniques and management were already making capital more fruitful, and it is certain that over the whole period the rate of growth of output depended as much on the rate of technical progress as on the rate of capital accumulation, on the quality as much as on the quantity of investment. The productivity effect of better machinery during the industrial revolution was both large and rapid in impact, and the growth of output, because the output increment per unit of investment was large, was rapid. As Robert Owen declared in 1816: 'in my establishment at New Lanark . . . mechanical powers and operations super-intended by about two thousand young persons and adults . . . now completed as much work as sixty years before would have required the entire working population of Scotland'.[1]

[1] R. Owen, *The Life of Robert Owen. Written by Himself* (London, 1857), I, p. 125.

The employment effect, however, was also potentially large. Many of the new machines required less labour per unit of output, so that, theoretically, the consequent labour displacement could have been large enough to have prevented real wages from rising. On the other hand, because the new machines generally reduced costs, including the cost of goods consumed by the workers, there was at the same time a tendency for real wages to rise. It is because of this tendency, J. R. Hicks has suggested, that capital accumulation in the nineteenth century was so favourable to the standard of living.[1] Moreover, money wages were stable between 1820 and 1850, a period of falling prices, indicating that there was insufficient competition from underemployed and unemployed labour to pull down wages. In spite of pockets of technological underemployment,[2] the displacement of labour by machinery did not result in a decline in average real wages. And the existence of groups of wage-earners whose real wages were stable or declining – industrial groups like the handloom weavers, or national groups like the Irish – bias the averages downwards and disguise the gains in the growing sectors of the economy. Indeed, to some extent, the displacement of labour was theoretical: the new machines required less labour per unit of output than did old plant making the same products; but much new plant was an

---

[1] J. R. Hicks, *Value and Capital* (Oxford University Press, 1939), p. 292. 'The fact that the things whose production has been facilitated have been particularly articles of mass consumption has worked in the same direction. If there are any goods in terms of which wages have fallen as a result of the accumulation of capital, they are not goods of much importance to the wage-earner.'

[2] *Report of the Commissioners for Inquiry into the Conditions of Unemployed Hand-Loom Weavers in the United Kingdom* (*Parliamentary Papers*, 1841 (296) X), showed that handloom weaving was not only a dying trade, but that, because it was an easy trade to learn and had early relaxed apprenticeship rules, it had become 'the refuge of the surplus numbers from nearly all other trades' and from Ireland, and that 'wages had begun to decline before any machinery was introduced'. Wages were higher and employment more constant in England than in Ireland, but Irish social habits often remained unchanged by emigration. (*Reports of Commissioners* (15) *Poor Laws (Ireland)*, *Parliamentary Papers*, XXXIV (1836), Appendix G, pp. ix–xii.) The Irish, therefore, although they *improved* their lot by emigration to Lancashire, often provided contemporary critics of industrialism with their best examples. Thus Place declared that Kay-Shuttleworth's horrifying picture of squalor and disease in Manchester in 1832 was based almost exclusively on Irish immigrants. (M. D. George, *London Life in the Eighteenth Century*, London, 1951 edn, p. 323.)

addition to total plant, not a displacement of existing plant, and when this was so, the net effect on the total demand for labour was an absolute increase. Thus, for example, railways did gradually displace canals, but the displacement effect on canal labour was insignificant compared with the massive labour requirements for railway construction and maintenance.[1] There was in this period a continually increasing demand for industrial labour, a demand that caused a differential between agricultural and industrial wages, and a consequent continuous migration towards the industrial areas.[2] As a spokesman of the agricultural labourers declared bitterly, 'it is well known that in the great trading towns, such as Manchester, Sheffield, Birmingham, etc., four days work in a week amply supply the dissolute and the drunken'.[3]

But factories have to be administered, and machines have to be tended, and even the best equipment is of little value without able entrepreneurs and skilled labourers. The industrial revolution was as much a revolution in industrial organization as in technology. Entrepreneurs increasingly centralized production into factories, worked out the problems of factory management, accounting, financing, merchanting and labour-relations. Not the least problem was to change craft and agricultural labourers into factory workers, with their different skills, different rhythm of work, different incentives, different social attitudes, and different way of life. This necessary transformation was certainly painful, but it was gradually achieved without political

---

[1] T. Tooke and W. Newmarch (*A History of Prices, and of the State of Circulation, during the nine years 1848–1856*, London, 1857, p. 368) estimated that 'the population supported by the Railway Works [in 1847–8] was nearly . . . as large . . . as the total population employed in the whole of the Factories of the United Kingdom'. T. Brassey (*On Work and Wages*, London, 1873, p. 39) tells how, in the period of the railway boom, when admittedly the demand for labour was 'excessive', 'look-outs [were] placed on the roads to intercept men tramping, and take them to the nearest beershop to be treated and induced to start work'.

[2] See E. W. Gilboy, *Wages in Eighteenth Century England* (Harvard University Press, 1934) and A. Redford, *Labour Migration in England, 1800–50* (Manchester University Press, 1926).

[3] D. Davies, *The Case of Labourers in Husbandry* (Bath, 1795), p. 163. Compare C. D. Brereton (*A Practical Inquiry into the Number, Means of Employment, and Wages, of Agricultural Labourers*, Norwich, 1826, p. 1) who contrasted the 'improving . . . knowledge, comfort, and conduct' of town workers with the depression of 'the peasantry'.

revolution, and with labour simultaneously increasing its opportunities, its industrial skill and its bargaining strength. The quantitative effect of such changes on output cannot be measured accurately, but they certainly tended to increase productivity.

Ricardo, who regarded economics as 'an inquiry into the laws which determine the division of industry amongst the classes who concur in its formation', argued that the combination of the laws of population and of diminishing returns to land determined wages at subsistence according to the price of corn, and thus limited economic progress because of the tendency of profits to decline as rents increased.[1] Thus was established the theory that wages inevitably stabilize at subsistence, which so influenced the early socialists and Marx, and all since then who have cherished the theory of exploitation. 'By the present constitution of society, the millions are a doomed class,' wrote J. F. Bray in 1839, 'from the position in which they stand with regard to capital and the capitalist, their condition is unimprovable and their wrongs irremediable'.[2] After 1830, however, it became increasingly difficult for the classical economists to reconcile theory with facts, and, in particular, with the facts that corn production was more than keeping pace with population, and that real wages were rising.[3] Theoretically it is possible that economic growth could result in reduced real incomes in the short run, but it is quite unreasonable to assume, over a long period of a half century, during which *per capita* national income was rising, that the rich were getting richer and the poor poorer.

There is some evidence that the distribution of income in England in 1850 was less unequal than it had been in 1800. C. Clark, for example, by estimating Pareto coefficients, reckons

[1] Ricardo to Malthus, 9 October 1820. *The Works and Correspondence of David Ricardo* (edited by P. Sraffa. Cambridge University Press, 1952), vol. VIII, p. 278. Even so, Ricardo was conscious of progress, remarking in *The Principles* that 'Many of the conveniences enjoyed in an English cottage, would have been thought luxuries at an earlier period of our history'. Ibid. vol. I, *On the Principles of Political Economy and Taxations*, p. 97.

[2] J. F. Bray, *Labour's Wrongs and Labour's Remedy* (Leeds, 1839), p. 67.

[3] This difficulty has been extremely well surveyed by M. Blaug in 'The Empirical Content of Ricardian Economics', *Journal of Political Economy*, February 1956.

that income distribution was more unequal in 1812 than in 1848;[1] income tax assessments of 1812 and 1848 show, also, that the number of assessments between £150 and £500 increased more than those over £500; a comparison of fund-holders of 1831 and 1848 reveals that the largest increase was in those receiving dividends of under £5.[2] These figures, how-ever, are no conclusive proof of a significant change in distri-bution. In any case, as E. H. Phelps Brown points out, 'the changes in real wages due to distributive shifts have been very small compared with those associated with the movements of productivity'.[3] There has been generally the simultaneous rise, at not dissimilar rates of growth, of capital stock, output and real incomes.[4] Study of the long-term trends in the wage-share of the national income show that since about 1860 that share has remained almost constant.[5] If this stability has a longer history, the wage bill would have been increasing proportionately with the national income from some earlier date, possibly from the beginning of the industrial revolution.

[1] C. Clark, *The Conditions of Economic Progress* (London: Macmillan, 2nd edn, 1951), pp. 534, 538.

[2] W. R. Greg, *Essays on Political and Social Science* (London, 1853), vol. I, pp 318–19.

[3] E. H. Phelps Brown, 'The Long-Term Movement of Real Wages' in J. T. Dunlop (ed.), *The Theory of Wage Determination* (London, 1957), p. 53.

[4] See P. H. Douglas, *The Theory of Wages* (New York: Macmillan, 1934, Ch. VII), showing the close correlation between productivity and wages; also his 'An Estimate of the Growth of Capital in the United Kingdom, 1865–1909', *Journal of Economic and Business History*, August 1930, p. 683. See also E. H. Phelps Brown, op. cit., showing how real wages per worker have usually moved in step with both capital accumulation and productivity; for example, the doubling of real capital per head and real income per head in the United Kingdom between 1870 and 1938. A. K. Cairncross ('The Place of Capital in Economic Progress', *Economic Progress*, edited by L. H. Dupriez, Louvain, 1955) argues also that 'capital and income do tend to increase at about the same rate' (p. 238), and notes the stability over a long period of the ratio between the two.

[5] The literature on this subject is large, 'partly because of the general interest in the fortunes of labor in a class-conscious society; . . . partly because of an attempt to use the wage share as a measure of the degree of monopoly' (S. Kuznets, 'Distribution of National Income by Factor Shares', *Economic Development and Cultural Change*, April 1959, p. 55), but no adequate explanation of the phenom-enon exists. See A. L. Bowley, *Wages and Income in the United Kingdom since 1860* (Cambridge University Press, 1937) for basic statistics, and the following for comment on the phenomenon: J. M. Keynes, 'Relative Movements of Real Wages and Output', *Economic Journal*, March 1939; J. H. Richardson, 'Real Wage Movements', *Economic Journal*, September 1939; and E. H. Phelps Brown and P. E. Hart, 'The Share of Wages in National Income', *Economic Journal*, June 1952.

It is not unlikely, however, that the share of wages was less in 1780–1800 than in 1860, and thus, that wages were rising between those dates more quickly than national income. That this was probable is indicated by the continuous increase over the period of those employed in manufacturing industry. Agricultural wages lagged behind industrial wages, and as more workers transferred to higher productivity occupations, average real wages increased. Census figures show that the percentage proportions of agricultural to all families in 1811 and 1831 were 35·2 and 28·2, and that the percentage proportions of adult males employed in agriculture to all male workers in 1831, 1841 and 1851 were 31·7, 25·7 and 21·1.[1] Further confirmation is provided by the increasing proportion over these years of total population engaged in commerce, finance and the professions, 'a fairly precise measurement of the degree of economic advancement'.[2] Occupational statistics before 1841, except in broad categories, are not very helpful, but other evidence shows that there were large increases in the numbers employed in services – in transport, commerce and finance, in government and in the professions – between 1780 and 1850.[3] Between 1841 and 1851 the census figures show an increase in services, excluding domestic service, of from 9·1 to 12·2 per cent of the population, or, as corrected by C. Booth, of from 14 to 16·5 per cent.[4] At the same time the proportion of gainfully occupied in the population increased, as the under-employed labour of the predominantly agricultural economy of pre-industrial Britain was gradually absorbed into fuller employment in industry and services. Thus, for example, the much publicized and criticized employment of women and children, though common in the farms and domestic industries of pre-industrial revolution England, was certainly more productive and generally more humane during the industrial revolution.

The workers' standard of living is affected by the redistribu-

---

[1] G. R. Porter, *The Progress of the Nation* (London, 1847), pp. 53 and 64.

[2] C. Clark, op. cit. pp. 397, 401.

[3] See, for example, A. M. Carr-Saunders and P. A. Wilson, *The Professions* (Oxford: at the Clarendon Press, 1933), pp. 294–7.

[4] C. Clark, op. cit. p. 408; E. A. G. Robinson, op. cit. p. 459. The Booth estimates also come from Clark quoting Booth's estimates in *The Journal of the Royal Statistical Society*, 1886.

tion of income by government, especially through taxation and expenditure on social welfare. The tax structure between 1800 and 1850 was certainly regressive, although there was income tax during the war (the heaviest of the century) and again after 1842 when it yielded £5 millions annually. Government revenue came mainly from indirect taxation, of which customs revenue provided an increasing proportion until 1840, and thereafter a stable one. The reduction of tariffs after 1824, and especially after 1840, gave general benefit by lowering the price of many goods of common consumption and by encouraging the demand for goods which hitherto had been considered luxuries. Other taxation, also mainly indirect, was reduced after the war, and remained relatively stable at £3–4 millions between 1825 and 1856. Total government revenue also declined after 1815 both absolutely (until 1843) and as a proportion of national income, and in terms of average *per capita* contributions. On the expenditure side, the national debt service was the largest and most regressive item, but its incidence remained stable in money terms, varying from £33·9 to £28·1 millions between 1815 and 1845, so that it was a decreasing proportion of national income even though in real terms its incidence increased in the period of falling prices. The civil and pensions list, to which *The Black Book* gave so much publicity, was a small item and it decreased absolutely. 'Social services' cost from £2 to £5 millions, increasing after 1830, but the benefit to the worker must have been very small. Much more important was the expenditure for the relief and maintenance of the poor through the poor and county rates, which increased to £7·9 millions in 1818, varied from £5·7 to £7·0 millions from 1818 to 1832, fell to £4·0 millions in 1834 and increased to £6·2 millions in 1848.[1] All that can be said in summary about these collections and disbursements of government is that there was no marked trend, although there was a reduction in the average contributions, and an increase in the average receipts, of the labouring poor. In another way, however, government action was important. Government legislation which involved private expenditure in improving the condition of the working classes was considerable. Such legis-

[1] G. R. Porter, op. cit. section IV.

lation included protective acts like the factory and truck acts, enabling acts such as the legislation for savings banks and friendly societies, and acts of general benefit such as those improving municipal government. Under such legislation, for example, hours of work were reduced in factories and limits were set to the age at which children were allowed to work, women and children were excluded from mines, some educational facilities were enforced for factory children, and the provision of water and the disposal of sewage by municipal authorities were facilitated. Such legislation, J. M. Ludlow and L. Jones declared, secured 'the primary elements of health, safety and well-being' for the people at large, and enabled them 'to become a better fed, better clothed, better housed, more healthy, more orderly, more saving, more industrious, more self-reliant, better educated population'.[1] There is no doubt that humanitarian and legislative pressure increased the social-overhead cost of industry, directly benefiting the workers, and driving out of business those employers at the margin whose efficiency had previously been protected by the exploitation of labour.

III

Evidence of the condition of the working class during the industrial revolution can be found also in the statistics of savings, wages and consumption. After the establishment of savings banks in 1817 deposits increased to £14·3 millions by 1829, and to almost £30 millions by 1850, when the number of depositors totalled 1,112,999. 'The £30 millions of deposits in 1847 were predominantly the savings of wage-earners, among whom domestic servants and artisans occupied the most prominent places.'[2] Friendly and Benefit Societies, of which

[1] J. M. Ludlow and L. Jones, *Progress of the Working Class 1832–1867* (London, 1867), pp. 69, 82.

[2] H. O. Horne, *A History of Savings Banks* (Oxford University Press, 1947), p. 116. The trend of savings was upwards except for the years 1828–9, 1830–2 and 1847–8. The range of depositors is best seen in examples: of the 14,937 depositors of the Manchester and Salford Savings Bank in 1842, 3,063 were domestic servants, 3,033 were children whose parents saved for them, 2,372 were tradesmen, clerks, warehousemen, porters, artists and teachers, and the remainder were labourers and industrial workers (W. R. Greg, op. cit. p. 318).

there were 20,000 in 1858 with a membership of about two millions, had also accumulated £9 millions.[1] Other societies catering for working-class savings, such as Building and Land Societies (after 1816) and Co-operative Societies (after 1844), did not advance with such rapidity, although their foundation in this period is evidence of the increasing ability of the working class to save.[2]

A large and long economic expansion like the industrial revolution was possible only with a large extension of the market, with the creation or discovery of increasing and accessible markets with consumers willing and able to buy the expanding output of goods and services. For a shorter period, however, it is relevant, in an inquiry into living standards, to know how much of the increased production went into savings and investment rather than into consumption, and how much went abroad without immediate repayment in other goods. But, whatever the amount of savings and exports in the short run, in the long run capital accumulation would have increased productivity, and sales abroad would have resulted in increased imports.[3] In any case neither capital accumulation nor exports, nor the two together, could have completely absorbed the increase in production in this period: capital accumulation was not so large as to make exorbitant demands on current output; and exports, as a proportion of national income, increased from 12 per cent in 1820 to 15 per cent in 1850 (retained imports meantime increasing from 12 to 18 per cent), while the balance of merchandise trade became increasingly *unfavourable* (averaging £8·66 millions in 1816–20, about 3 per cent of national

[1] C. Hardwick, *The History, Present Position, and Social Importance of Friendly Societies* (Manchester: Heywood, 2nd edn, 1869, p. 22).

[2] J. M. Ludlow and L. Jones, op. cit. p. 125 *et seq.*; G. J. Holyoake, *The History of Co-operation* (London: Unwin, 1906), vol. 1, 266 *et seq.* Thus for example, the deeds for houses registered by Building Societies in the West Riding totalled 192 between 1843 and 1847, 1,372 between 1848 and 1852, and 3,044 between 1853 and 1857.

[3] Unless, of course, the terms of trade deteriorated so much that the increase in productivity was exported. The quantum (at 1694 prices) of imports increased from 4 (1811–18) to 15 (1847–53) and exports from 4 to 15; the terms of trade (export prices divided by import prices, 1913 = 100) fell from 123 to 90. Thus, although some of the increase in productivity went abroad, imports increased at much the same rate as exports (W. A. Lewis, *Economic Survey, 1919–1939*, London: Allen and Unwin, 1949, pp. 195, 202).

income, and £26·8 millions in 1846–50, about 5 per cent of national income).[1] There was, however, the period of the war, when much production went either into unproductive war effort at home, or into loans and subsidies for allies abroad. As G. W. Daniels has pointed out, 'the increased power of production, instead of improving the material welfare of the community, had to be devoted to the prosecution of the war'.[2] The failure of living standards to rise much before 1815 was due, therefore, not to industrialization, but to war.

The extension of the market was made possible more by reduced prices than by increased money wages.[3] While money wages after the war remained relatively constant, the prices of manufactured and agricultural goods declined. The goods of the industrial and agricultural revolutions tended to be cheap and plentiful, for the new entrepreneurs were fully aware that great expansion of production was possible only by supplying goods suitable for mass markets. Thus, Robert Bakewell's object in breeding new sheep was 'not to produce meat for the tables of the rich, but to supply substantial nourishment for the working classes'. 'I do not breed mutton for gentlemen,' he said, 'but for the public.'[4] Similarly A. Redgrave of Yorkshire reported that 'the efforts of the majority of West Riding manu-

---

[1] Percentages reckoned from the figures of E. A. G. Robinson, op. cit.; P. Deane, op. cit.; and L. Levi, *History of British Commerce* (London, 1872).

[2] G. W. Daniels, *The Early English Cotton Industry* (Manchester University Press, 1920), pp. 147–8. The memory of war hardships persisted throughout the nineteenth century resulting, for example, in such statements as that of J. E. Thorold Rogers: 'Thousands of homes were starved in order to find the means for the great war . . . the resources on which the struggle was based, and without which it would have speedily collapsed, were the stint and starvation of labour, the overtaxed and underfed toils of childhood, the underpaid and uncertain employment of men' (*Six Centuries of Work and Wages*, London, 1884, p. 505). See also Sir George Nicholls, *A History of the English Poor Law* (First edition 1860. New edition by H. G. Willink, London, 1904), vol. II, 165–6; and W. Cunningham, *The Growth of English Industry and Commerce in Modern Times* (First edition 1882. Cambridge University Press, 1925 edition), vol. III, section III.

[3] For example, G. R. Porter, op. cit. p. 459: 'the diminution in the weekly earnings . . . has been but small in any case, and certainly not commensurate with the diminished cost of most of the necessaries of life, comprehending in this list most articles of food, and every article of clothing'.

[4] A. Rees, *The Cyclopaedia* (London, 1819), vol. 32, article on 'Sheep'; R. Wallace, *Farm Live Stock of Great Britain* (Edinburgh, 4th edn 1907), p. 575.

facturers have been chiefly directed to the production of cheap cloth; they can unquestionably sell a moderately well got up cloth at a low price; . . . they can also produce in enormous quantity'.[1] If only manufactured goods had fallen in price, however, the gain in real wages to a working class that spent a high proportion of its income on food and fuel would not have been large. But food prices also declined after 1815, along with the prices of most other consumer goods. R. S. Tucker's index of consumer goods prices – for food, fuel and light, and clothing, the most important items in working-class budgets – shows a downward trend from 1813–15 to 1845, as also does Miss E. B. Schumpeter's index for twenty-two articles of food and drink, and nine articles of fuel, light and clothing.[2] Money wages, in contrast, rose slightly less than prices during the war, and remained stable, or fell less than prices after the war, as the wages indices that have been compiled for this period show.[3] The facts that aggregate money national income increased substantially, money wages remained stable, and prices of key foodstuffs remained stable or fell, suggest clearly that food supplies at least kept pace with population. When other commodities are taken into consideration, the implication is clear: an increase in real wages, at least after 1815, which it

[1] A. Ure, *Philosophy of Manufactures* (revised edition by P. L. Simmonds, London, 1861), p. 710.

[2] R. S. Tucker, 'Real Wages of Artisans in London, 1729–1935', *Journal of the American Statistical Society*, 1936. E. B. Schumpeter, 'English Prices and Public Finance, 1660–1822', *Review of Economic Statistics*, 1938.

[3] For example, see the articles of A. L. Bowley in *The Journal of the Statistical Society* (1895, 1898, 1899, 1902) and *The Economic Journal* (1895, 1896) and his book *Wages in the United Kingdom in the Nineteenth Century* (Cambridge University Press, 1900); G. H. Wood, 'The Course of Average Wages between 1790 and 1860', *The Economic Journal*, 1899; N. D. Kondratieff, 'Die Preisdynamic der Industriellen und Landwirtschaftlichen Waren', *Archiv für Sozialwissenschaft und Sozialpolitik*, 1930; E. H. Phelps Brown and S. V. Hopkins, 'Seven Centuries of Building Wages', *Economica*, 1955; R. S. Tucker, op. cit. Moreover, those who have argued for deterioration have too often depended, not on indices, but on individual statements of hardship that were exaggerated; thus W. Felkin (*Remarks upon the Importance of an Inquiry into the Amount and Appropriation of Wages by the Working Classes*, London, 1837, p. 7), comparing workers' statements about wages received with wages actually received as recorded in employers' account books, wrote, 'The results are, No. 1 says 16*s*., he received 18*s*.; No. 2 says 15*s*., he received 18*s*.; No. 3 says 16*s*., he received 20*s*.; No. 4 says 18*s*., he received 26*s*.; No. 5 says 15*s*., he received 25*s*.'

would be irresponsible to deny, and which, indeed, has been confirmed by the industrial histories of the period.[1]

Although consumption statistics before 1850 are inadequate and unreliable, they do indicate modest though fluctuating increases in the consumption of most foodstuffs and other consumption goods.[2] M. G. Mulhall, for example, has reckoned that between 1811 and 1850 the *per capita* consumption of meat, sugar, tea, beer and eggs increased, while that of wheat decreased somewhat between 1830 and 1850, increasing thereafter.[3] Import statistics are the most accurate of the measures of consumption in this period, and these show important long-term gains in a wide range of commodities; for example, in tea, 'from about 1815 there is a secular rise, notably accelerated in the last decade of the period'; in tobacco, also a 'persistent upward trend'; and in sugar, 'the trend movement is upward'.[4] By 1840, to take one source of imports, steamships were pouring into England an almost daily stream of Irish livestock,

[1] For example, S. J. Chapman, *The Lancashire Cotton Industry* (Manchester University Press, 1904), p. 75; T. S. Ashton, *Iron and Steel in the Industrial Revolution* (Manchester University Press, 1924), p. 75; T. S. Ashton and J. Sykes, *The Coal Industry of the Eighteenth Century* (Manchester University Press, 1929), p. 141; F. A. Wells, *The British Hosiery Trade* (London, 1935), pp. 128–9. See also A. D. Gayer, W. W. Rostow and A. J. Schwartz, *The Growth and Fluctuation of the British Economy 1790–1850* (Oxford: at the Clarendon Press, 1953), vol. II, ch. XI, 'Cyclical Patterns Relating to the Condition of Labour'. See also the contemporary general books: for example, G. R. Porter, op. cit. p. 459; P. Gaskell, *The Manufacturing Population of England* (London, 1833); J. Ward, *Workmen and Wages at Home and Abroad* (London, 1868); S. Smiles, *Workmen's Earnings, Strikes and Savings* (London, 1861); J. R. McCulloch, *The Principles of Political Economy* (London, 4th edn, 1849).

[2] E. J. Hobsbawm argues that the case for deterioration, if it can be established, 'will be done on the basis of consumption data' and declares that 'there is no evidence of any major rise in the *per capita* consumption of several foodstuffs, and in some instances evidence of a temporary fall' (op. cit. p. 57). The use of 'major' makes this statement difficult to refute, but Dr Hobsbawm's evidence about the consumption of meat, wheat, milk, cheese, butter, eggs, tea, sugar and tobacco (the commodities he considers) is ambiguous: he admits increases in the last three items; bases his figures of meat and wheat consumption on very dubious statistics (see below); argues that consumption of dairy produce must have declined because 'cow-keeping must have declined with urbanization' (no statistics provided), and that they were, in any case, inferior substitutes for meat; states that consumption of eggs 'can hardly have risen' (no evidence).

[3] M. G. Mulhall, *The Dictionary of Statistics* (London, 1892), pp. 120, 158, 281, 286, 354, 544. Mulhall also gives statistics for increasing *per capita* consumption of soap, leather, linen, cotton and coal.

[4] Gayer, Rostow and Schwartz, op. cit. vol. II, pp. 957–65.

poultry, meat and eggs. During 'the hungry 'forties' there were increases in the average *per capita* consumption of a number of imported foodstuffs: butter, cocoa, cheese, coffee, rice, sugar, tea, tobacco, currants.[1] For this reason Peel, in his election letter to the electors of Tamworth in July 1847, noting the large increase in the import of non-essential foodstuffs between 1841 and 1846, declared: 'Can there be a doubt that if the consumption of articles of a second necessity has been thus advancing, the consumption of articles of first necessity, of meat and of bread for instance, has been making at least an equally rapid progress?'[2] Certainly, when P. L. Simmonds considered national eating habits in the 1850s he concluded 'how much better an Englishman is fed than anyone else in the world'.[3]

There are, unfortunately, no adequate statistics for bread and meat consumption. The main statistical uncertainties in the case of bread are the acreage and the yield of cereal crops, especially wheat. There is no convincing evidence for Dr Hobsbawm's statement that, 'The fundamental fact is that, as contemporaries already knew, wheat production and imports did not keep pace with the growth of population so that the amount of wheat available *per capita* fell steadily from the late eighteenth century until the 1850s, the amount of potatoes available rising at about the same rate'.[4] On the contrary, as T. Tooke, G. R. Porter, J. R. McCulloch and even J. S. Mill pointed out, agricultural output increased faster than population.[5] When F. M. Eden

[1] L. Levi, op. cit. p. 497. It could be argued that food imports increased to compensate for inadequate home supplies, without any *per capita* increase in total food supply. More plausibly, however, it can be argued that Britain increasingly specialized to benefit from her comparative advantages in industrial production. That such specialization increased living standards, even in this period, is indicated by the 'luxury' character of many of the food imports. An absolute increase in demand occurred both when tariffs, and hence prices, were reduced (for example, tea prices were reduced from 2s. 9d. per lb. in 1831 to 1s. in 1853), and also when prices remained relatively stable (for example, with sugar and coffee).

[2] *Memoirs by the Right Honourable Sir Robert Peel* (London, 1857), vol. II, p. 104.

[3] P. L. Simmonds, *The Curiosities of Food* (London, 1859), p. 2.

[4] E. J. Hobsbawm, op. cit. p. 59. Dr Hobsbawm's wheat statistics come from R. N. Salaman (*The History and Social Influence of the Potato*, Cambridge University Press, 1949, Appendix IV) who took them from Lord Ernle (*English Farming Past and Present*, London: Longmans, Green, 1st edn, 1912).

[5] Thus, for example, J. S. Mill, who probably believed that living standards had been lowered by industrialization, argued that, 'In England and Scotland

wrote in 1797, barley, oat and rye breads were common, especially in the north; when McCulloch discussed bread in his commercial dictionary in 1859 he commented on the disappearance of barley and oat breads, the inconsiderable use of rye bread, and the universal consumption in towns and villages, and almost everywhere in the country, of wheat bread.[1] Such a substitution in a rapidly growing population – and one usually associated with increasing living standards – would not have been possible without a large increase in the home production of wheat, for it cannot be accounted for by the increase in imports. In the century of the agricultural revolution, however, this is not surprising: between 1760 and 1864 the common fields and wastes of England were enclosed, increasing both the area of, and yield from, arable. Even without other improvements, enclosure generally increased yields substantially. The largest increase in cultivation was during the war, and exactly how much increase there was after 1815 is not known.[2] Drescher estimated, however, that wheat cultivation in England and Wales increased from 3 to 3·8 million acres between 1798 and 1846, and that yields increased from 20–24 bushels per acre to 32–34 bushels. In a study of wheat yields over seven centuries, M. K. Bennett showed that 'the most rapid rate of

---

agricultural skill has of late increased considerably faster than population, insomuch that food and other agricultural produce, notwithstanding the increase of people, can be grown at less cost than they were thirty years ago.' (Written in 1848.) (*Principles of Political Economy*, edited by W. J. Ashley, London: Longman's Green, 1915, p. 704.)

[1] F. M. Eden, *The State of the Poor* (Edited by A. G. L. Rogers, London: Routledge, 1928), pp. 103–4; J. R. McCulloch, *A Dictionary, Practical, Theoretical and Historical of Commerce and Commercial Navigation* (Edited by H. G. Reid, London, 1869), p. 197. Even as early as 1795 Count Rumford (*An Essay on Food and Particularly on Feeding the Poor*, new edition, Dublin, 1847, p. 48) commented on the 'strange dislike' of rye bread in England.

[2] Agricultural historians of this period do agree, however, that the area of cultivation expanded after 1815; for example, W. H. R. Curtler, *The Enclosure and Redistribution of our Land* (Oxford: at the Clarendon Press, 1920), pp. 231–2; A. H. Johnson, *The Disappearance of the Small Landowner* (Oxford: at the Clarendon Press, 1909), p. 99; J. A. Venn, *Foundations of Agricultural Economics* (Cambridge University Press, 1923), p. 314; G. E. Fussell and M. Compton, 'Agricultural Adjustments after the Napoleonic Wars', *Economic History*, February 1939, p. 202; L. Drescher, 'The Development of Agricultural Production in Great Britain and Ireland from the early nineteenth Century', *The Manchester School*, May 1955, p. 167.

increase in British wheat yield was probably in the century between 1750 and 1850', that whereas 15 bushels was 'broadly representative of British wheat yield per acre in the middle of the eighteenth century', the representative yield in 1850 was 26–28 bushels.[1] On Drescher's estimates, wheat production just failed to keep pace with population. On other and reasonably plausible assumptions – for example, that yields were under 20 bushels per acre in 1800, and nearly 30 bushels in 1850 – domestic wheat production (without wheat imports) was keeping pace with population.[2] Wheat and bread prices certainly support the view that there was no long-term shortage of wheat and flour. Wheat prices fell sharply after 1815 and were relatively stable, though with a discernible downward trend after 1822, the yearly average reaching 70s. only on one occasion, 1839, before 1850, and the price in 1835, 39s. 4d., being the lowest for half a century.[3] The price of bread was also relatively stable in these years; for example, the London four lb. loaf fluctuated from 6·8d. to 11·5d. between 1820 and 1850, but with a range of 6·8d. to 10·5d. in all but seven years, and with decade averages of 9·7d., 9·1d. and 9·3d.[4]

Far less is known about potato consumption than wheat consumption, although R. N. Salaman reckoned that *per capita* daily consumption in England and Wales increased from 0·4 to 0·6 lb. between 1795 and 1838.[5] The theory that this increase was not a net addition to total diet, associated after 1815 with the increasing use of allotments by the working class, but a necessary substitution of an inferior vegetable for wheat bread,

[1] M. K. Bennett, 'British Wheat Yield per acre for Seven Centuries', *Economic History*, February 1935, p. 28.

[2] T. Tooke and W. Newmarch (op. cit. vol. V, p. 132) wrote in 1857 that 'during the last thirty years, the increase in England on the Average Acreable Produce of Wheat is very much greater than it is the habit to suppose', with supporting evidence. Compare J. R. McCulloch's statement (1869) that 'the produce of the wheat crops has been, at the very least *quadrupled* since 1760' (op. cit. p. 197).

[3] W. Page (ed.), *Commerce and Industry* (London: Constable, 1919), vol. II, p. 216; T. H. Baker, *Records of the Seasons, Prices of Agricultural Produce, and Phenomena observed in the British Isles* (London, 1883), p. 249 *et seq.*

[4] *Wheat*, Return to House of Commons, 7 August 1912.

[5] R. N. Salaman, op. cit. p. 613. It is interesting that consumption of potatoes today is almost exactly the same as in 1838, between 3 and 4 lb. per person per week (*Economic Trends*, no. 59, September 1958, p. xvii; and *The Times*, 21 April 1959).

is based on the doubtful assumptions that bread consumption was declining, and that the potato was an inferior food. Prejudice against the potato stemmed partly from dislike of the Irish, and certainly the half million Irish in England in 1850 help to explain the increasing popularity of the root. But increasing consumption was due also to the simple facts that people liked potatoes and that they were good food, as Adam Smith demonstrated.[1] Moreover the potato was but one of many vegetables and fruits whose consumption was increasing.[2] Vegetables that in 1800 had only been grown casually, like water-cress, were by 1850 commercialized; fruits that were not imported at all, or in very small quantities in 1800, were regularly imported by the 1830s – for example, cherries and apples – and in large quantities by 1850.[3] In London, Covent Garden was rebuilt in 1827, and by 1850 there were in addition five other important markets supplying the metropolis with fruit and vegetables. By 1850 every large town had its market gardens and orchards, and for London, the largest and richest market, the movement was well under way which by 1870 had almost filled the Thames Valley with fruit trees and vegetable crops.[4]

'Next to the *Habeas Corpus* and the Freedom of the Press,' Charles Dickens wrote, 'there are few things that the English people have a greater respect for and livelier faith in than beef.' In the first fifty years of the nineteenth century, the English

[1] Adam Smith, *The Wealth of Nations* (Cannan edition, New York: The Modern Library, 1937, p. 161): 'The Chairmen, porters, and coal-heavers in London, and those unfortunate women who live by prostitution, the strongest men and the most beautiful women perhaps in the British dominions, are said to be, the greater part of them, from the lowest rank of people in Ireland, who are generally fed with this root. No food can afford a more decisive proof of its nourishing quality, or of its being peculiarly suitable to the health of the human constitution.'

[2] See G. Dodd (*The Food of London*, London, 1856), H. Mayhew (*London Labour and the London Poor*, London, 1851), B. Poole (*Statistics of British Commerce*, London, 1852), and *The Commissariat of London* (*The Quarterly Review*, September 1854), for the fruit and vegetable markets of London.

[3] Dodd, op. cit. pp. 377–8.

[4] See, for example, J. Cuthill, *Market Gardening round London* (London 1851) and C. W. Shaw, *The London Market Gardens* (London, 1879), for a description of the Thames Valley gardens and orchards. Shaw commented that 'the price paid now for fruits deviates but slightly from that paid half a century ago; although the quantity which we receive is fifty times greater, yet the demand has increased accordingly, and thus the price has been kept up' (pp. 82–3).

working class came to expect meat as a part of the normal diet.[1]
Above all other foods, wheat bread and meat were to them the
criteria of increasing living standards and superiority over
foreigners. 'Until the "Roast beef of old England" shall cease
to be one of the institutions of the country – one of the
characteristics whereby foreigners believe, at any rate, that they
may judge us as a nation – butchers' meat will continue to be
(with the exception of bread) the chief article in our commissariat', G. Dodd declared in 1856.[2] The fifty years before
had been a period of widespread livestock improvement. For
example, the story of the English sheep in this period was one
of substituting mutton for wool as the main criterion of
breeding, a substitution firmly based on economic incentives;
the flock owners were turning away from the ancient breeds to
larger, stronger and quickly maturing breeds like the New
Leicester and the Southdown.[3] As with sheep, so with cattle
and pigs.

The only detailed statistics of meat consumption, however,
are for London, based on killings at Smithfield, where, between
1800 and 1850, the slaughter of cattle increased 91 per cent and
sheep 92 per cent while London population meantime increased
173 per cent.[4] But these figures ignore any increase in carcass
weight, and also the supply from other markets. Smithfield
killings cannot be accepted as a reliable index for London meat
consumption – as E. J. Hobsbawm does – for there were other
fast growing markets – Newgate, Leadenhall, Farringdon and
Whitechapel – in addition to a number of smaller markets, all
of which were largely dependent on country-killed meat and on

---

[1] *Reports from Commissioners* (13), *Poor Laws (Ireland)*, *Parliamentary Papers*,
1836 (XXXIV), p. xii, comments that the English working class have meat most
days, in contrast to the Irish. See also C. S. Peel, 'Homes and Habits' (*Early
Victorian England 1830–1865*, Oxford, 1934, vol. I, pp. 126–43) showing working-
class budgets 1824–59, all with meat.

[2] Dodd, op. cit. p. 211.

[3] Lord Ernle, op. cit. p. 371; R. Trow-Smith, *A History of British Livestock
Husbandry 1700–1900* (London: Routledge and Kegan Paul, 1959), pp. 156–8;
J. Bischoff, *A Comprehensive History of the Woollen and Worsted Manufactures*
(London, 1842), vol. II, 255. Bischoff reckoned that by 1850 eight million sheep
were slaughtered annually to give the Englishman his mutton.

[4] Averaging 1798–1802 and 1848–1852.

[5] Hobsbawm, op. cit. p. 65.

imported 'preserved' meats, like bacon and salt pork.[1] Even in the mid-eighteenth century, when London was smaller and Smithfield relatively more important, perhaps only two-thirds of the fresh meat for London went through Smithfield, 'because the London butchers bought at the country markets and at fairs in Cambridge, Northampton and Norfolk as well as bringing carcases in'.[2] In the nineteenth century the limitations of Smithfield[3] and the growth of London led inevitably to the development of other sources of supply, other markets that increased in size more rapidly than Smithfield. Newgate had thirteen principal salesmen in 1810, and by 1850, two hundred, who were handling half as many sheep, three-quarters as many cattle and more calves and pigs than Smithfield; in 1850, 800 tons of country-killed meat arrived there weekly, mainly by railway. In the same year Poole estimated that the yearly sales at Newgate and Leadenhall amounted to 76,500 tons.[4] Certainly the railways much increased the supply of country-killed meat to London, but well before their time increasing quantities had been transported in wagons and carts. At the same time the import of bacon, ham and salt pork increased. Little wonder, therefore, that McCulloch concluded that 'the . . . extraordinary increase in the supply of butchers' meat' was evidence of 'a very signal improvement . . . in the condition of the population, in respect of food'.[5] Nor, of course, was the increased supply confined to London. As a farmer noted significantly in 1836, the fat stock of Gloucestershire and Cumberland were then going, not to London as before, but increasingly

[1] Dodd, op. cit. p. 267 *et seq.*, p. 276 *et seq.*; *Report of the Commissioners Appointed to make Inquiries relating to Smithfield Market and the Markets in the City of London for the sale of Meat* (Reports of Commissioners (12), *Parliamentary Papers*, 1850, XXXI), pp. 16–18; *The Commissariat of London*, op. cit. pp. 280–7.

[2] G. E. Fussell and C. Goodman, 'Eighteenth-Century Traffic in Live-Stock', *Economic History*, February 1936, p. 231.

[3] In 1854 Smithfield market occupied under seven acres. *The Commissariat of London*, op. cit. p. 280.

[4] Dodd, op. cit. p. 273; B. Poole, op. cit. p. 225; McCulloch, *Dictionary*, op. cit. pp. 281–3; Levi, op. cit. p. 497; *Report of Commissioners . . . for the sale of meat*, op. cit. p. 16; *The Commissariat of London*, op. cit. p. 287. See also, A. B. Robertson, 'The Suburban Food Markets of Eighteenth-Century London' (*East London Papers*, II, 1, p. 21 *et seq.*), for an account of the expansion of market facilities in London up to 1801.

[5] McCulloch, *Dictionary*, op. cit. p. 197.

to Birmingham, Liverpool and the other industrial towns.[1] Increased supply was reflected in prices, with steady prices generally from 1819 to 1841, and fluctuating prices in the 'forties.[2]

Another important food whose consumption was increasing at this time was fish.[3] Before 1815, except during gluts, fish was expensive, and appeared regularly only on the tables of the well-to-do. Early in the nineteenth century, consumption was small, partly because of religious prejudice,[4] partly because of the difficulty of transporting such a perishable commodity, partly because of a preference for meat. After 1815 increasing supply and decreasing prices (the average price for all fish at Billingsgate in 1833 was $2\frac{1}{2}d.$ per lb.)[5] led to a large increase in consumption; but even in 1833 the clerk of Billingsgate declared that 'the lower class of people entertain the notion that fish is not substantial food enough for them, and they prefer meat'.[6] Nevertheless the poor by this time were becoming large purchasers of fish, taking particular advantage of price fluctuations (which were much greater than for meat) to increase consumption. When, for example, mackerel and herring were cheap, the poor ate 'a great deal of them' and at any time the news of cheap fish spread throughout London 'with wonderful celerity'.[7] Official statistics, unfortunately, are confined mainly to the Scottish herring export industry. We know, however, that 'a large proportion of the Fish caught upon the English coast [was] supplied by hand carriage to the London and Inland Markets', and, also, that the supply of fish increased after the

[1] *Parliamentary Papers* 1836 (465) VIII, part 2, pp. 181, 210; also, 1833 (612) V, p. 59, saying that meat 'sells well in the large towns', 'the mechanics having more money to lay out'.

[2] Tooke and Newmarch, op. cit. vol. II, pp. 85, 135, 257; vol. VI, pp. 454–60.

[3] *Commissariat of London*, op. cit. pp. 273–80; C. L. Cutting, *Fish Saving* (London, 1955), pp. 207–30.

[4] 'The Reformation seems almost to have abolished the use of fish among this class of the community; they have contracted, I know not how, some obstinate prejudice against a kind of food at once wholesome and delicate, and everywhere to be obtained cheaply and in abundance, were the demand for it as general as it ought to be.' R. Southey, *Sir Thomas More, or Colloquies on the Progress and Prospects of Society* (London, 1829), vol. I, p. 175.

[5] *Parliamentary Papers* 1833 (676), XIV, p. 95.

[6] Ibid. p. 94.

[7] Ibid. pp. 94, 100.

abolition of the salt tax in 1825, and, after 1830, with technical innovations in fishing that increased yields, particularly the development of deep-sea trawling and of drift fishing; with improvements in the handlings of fish, for example, the use of fast cutters, walled steamers and the railways, and the increasing use of ice; and with the discovery of new fishing waters, for example, the Great Silver Pitt, south of the Dogger, in 1837.[1] By 1840 ice and fast transport were enabling trawlers to fish farther north, and were opening up new markets in the inland towns.[2] The kipper was invented in 1843.[3] By 1850 steamship and railway combined to transport catches quickly to the centres of consumption all over England: steamships linked the Channel, North and German Seas to the English ports; railways linked the ports to the internal towns and London. In season, herrings alone were arriving in London from Yarmouth at the rate of 160 tons an evening, and even the humble periwinkle, Simmonds estimated, was consumed at the rate of 76,000 baskets (or 1,900 tons) annually.[4]

The conclusion from consumption figures is unquestionably that the amount and variety of food consumed increased between 1800 and 1850. Even an uncritical reading of those entertaining and informative volumes of G. R. Dodd (*The Food of London*) and H. Mayhew (*London Labour and the London Poor*), and of the article 'The Commissariat of London' in *The Quarterly Review* (1854), will reveal the size, range and quality of London's food supplies. By 1850, using the admittedly rough calculations of Dodd, McCulloch, Mayhew, Poole, Mulhall and Levi, the Londoner was consuming each week 5 oz. of butter, 30 oz. of meat, 56 oz. of potatoes, and 16 oz. of fruit, compared with an English consumption today of 5 oz.

---

[1] *Parliamentary Papers* 1833 (676), XIV, p. 12; J. T. Jenkins, *The Sea Fisheries* (London, 1920), p. 145, and chapters II and V; *The Commissariat of London*, op. cit. pp. 278–9.

[2] Cutting, op. cit. p. 220.　　　　[3] Ibid. p. 277.

[4] Simmonds, op. cit. p. 345; Dodd, op. cit. p. 341 *et seq*. London streets in the 'forties were crowded with barrows. When Jorrocks and the Yorkshireman went from Covent Garden to Surrey they met, among others, 'an early breakfast and periwinkle stall', 'three water-cress women', 'one pies-all-ot! -all-ot man', 'a whole covey of Welsh milk-maids'. (*Jorrocks's Jaunts and Jollities*, 1843.) By 1854 there were probably 30,000 costermongers, hawkers and stall-keepers in London (*The Commissariat of London*, op. cit. p. 307).

of butter, 35 oz. of meat, 51 oz. of potatoes and 32 oz. of fruit.[1]
Even allowing for contemporary exaggeration and enthusiasm,
the consumption of *basic* foods in 1850 London was not wildly
inferior to that of modern England.[2]

IV

What conclusion follows from the evidence so far presented?
Surely, since the indices point in the same direction, even
though the change cannot be measured with accuracy, that the
standard of living of the mass of the people of England was
improving in the first half of the nineteenth century, slowly
during the war, more quickly after 1815, and rapidly after 1840.
And, if expectation of life depends partly on living standards,
the increase in average life over these years is further proof of
increasing well-being. As Macaulay argued, 'that the lives of
men should become longer while their bodily condition during
life is becoming worse, is utterly incredible'. The expectation
of life at birth in 1840–50 was higher than in 1770–80; by the
1840s infantile mortality rates had been reduced from 'the
terrifying levels of the eighteenth century', and 'the death
rate for ages 0–4 . . . was very low, at least for a highly urban-
ized country at that time'.[3] McKeown and Brown have shown

[1] The 1850 calculations are made by simple division of yearly totals, when
given, by London population; the modern figures come from *The Times*, 21 April
1959.

[2] Of other foodstuffs mentioned by Dr Hobsbawm, milk and eggs deserve
some attention. Of milk, he wrote, 'it is difficult to see anything but a decline . . .
because cow-keeping must have declined with urbanisation' (p. 59). But this was
a period of 'a new race of enlightened cowkeepers' when the railway enabled 'the
evening's milk from the country to be on the London doorstep the next morning'.
As Trow Smith points out: by 1853 on some farms in Surrey '100 to 150 cows
are kept and the milk sent to the Waterloo terminus of the South Western Railway'
(op. cit. pp. 305, 309). There were, in any case, about 20,000 cows in metropolitan
and suburban dairies in 1854 (*The Commissariat of London*, op. cit. p. 287). Of
eggs, Simmonds wrote of 'the sixty wholesale egg merchants and salesmen in the
metropolis, whose itinerant carts are kept constantly occupied in distributing
their brittle ware' and the 'railways and steamers bring up large crates, and carefully packed boxes of eggs, for the ravenous maws of young and old' (op. cit.
p. 138). Mayhew also refers to the change in the egg trade due to the 'immense
quantities from France and Belgium' (op. cit. vol. i, p. 129).

[3] H. J. Habakkuk, 'The Economic History of Modern Britain', *Journal of
Economic History*, December 1958, p. 496; J. T. Krause, 'Changes in English
Fertility and Mortality', *Economic History Review*, August 1958, pp. 66–7.

that medical improvements could have had little effect on life expectation before 1850, and suggest that it was an improvement in the economic and social environment that lengthened life.[1] People lived longer because they were better nourished and sheltered, and cleaner, and thus were less vulnerable to infectious and other diseases (like consumption) that were peculiarly susceptible to improved living standards.[2] Factory conditions also improved. R. Baker, one of the early factory inspectors, in a paper to the Social Science Association at Bradford in 1859, declared of the years 1822 to 1856 that 'all the diseases which were specific to factory labour in 1822 have as nearly as possible disappeared', and, quoting a Dr Smith of Leeds, referred particularly to 'the wonderful change in the condition of the female part of the population . . . So striking a difference in twenty-five years I could not have believed, had I not marked and seen it with my own eyes.'

But increasing life expectation and increasing consumption are no measures of ultimate well-being, and to say that the standard of living for most workers was rising, is *not* to say that it was high, *nor* is it to affirm that it was rising fast, *nor* that there was no dire poverty, and cyclical fluctuations and technological unemployment of a most distressing character. It is as foolish to ignore the sufferings of this period as to deny the wealth and

[1] T. McKeown and R. G. Brown, 'Medical Evidence Related to English Population Changes in the Eighteenth Century', *Population Studies*, November 1955. In so far as the population increase was due to an increased birth rate, whether from a lower marriage age, or from increasing fertility without a change in the age of marriage, economic factors again were probably important. Improved conditions, also, would help to explain 'the failure of births to fall as soon as one would have expected under the pressure of population' (Habakkuk, op. cit. p. 495), a phenomenon puzzling to those who take for granted a Malthusian situation in England at this period.

[2] Dr Hobsbawm argues that a greater regularity of supply in *per capita* consumption does not imply a rise in living standards, even though it causes a reduction in mortality. 'It is quite possible for the industrial citizen to be worse fed in a normal year than his predecessor, so long as he is more regularly fed.' (p. 46.) This is double talk; the final criterion is surely death? Some people may prefer a combination of feasts and famine, with an uncertain expectation of life, but surely most people would prefer regular consumption, the certainty of longer life, and the hope of improved conditions. And, in any case, there were no feasts in pre-industrial, or modern non-industrial societies: the alternatives were (and are) subsistence, and, when crops fail, less than subsistence. In the classic definition of welfare, a person is better off if his income is larger, or more evenly distributed over time.

opportunities created by the new industry. Moreover little understanding comes from trying to attribute blame for the suffering that did exist. The discomfort of the period was due in large part to an inability to handle new problems or old problems enormously magnified; problems of increasing population, of urbanization, of factory conditions, of fluctuating trade and employment. And the tensions of the period arose naturally from the rapidly changing social and economic relationships. As the Hammonds point out: 'When . . . society is passing through changes that destroy the life of custom, the statesman who seeks . . . to command man's will and not merely his deeds and services has a specially difficult task, for these changes bring into men's minds the dreaded questions that have been sleeping beneath the surface of habit.'[1] On the easier practical problems, to take an example, municipal authorities did not have the knowledge, and usually not the adequate authority, to deal with the various problems of sanitation in rapidly growing cities. Such problems required study, experiment and experience, as well as a change of attitudes, before they could be solved, so that it was ignorance rather than avarice that was often the cause of misery. In any case, much of the ill that has been attributed solely to the industrial revolution existed also in the pre-industrial age. 'Appalling as was the state of things revealed by the nineteenth-century reports (1840–45) on the sanitary state of towns it can hardly be doubted that the state of London was far worse in the eighteenth century.'[2] And by 1854 London was 'the healthiest metropolis in Europe'.[3]

Thus much misunderstanding has arisen because of assumptions – mainly misconceptions – about England before the industrial revolution; assumptions, for example, that rural life was naturally better than town life, that working for oneself was better and more secure than working for an employer, that child and female labour was something new, that the domestic system (even though it often involved a house crammed with

[1] J. L. and B. Hammond, *The Bleak Age* (Pelican edition, 1947), p. 30.
[2] M. D. George, *London Life in the Eighteenth Century* (London, 1925), p. 103. See also, T. S. Ashton, 'Changes in the Standard of Comfort in Eighteenth-Century England' (*Proceedings of the British Academy*, 1955).
[3] D. Roberts, *Victorian Origins of the British Welfare State* (Yale University Press, 1960), p. 325.

industrial equipment) was preferable to the factory system, that slums and food adulteration were peculiar products of industrialization, and so on; in other words, the perennial myth of the golden age, the belief that since conditions were bad, and since one did not approve of them, they could not have been worse, and, indeed, must once have been better! But, as Alfred Marshall pointed out: 'Popular history underrates the hardships of the people before the age of factories'.[1]

Rural life was just as appalling as urban life: on the estates of the Marquis of Ailesbury much later cottage conditions exhibited 'a violation of all decency', 'altogether filthy and disgusting', with, in extreme cases, twelve persons in one room and 'depravity which the towns could scarcely have rivalled'.[2] Insecurity, as T. S. Ashton has demonstrated, was as much a characteristic of the eighteenth as of the nineteenth century, with regular cycles of trade complicated by harvest failures for which there was no adequate redress.[3] In any case, already before the industrial revolution, large numbers of employees worked as wage-labourers for clothiers, ironmongers, hosiers and the government. 'In the textile trades, in particular, there must have been thousands of workers who never set eyes on their employer. The notion that the coming of factories meant a "depersonalization" of relations to industry is the reverse of the truth.'[4] Again, in the eighteenth century the domestic system and agriculture (the largest employer before the coming of the factories) depended heavily on the labour of women and children.

Similarly, food adulteration, which Dr Hobsbawm seems to think was suddenly discovered in the 1850s, was well known to Smollett in 1771, when he complained that: 'The bread I eat in London, is a deleterious paste, mixed up with chalk, alum, and bone-ashes; insipid to the taste and destructive to the constitution.' 'I need not dwell upon the pallid contaminated mash,

[1] A. Marshall, *Industry and Trade* (London, 1920, 3rd edn), p. 73 n.

[2] F. M. L. Thompson, 'English Landownership: The Ailesbury Trust, 1832–56', *Economic History Review*, August 1958, p. 128.

[3] T. S. Ashton, *Economic Fluctuations in England 1700–1800* (Oxford: at The Clarendon Press, 1959).

[4] T. S. Ashton, *An Economic History of England: The 18th Century* (London: Methuen, 1955) pp. 102–3.

which they call strawberries; soiled and tossed by greasy paws through twenty baskets crusted with dirt; and then presented with the worst milk, thickened with the worst flour, into a bad likeness of cream.' 'The milk . . . the produce of faded cabbage-leaves and sour draff, lowered with hot water, frothed with bruised snails, carried through the streets in open pails.'[1] Like-wise with morals. It cannot be assumed that the moral standards of the working class had deteriorated, or, indeed, that they were worse than those of their betters. The Webbs were certainly shocked by the morals of the eighteenth century where they discovered 'a horrifying mass of sensual and sordid delin-quency' and 'private licentiousness'.[2] Moreover, the evidence about morals is, to say the least, ambiguous; and, in any case, immorality in the slums was no worse, in quantity or kind, than immorality in high society.

But if misery was not a new phenomenon, the range and possibility of opportunities for workmen were new. As A. Toynbee admitted: 'The artisan's horizon became indistinct; there was no visible limit to subsistence.'[3] Economy and society were in process of rapid change, and the opportunities for wealth and social advancement were greater than they had ever been before. The result was the increasing self-respect of the poor that so pleased Francis Place and the young Edwin Chadwick.[4] One might well ask, however, as did the Hammonds: 'Why did this age with all its improvements create

[1] T. Smollett, *The Expedition of Humphry Clinker* (1771: World Classics Edition, Oxford, 1938), pp. 144, 146.

[2] Webb Local Government Collection, London School of Economics and Political Science, report (unpublished) by Ruth Atkins.

[3] A. Toynbee, *Lectures on the Industrial Revolution of the Eighteenth Century in England* (London, 1913 edn), 'Malthus and the Law of Population', p. 91.

[4] See M. D. George, *London Life in the Eighteenth Century*, op. cit. pp. 103, 105; quoting Chadwick commenting in 1828 on 'considerable improvements . . . in the domestic habits of artisans; they are more cleanly and regular, their houses are better constructed, they have acquired some notions that fresh air is conducive to health, and the streets where they reside are less filthy and pestilential than formerly'. Professor Schultes of Baden, visiting London in 1824, also noted a habit that showed the increasing refinement of the poor: 'the poor Londoner who cannot afford to buy what is beautiful, will still obtain . . . something green to decorate the window of his dark little attic, and give his last farthing for a bit of verdure . . . the poor artisan of the French capital, he only thinks of vegetable productions as they are fit for culinary uses.' (Sir W. J. Hooker, *Botanical Miscel-lany*, London, 1831–3, vol. I, 72–3.)

such violent discontent?'[1] But discontent is not merely a simple product of living standards. The vision of an age of plenty, stimulated by the obvious productivity of new machines that seemed to compete with labour, roused both anger and ambition. The breaking-up of the old social relationships was a liberating and stimulating experience that made possible, for the first time, an effective working-class movement. And although the standard of living was rising, it was not rising quickly, and the individual was aware only that his wages were meagre and not sufficient to satisfy his wants and needs. As A. L. Bowley has pointed out: 'The idea of progress is largely psychological and certainly relative; people are apt to measure their progress not from a forgotten position in the past, but towards an ideal, which, like an horizon, continually recedes. The present generation is not interested in the earlier needs and successes of its progenitors, but in its own distresses and frustration considered in the light of the presumed possibility of universal comfort or riches.'[2] Discontent, even disorder, were indeed understandable, and both, like suffering, it must be remembered, were also characteristic of the previous age. But the disorder of the 'forties was far less violent and destructive than the Gordon Riots, and this restraint was due, not only to better police, but 'to the fact that the English industrial working class was on the whole better housed, better fed, better educated, and far less degraded than in preceding years'.[3] And the important thing about suffering during the industrial revolution was that it brought with it its own solution: increasing productivity in industry and agriculture, and, in society, faith that social conditions should and could be improved, and that economic progress was inevitable. 'Amidst

---

[1] J. L. Hammond, 'The Industrial Revolution and Discontent', *Economic History Review*, January 1930, p. 215. A. V. Dicey (*Law and Public Opinion in England during the Nineteenth Century*, London, 2nd edn, 1914, pp. lxviii–lxix) argued that discontent 'is often due far less to the absolute amount of the suffering endured among men . . . than to the increased vividness of the contrast between given institutions and the desires of persons who suffer, or think they suffer, from the existing state of things'.

[2] A. L. Bowley, *Wages and Income in the United Kingdom since 1860* (Cambridge University Press, 1937), p. x.

[3] F. C. Mather, *Public Order in the Age of the Chartists* (Manchester University Press, 1959), pp. 12–13.

the varied reflections which the nineteenth century is in the
habit of making on its condition and its prospects', wrote
J. A. Froude later in the century, 'there is one common
opinion in which all parties coincide – that we live in an era of
progress . . . in every department of life – in its business and in
its pleasures, in its beliefs and in its theories, in its material
developments and in its spiritual convictions – we thank God
that we are not like our fathers. And while we admit their
merits, making allowance for their disadvantages, we do not
blind ourselves in mistaken modesty to our own immeasurable
superiority.'[1] The new attitude to social problems that emerged
with the industrial revolution was that ills should be identified,
examined, analysed, publicized and remedied, either by
voluntary or legislative action. Thus evils that had long existed
– child labour, for example – and had long been accepted as
inevitable, were regarded as new ills to be remedied rather than
as old ills to be endured. It was during the industrial revolution,
moreover, and largely because of the economic opportunities
it afforded to working-class women, that there was the beginning of that most important and most beneficial of all the social
revolutions of the last two centuries, the emancipation of
women.

[1] J. A. Froude, *Short Studies on Great Subjects* (London, 1907 edn), vol. III,
'On Progress', pp. 149–50.

6 Standards and Experiences

E. P. THOMPSON

[First published *The Making of the English Working Class*, Victor Gollancz Ltd, London, 1963.]

An aristocratic traveller who visited the Yorkshire Dales in 1792 was alarmed to find a new cotton-mill in the 'pastoral vale' of Aysgarth – 'why, here now is a great flaring mill, whose back stream has drawn off half the water of the falls above the bridge':

> With the bell ringing, and the clamour of the mill, all the vale is disturb'd; treason and levelling systems are the discourse; and rebellion may be near at hand.

The mill appeared as symbol of social energies which were destroying the very 'course of Nature'. It embodied a double threat to the settled order. First, from the owners of industrial wealth, those upstarts who enjoyed an unfair advantage over the landowners whose income was tied to their rent-roll:

> If men thus start into riches; or if riches from trade are too easily procured, woe to us men of middling income, and settled revenue; and woe it has been to all the Nappa Halls, and the Yeomanry of the land.

Second, from the industrial working population, which our traveller regarded with an alliterative hostility which betrays a response not far removed from that of the white racialist towards the coloured population today:

> The people, indeed, are employ'd; but they are all abandon'd to vice from the throng. . . . At the times when people work not in the mill, they issue out to poaching, profligacy and plunder . . .[1]

[1] *The Torrington Diaries*, ed. C. B. Andrews (1936), III, pp. 81–2.

The equation between the cotton-mill and the new industrial society, and the correspondence between new forms of productive and of social relationship, was a commonplace among observers in the years between 1790 and 1850. Karl Marx was only expressing this with unusual vigour when he declared: 'The hand-mill gives you society with the feudal lord: the steam-mill, society with the industrial capitalist.' And it was not only the mill-owner but also the working population brought into being within and around the mills which seemed to contemporaries to be 'new'. 'The instant we get near the borders of the manufacturing parts of Lancashire,' a rural magistrate wrote in 1808, 'we meet a fresh race of beings, both in point of manners, employments and subordination . . .'; while Robert Owen, in 1815, declared that 'the general diffusion of manufactures throughout a country generates a new character in its inhabitants . . . an essential change in the general character of the mass of the people'.

Observers in the 1830s and 1840s were still exclaiming at the novelty of the 'factory system'. Peter Gaskell, in 1833, spoke of the manufacturing population as 'but a Hercules in the cradle'; it was 'only since the introduction of steam as a power that they have acquired their paramount importance'. The steam-engine had 'drawn together the population into dense masses' and already Gaskell saw in working-class organizations an ' "imperium in imperio" of the most obnoxious description'.[1] Ten years later Cooke Taylor was writing in similar terms:

> The steam-engine had no precedent, the spinning-jenny is without ancestry, the mule and the power-loom entered on no prepared heritage: they sprang into sudden existence like Minerva from the brain of Jupiter.

But it was the human consequence of these 'novelties' which caused this observer most disquiet:

> As a stranger passes through the masses of human beings which have accumulated round the mills and print works . . . he cannot contemplate these 'crowded hives' without feelings

[1] P. Gaskell, *The Manufacturing Population of England* (1833), p. 6; Asa Briggs, 'The Language of "Class" in Early Nineteenth-century England', in *Essays in Labour History*, ed. Briggs and Saville (1960), p. 63.

of anxiety and apprehension almost amounting to dismay. The population, like the system to which it belongs, is NEW; but it is hourly increasing in breadth and strength. It is an aggregate of masses, our conceptions of which clothe themselves in terms that express something portentous and fearful . . . as of the slow rising and gradual swelling of an ocean which must, at some future and no distant time, bear all the elements of society aloft upon its bosom, and float them Heaven knows whither. There are mighty energies slumbering in these masses. . . . The manufacturing population is not new in its formation alone: it is new in its habits of thought and action, which have been formed by the circumstances of its condition, with little instruction, and less guidance, from external sources . . .[1]

For Engels, describing the *Condition of the Working Class in England in 1844* it seemed that 'the first proletarians were connected with manufacture, were engendered by it . . . the factory hands, eldest children of the industrial revolution, have from the beginning to the present day formed the nucleus of the Labour Movement'.

However different their judgments of value, conservative, radical and socialist observers suggested the same equation: steam power and the cotton-mill = new working class. The physical instruments of production were seen as giving rise in a direct and more-or-less compulsive way to new social relationships, institutions and cultural modes. At the same time the history of popular agitation during the period 1811–50 appears to confirm this picture. It is as if the English nation entered a crucible in the 1790s and emerged after the Wars in a different form. Between 1811 and 1813, the Luddite crisis; in 1817 the Pentridge Rising; in 1819, Peterloo; throughout the next decade the proliferation of trade union activity, Owenite propaganda, Radical journalism, the Ten Hours Movement, the revolutionary crisis of 1831–2; and, beyond that, the multitude of movements which made up Chartism. It is, perhaps, the scale and intensity of this multiform popular agitation which

[1] W. Cooke Taylor, *Notes of a Tour in the Manufacturing Districts of Lancashire* (1842), pp. 4–6.

has, more than anything else, given rise (among contemporary observers and historians alike) to the sense of some catastrophic change.

Almost every radical phenomenon of the 1790s can be found reproduced tenfold after 1815. The handful of Jacobin sheets gave rise to a score of ultra-Radical and Owenite periodicals. Where Daniel Eaton served imprisonment for publishing Paine, Richard Carlyle and his shopmen served a total of more than 200 years imprisonment for similar crimes. Where Corresponding Societies maintained a precarious existence in a score of towns, the post-war Hampden Clubs or political unions struck root in small industrial villages. And when this popular agitation is recalled alongside the dramatic pace of change in the cotton industry, it is natural to assume a direct causal relationship. The cotton-mill is seen as the agent not only of industrial but also of social revolution, producing not only more goods but also the 'Labour Movement' itself. The Industrial Revolution, which commenced as a description, is now invoked as an explanation.

From the time of Arkwright through to the Plug Riots and beyond, it is the image of the 'dark, Satanic mill' which dominates our visual reconstruction of the Industrial Revolution. In part, perhaps, because it is a dramatic visual image – the barrack-like buildings, the great mill chimneys, the factory children, the clogs and shawls, the dwellings clustering around the mills as if spawned by them. (It is an image which forces one to think first of the industry, and only secondly of the people connected to it or serving it.) In part, because the cotton-mill and the new mill-town – from the swiftness of its growth, ingenuity of its techniques, and the novelty or harshness of its discipline – seemed to contemporaries to be dramatic and portentous: a more satisfactory symbol for debate on the 'condition-of-England' question than those anonymous or sprawling manufacturing *districts* which figure even more often in the Home Office 'disturbance books'. And from this both a literary and an historical tradition is derived. Nearly all the classic accounts by contemporaries of conditions in the Industrial Revolution are based on the cotton industry – and, in the main, on Lancashire: Owen, Gaskell, Ure, Fielden, Cooke

Taylor, Engels, to mention a few. Novels such as *Michael Armstrong* or *Mary Barton* or *Hard Times* perpetuate the tradition. And the emphasis is markedly found in the subsequent writing of economic and social history.

But many difficulties remain. Cotton was certainly the pacemaking industry of the Industrial Revolution,[1] and the cotton-mill was the pre-eminent model for the factory system. Yet we should not assume any automatic, or over-direct, correspondence between the dynamic of economic growth and the dynamic of social or cultural life. For half a century after the 'breakthrough' of the cotton-mill (around 1780) the mill workers remained as a minority of the adult labour force in the cotton industry itself. In the early 1830s the cotton handloom weavers alone still outnumbered all the men and women in spinning and weaving mills of cotton, wool and silk combined.[2] Still, in 1830, the adult male cotton-spinner was no more typical of that elusive figure, the 'average working man', than is the Coventry motor-worker of the 1960s.

The point is of importance, because too much emphasis upon the newness of the cotton-mills can lead to an underestimation of the continuity of political and cultural traditions in the making of working-class communities. The factory hands, so far from being the 'eldest children of the industrial revolution', were late arrivals. Many of their ideas and forms of organization were anticipated by domestic workers, such as the woollen workers of Norwich and the West Country, or the small-ware weavers of Manchester. And it is questionable whether factory hands – except in the cotton districts – 'formed the nucleus of the Labour Movement' at any time before the late 1840s (and, in some northern and Midland towns, the years 1832–4, leading up to the great lock-outs). Jacobinism, as we have seen, struck root most deeply among artisans. Luddism was the work of skilled men in small workshops. From 1817 onwards to Chartism, the outworkers in the north and the Midlands were as prominent in every radical agitation as the factory hands. And

---

[1] For an admirable restatement of the reasons for the primacy of the cotton industry in the Industrial Revolution, see E. J. Hobsbawm, *The Age of Revolution* (1962), ch. 2.

[2] Estimates for U.K., 1833. Total adult labour force in all textile mills, pp. 191, 671. Number of cotton handloom weavers, 213,000.

in many towns the actual nucleus from which the labour movement derived ideas, organization and leadership, was made up
of such men as shoemakers, weavers, saddlers and harness-
makers, booksellers, printers, building workers, small tradesmen, and the like. The vast area of Radical London between
1815 and 1850 drew its strength from no major heavy industries
(shipbuilding was tending to decline, and the engineers only
made their impact later in the century) but from the host of
smaller trades and occupations.[1]

Such diversity of experiences has led some writers to question
both the notions of an 'industrial revolution' and of a 'working
class'. The first discussion need not detain us here.[2] The term
is serviceable enough in its usual connotations. For the second,
many writers prefer the term working *classes*, which emphasizes
the great disparity in status, acquisitions, skills, conditions,
within the portmanteau phrase. And in this they echo the
complaints of Francis Place:

> If the character and conduct of the working-people are to
> be taken from reviews, magazines, pamphlets, newspapers,
> reports of the two Houses of Parliament and the Factory
> Commissioners, we shall find them all jumbled together as
> the 'lower orders', the most skilled and the most prudent
> workman, with the most ignorant and imprudent labourers
> and paupers, though the difference is great indeed, and
> indeed in many cases will scarce admit of comparison.[3]

Place is, of course, right: the Sunderland sailor, the Irish navvy,
the Jewish costermonger, the inmate of an East Anglian village
workhouse, the compositor on *The Times* – all might be seen by
their 'betters' as belonging to the 'lower classes' while they
themselves might scarcely understand each other's dialect.

Nevertheless, when every caution has been made, the outstanding fact of the period between 1790 and 1830 is the
formation of 'the working class'. This is revealed, first, in the
growth of class-consciousness: the consciousness of an identity

---

[1] Cf. Hobsbawm, op. cit., ch. 2.

[2] There is a summary of this controversy in E. E. Lampard, *Industrial Revolution*
(American Historical Association, 1957). See also Hobsbawm, op. cit., ch. 2.

[3] Cit. M. D. George, *London Life in the Eighteenth Century* (1930), p. 210.

of interests as between all these diverse groups of working people and as against the interests of other classes. And, second, in the growth of corresponding forms of political and industrial organization. By 1832 there were strongly based and self-conscious working-class institutions – trade unions, friendly societies, educational and religious movements, political organizations, periodicals – working-class intellectual traditions, working-class community-patterns, and a working-class structure of feeling.

The making of the working class is a fact of political and cultural, as much as of economic, history. It was not the spontaneous generation of the factory system. Nor should we think of an external force – the 'industrial revolution' – working upon some nondescript undifferentiated raw material of humanity, and turning it out at the other end as a 'fresh race of beings'. The changing productive relations and working conditions of the Industrial Revolution were imposed, not upon raw material, but upon the free-born Englishman – and the free-born Englishman as Paine had left him or as the Methodists had moulded him. The factory hand or stockinger was also the inheritor of Bunyan, of remembered village rights, of notions of equality before the law, of craft traditions. He was the object of massive religious indoctrination and the creator of political traditions. The working class made itself as much as it was made.

To see the working class in this way is to defend a 'classical' view of the period against the prevalent mood of contemporary schools of economic history and sociology. For the territory of the Industrial Revolution, which was first staked out and surveyed by Marx, Arnold Toynbee, the Webbs and the Hammonds, now resembles an academic battlefield. At point after point, the familiar 'catastrophic' view of the period has been disputed. Where it was customary to see the period as one of economic disequilibrium, intense misery and exploitation, political repression and heroic popular agitation, attention is now directed to the rate of economic growth (and the difficulties of 'take-off' into self-sustaining technological reproduction). The enclosure movement is now noted, less for its harshness in displacing the village poor, than for its success in feeding a rapidly growing population. The hardships of the period are seen as being due to the dislocations consequent upon the Wars, faulty communications, immature banking and exchange, uncertain markets, and the trade-cycle, rather than to exploitation or cut-throat competition. Popular unrest is seen as consequent upon the unavoidable coincidence of high wheat prices and trade depressions, and explicable in terms of an elementary 'social tension' chart derived from these data.[1] In general, it is suggested that the position of the industrial worker in 1840 was better in most ways than that of the domestic worker of 1790. The Industrial Revolution was an age, not of catastrophe or acute class-conflict and class oppression, but of improvement.[2]

The classical catastrophic orthodoxy has been replaced by a new anti-catastrophic orthodoxy, which is most clearly distinguished by its empirical caution and, among its most notable exponents (Sir John Clapham, Dr Dorothy George, Professor Ashton) by an astringent criticism of the looseness of certain writers of the older school. The studies of the new orthodoxy have enriched historical scholarship, and have qualified and revised in important respects the work of the classical school. But as the new orthodoxy is now, in its turn, growing old and entrenched in most of the academic centres, so it becomes open to challenge in its turn. And the successors of the great empiricists too often exhibit a moral complacency, a narrowness of reference, and an insufficient familiarity with the actual movements of the working people of the time. They are more aware of the orthodox empiricist postures than of the changes in social relationship and in cultural modes which the Industrial Revolution entailed. What has been lost is a sense of the whole process – the whole political and social context of the period. What arose as valuable qualifications have passed by imperceptible stages to new generalizations (which the evidence can rarely sustain) and from generalizations to a ruling attitude.

[1] See W. W. Rostow, *British Economy in the Nineteenth Century* (1948), esp. pp. 122–5.

[2] Some of the views outlined here are to be found, implicitly or explicitly, in T. S. Ashton, *Industrial Revolution* (1948) and A. Redford, *The Economic History of England* (2nd edn 1960). A sociological variant is developed by N. J. Smelser, *Social Change in the Industrial Revolution* (1959), and a knockabout popularization is in John Vaizey, *Success Story* (W.E.A., n.d.).

The empiricist orthodoxy is often defined in terms of a running critique of the work of J. L. and Barbara Hammond. It is true that the Hammonds showed themselves too willing to moralize history, and to arrange their materials too much in terms of 'outraged emotion'.[1] There are many points at which their work has been faulted or qualified in the light of subsequent research, and we intend to propose others. But a defence of the Hammonds need not only be rested upon the fact that their volumes on the labourers with their copious quotation and wide reference, will long remain among the most important source-books for this period. We can also say that they displayed throughout their narrative an understanding of the political context within which the Industrial Revolution took place. To the student examining the ledgers of one cotton-mill, the Napoleonic Wars appear only as an abnormal influence affecting foreign markets and fluctuating demand. The Hammonds could never have forgotten for one moment that it was also a war against Jacobinism. 'The history of England at the time discussed in these pages reads like a history of civil war.' This is the opening of the introductory chapter of *The Skilled Labourer*. And in the conclusion to *The Town Labourer*, among other comments of indifferent value, there is an insight which throws the whole period into sudden relief:

> At the time when half Europe was intoxicated and the other half terrified by the new magic of the word citizen, the English nation was in the hands of men who regarded the idea of citizenship as a challenge to their religion and their civilization; who deliberately sought to make the inequalities of life the basis of the state, and to emphasize and perpetuate the position of the workpeople as a subject class. Hence it happened that the French Revolution has divided the people of France less than the Industrial Revolution has divided the people of England . . .

'Hence it happened . . .' The judgment may be questioned. And yet it is in this insight – that the revolution which did *not* happen in England was fully as devastating, and in some features more divisive, than that which did happen in France –

[1] See E. E. Lampard, op. cit., p. 7.

that we find a clue to the truly catastrophic nature of the period. Throughout this time there are three, and not two, great influences simultaneously at work. There is the tremendous increase in population (in Great Britain, from 10·5 millions in 1801 to 18·1 millions in 1841, with the greatest rate of increase between 1811–21). There is the Industrial Revolution, in its technological aspects. And there is the political *counter*-revolution, from 1792–1832.

In the end, it is the political context as much as the steam-engine, which had most influence upon the shaping consciousness and institutions of the working class. The forces making for political reform in the late eighteenth century – Wilkes, the city merchants, the Middlesex small gentry, the 'mob' – or Wyvill, and the small gentry and yeomen, clothiers, cutlers, and tradesmen – were on the eve of gaining at least some piecemeal victories in the 1790s: Pitt had been cast for the rôle of reforming Prime Minister. Had events taken their 'natural' course we might expect there to have been some show-down long before 1832, between the oligarchy of land and commerce and the manufacturers and petty gentry, with working people in the tail of the middle-class agitation. And even in 1792, when manufacturers and professional men were prominent in the reform movement, this was still the balance of forces. But, after the success of *Rights of Man*, the radicalization and terror of the French Revolution, and the onset of Pitt's repression, it was the plebeian Corresponding Society which alone stood up against the counter-revolutionary wars. And these plebeian groups, small as they were in 1796, did nevertheless make up an 'underground' tradition which ran through to the end of the Wars. Alarmed at the French example, and in the patriotic fervour of war, the aristocracy and the manufacturers made common cause. The English *ancien régime* received a new lease of life, not only in national affairs, but also in the perpetuation of the antique corporations which misgoverned the swelling industrial towns. In return, the manufacturers received important concessions: and notably the abrogation or repeal of 'paternalist' legislation covering apprenticeship, wage-regulation, or conditions in industry. The aristocracy were interested in repressing the Jacobin 'conspiracies' of the people, the manufacturers were interested in defeating their 'conspiracies' to increase wages: the Combination Acts served both purposes.

Thus working people were forced into political and social *apartheid* during the Wars (which, incidentally, they also had to fight). It is true that this was not altogether new. What was new was that it was coincident with a French Revolution; with growing self-consciousness and wider aspirations (for the 'liberty tree' had been planted from the Thames to the Tyne); with a rise in population, in which the sheer sense of numbers, in London and in the industrial districts, became more impressive from year to year (and as numbers grew, so deference to master, magistrate, or parson was likely to lessen); and with more intensive or more transparent forms of economic exploitation. More intensive in agriculture and in the old domestic industries: more transparent in the new factories and perhaps in mining. In agriculture the years between 1760 and 1820 are the years of wholesale enclosure, in which, in village after village, common rights are lost, and the landless and – in the south – pauperized labourer is left to support the tenant-farmer, the landowner, and the tithes of the Church. In the domestic industries, from 1800 onwards, the tendency is widespread for small masters to give way to larger employers (whether manufacturers or middlemen) and for the majority of weavers, stockingers, or nail-makers to become wage-earning outworkers with more or less precarious employment. In the mills and in many mining areas these are the years of the employment of children (and of women underground); and the large-scale enterprise, the factory-system with its new discipline, the mill communities – where the manufacturer not only made riches out of the labour of the 'hands' but could be *seen* to make riches in one generation – all contributed to the transparency of the process of exploitation and to the social and cultural cohesion of the exploited.

We can now see something of the truly catastrophic nature of the Industrial Revolution; as well as some of the reasons why the English working class took form in these years. The people were subjected simultaneously to an intensification of two intolerable forms of relationship: those of economic exploitation and of political oppression. Relations between employer and labourer were becoming harsher and less personal; and while it is true that this increased the potential freedom of the worker, since the hired farm servant or the journeyman in domestic industry was (in Toynbee's words) 'halted half-way between the position of the serf and the position of the citizen', this 'freedom' meant that he felt his *un*-freedom more. But at each point where he sought to resist exploitation, he was met by the forces of employer or State, and commonly of both.

For most working people the crucial experience of the Industrial Revolution was felt in terms of changes in the nature and intensity of exploitation. Nor is this some anachronistic notion, imposed upon the evidence. We may describe some parts of the exploitive process as they appeared to one remarkable cotton operative in 1818 – the year in which Marx was born. The account – an Address to the public of strike-bound Manchester by 'A Journeyman Cotton Spinner' – commences by describing the employers and the workers as 'two distinct classes of persons':

First, then, as to the employers: with very few exceptions, they are a set of men who have sprung from the cotton-shop without education or address, except so much as they have acquired by their intercourse with the little world of merchants on the exchange at Manchester, but to counterbalance that deficiency, they give you enough of appearances by an ostentatious display of elegant mansions, equipages, liveries, parks, hunters, hounds, &c. which they take care to shew off to the merchant stranger in the most pompous manner. Indeed their houses are gorgeous palaces, far surpassing in bulk and extent the neat charming retreats you see round London . . . but the chaste observer of the beauties of nature and art combined will observe a woeful deficiency of taste. They bring up their families at the most costly schools, determined to give their offspring a double portion of what they were so deficient in themselves. Thus with scarcely a second idea in their heads, they are literally petty monarchs, absolute and despotic, in their own particular districts; and to support all this, their whole time is occupied in contriving how to get the greatest quantity of work turned off with the least expence. . . . In short, I will venture to say, without fear of contradiction, that there is a greater distance observed between the master there and the spinner, than there is between the first merchant in London and his lowest servant or the lowest artisan. Indeed there is no comparison. I know it to be a fact, that the greater part of the master spinners are anxious to keep wages low for the purpose of keeping the spinners indigent and spiritless . . . as for the purpose of taking the surplus to their own pockets.

The master spinners are a class of men unlike all other master tradesmen in the kingdom. They are ignorant, proud, and tyrannical. What then must be the men or rather beings who are the instruments of such masters? Why, they have been for a series of years, with their wives and their families, patience itself – bondmen and bondwomen to their cruel taskmasters. It is in vain to insult our common understandings with the observation that such men are free; that the law protects the rich and poor alike, and that a spinner can leave his master if he does not like the wages. True; so he can: but where must he go? why to another, to be sure. Well: he goes; he is asked where did you work last: 'did he discharge you?' No; we could not agree about wages. Well I shall not employ you nor anyone who leaves his master in that manner. Why is this? Because there is an abominable *combination existing amongst the masters,* first established at Stockport in 1802, and it has since become so general, as to embrace all the great masters for a circuit of many miles round Manchester, though not the little masters: they are excluded. They are the most obnoxious beings to the great ones that can be imagined. . . . When the combination first took place, one of their first articles was, that no master should take on a man until he had first ascertained whether his last master had discharged him. What then is the man to do? If he goes to the parish, that grave of all independence, he is there told – We shall not relieve you; if you dispute with your master, and don't support your family, we will send you to prison; so that the man is bound, by a combination of circumstances, to submit to his master. He cannot travel and get work in any town like a shoe-maker, joiner, or taylor; he is confined to the district.

The workmen in general are an inoffensive, unassuming, set of well-informed men, though how they acquire their information is almost a mystery to me. They are docile and tractable, if not goaded too much; but this is not to be wondered at, when we consider that they are trained to work from six years old, from five in a morning to eight and nine at night. Let one of the advocates for obedience to his master take his stand in an avenue leading to a factory a little before five o'clock in the morning, and observe the squalid appearance of the little infants and their parents taken from their beds at so early an hour in all kinds of weather; let him examine the miserable pittance of food, chiefly composed of water gruel and oatcake broken into it, a little salt, and sometimes coloured with a little milk, together with a few potatoes, and a bit of bacon or fat for dinner; would a London mechanic eat this? There they are (and if late a few minutes, a quarter of a day is stopped in wages) locked up until night in rooms heated above the hottest days we have had this summer, and allowed no time, except three-quarters of an hour at dinner in the whole day: whatever they eat at any other time must be as they are at work. The negro slave in the West Indies, if he works under a scorching sun, has probably a little breeze of air sometimes to fan him: he has a space of ground, and time allowed to cultivate it. The English spinner slave has no enjoyment of the open atmosphere and breezes of heaven. Locked up in factories eight stories high, he has no relaxation till the ponderous engine stops, and then he goes home to get refreshed for the next day; no time for sweet association with his family; they are all alike fatigued and exhausted. This is no over-drawn picture: it is literally true. I ask again, would the mechanics in the South of England submit to this?

When the spinning of cotton was in its infancy, and before those terrible machines for superseding the necessity of human labour, called steam engines, came into use, there were a great number of what were then called *little masters*; men who with a small capital, could procure a few machines, and employ a few hands, men and boys (say to twenty or thirty), the produce of whose labour was all taken to Manchester central mart, and put into the hands of brokers. . . . The brokers sold it to the merchants, by which means the master spinner was enabled to stay at home and work and attend to his workmen. The cotton was then always given out in its raw state from the bale to the wives of the spinners at home, when they heat and cleansed it ready for the spinners in the factory. By this they could earn eight, ten, or twelve shillings a week, and cook and attend to their families. But none are thus employed now; for all the cotton is broke up by a machine, turned by the steam engine, called a devil: so that the spinners' wives have no employment, except they go to work in the factory all day at what can be done by children for a few shillings, four or five per week. If a man then could not agree with his master, he left him, and could get employed elsewhere. A few years, however, changed the face of things. Steam engines came into use, to purchase which, and to erect buildings sufficient to contain them and six or seven hundred hands, required a great capital. The engine power produced a more marketable (though not a better) article than the little master could at the same price. The consequence was their ruin in a short time; and the overgrown capitalists triumphed in their fall; for they were the only obstacle that stood between them and the complete controul of the workmen.

Various disputes then originated between the workmen and masters as to the fineness of the work, the workmen being paid according to the number of hanks or yards of thread he produced from a given quantity of cotton, which was always to be proved by the overlooker, whose interest made it imperative on him to lean to his master, and call the material coarser than it was. If the workman would not submit *he must summon his employer before a magistrate*; the whole of the acting magistrates in that district, with the exception of two worthy clergymen, being gentlemen who have sprung from the same source with the master cotton spinners. The employer generally contented himself with sending his overlooker to answer any such summons, thinking it beneath him to meet his servant. The magistrate's decision was generally in favour of the master, though on the statement of the overlooker only. The workman dared not appeal to the sessions on account of the expense. . . .

These evils to the men have arisen from that dreadful monopoly which exists in those districts where wealth and power are got into the hands of the few, who, in the pride of their hearts, think themselves the lords of the universe.[1]

This reading of the facts, in its remarkable cogency, is as much an *ex parte* statement as is the 'political economy' of Lord Brougham. But the 'Journeyman Cotton Spinner' was describing facts of a different order. We need not concern ourselves with the soundness of all his judgments. What his address does is to itemize one after another the grievances felt by working people as to changes in the character of capitalist exploitation: the rise of a master-class without traditional authority or obligations; the growing distance between master and man; the transparency of the exploitation at the source of their new wealth and power; the loss of status and above all of independence for the worker, his reduction to total dependence on the master's instruments of production; the partiality of the law; the disruption of the traditional family economy; the discipline, monotony, hours and conditions of work; loss of leisure and amenities; the reduction of the man to the status of an 'instrument'.

That working people felt these grievances at all – and felt them passionately – is itself a sufficient fact to merit our attention. And it reminds us forcibly that some of the most bitter conflicts of these years turned on issues which are not encompassed by cost of living series. The issues which provoked the most intensity of feeling were very often ones in which such values as traditional customs, 'justice', 'independence', security or family economy were at stake, rather than straightforward 'bread-and-butter' issues. The early years of the 1830s are aflame with agitations which turned on issues in which wages were of secondary importance; by the potters, against the Truck System; by the textile workers, for the 10-Hour Bill; by

[1] *Black Dwarf*, 30 September 1818.

the building workers, for co-operative direct action; by all groups of workers, for the right to join trade unions. The great strike in the north-east coalfield in 1831 turned on security of employment, 'tommy shops', child labour.

The exploitive relationship is more than the sum of grievances and mutual antagonisms. It is a relationship which can be sent to take distinct forms in different historical contexts, forms which are related to corresponding forms of ownership and State power. The classic exploitive relationship of the Industrial Revolution is depersonalized, in the sense that no lingering obligations of mutuality – of paternalism or deference, or of the interests of 'the Trade' – are admitted. There is no whisper of the 'just' price, or of a wage justified in relation to social or moral sanctions, as opposed to the operation of free market forces. Antagonism is accepted as intrinsic to the relations of production. Managerial or supervisory functions demand the repression of all attributes except those which further the expropriation of the maximum surplus value from labour. This is the political economy which Marx anatomized in *Das Kapital*. The worker has become an 'instrument', or an entry among other items of cost.

In fact, no complex industrial enterprise could be conducted according to such a philosophy. The need for industrial peace, for a stable labour-force, and for a body of skilled and experienced workers, necessitated the modification of managerial techniques – and, indeed, the growth of new forms of paternalism – in the cotton-mills by the 1830s. But in the overstocked outwork industries, where there was always a sufficiency of unorganized 'hands' competing for employment, these considerations did not operate. Here, as old customs were eroded, and the old paternalism was set aside, the exploitive relationship emerged supreme.

This does not mean that we can lay all the 'blame' for each hardship of the Industrial Revolution upon 'the masters' or upon *laissez faire*. The process of industrialization must, in any conceivable social context, entail suffering and the destruction of older and valued ways of life. Much recent research has thrown light upon the particular difficulties of the British experience; the hazards of markets; the manifold commercial and financial consequences of the Wars; the post-war deflation; movements in the terms of trade; and the exceptional stresses resulting from the population 'explosion'. Moreover, twentieth-century preoccupations have made us aware of the overarching problems of economic growth. It can be argued that Britain in the Industrial Revolution was encountering the problems of 'take-off'; heavy long-term investment – canals, mills, railways, foundries, mines, utilities – was at the expense of current consumption; the generations of workers between 1790 and 1840 sacrificed some, or all, of their prospects of increased consumption to the future.[1]

These arguments all deserve close attention. For example, studies of the fluctuations in the demand of the South American market, or of the crisis in country banking, may tell us much about the reasons for the growth or retardation of particular industries. The objection to the reigning academic orthodoxy is not to empirical studies *per se*, but to the fragmentation of our comprehension of the full historical process. First, the empiricist segregates certain events from this process and examines them in isolation. Since the conditions which gave rise to these events are assumed, they appear not only as explicable in their own terms but as inevitable. The Wars had to be paid for out of heavy taxation; they accelerated growth in this way and retarded it in that. Since this can be shown, it is also implied that this was *necessarily* so. But thousands of Englishmen at the time agreed with Thomas Bewick's condemnation of 'this superlatively wicked war'.[2] The unequal burden of taxation, fund-holders who profited from the National Debt, paper-money – these were not accepted as given data by many contemporaries, but were the staple of intensive Radical agitation.

But there is a second stage, where the empiricist may put these fragmentary studies back together again, constructing a model of the historical process made up from a multiplicity of interlocking inevitabilities, a piecemeal processional. In the scrutiny of credit facilities or of the terms of trade, where

[1] See S. Pollard, 'Investment, Consumption, and the Industrial Revolution', *Econ. Hist. Review*, 2nd Series, XI (1958), pp. 215–26.

[2] T. Bewick, *Memoir* (1961 edn), p. 151.

each event is explicable and appears also as a self-sufficient cause of other events, we arrive at a *post facto* determinism. The dimension of human agency is lost, and the context of class relations is forgotten.

It is perfectly true that what the empiricist points to was there. The Orders in Council had in 1811 brought certain trades almost to a standstill; rising timber prices after the Wars inflated the costs of building; a passing change of fashion (lace for ribbon) might silence the looms of Coventry; the power-loom competed with the hand-loom. But even these open-faced facts, with their frank credentials, deserve to be questioned. Whose Council, why the Orders? Who profited most from corners in scarce timber? Why should looms remain idle when tens of thousands of country girls fancied ribbons but could not afford to buy. By what social alchemy did inventions for saving labour become engines of immiseration? The raw fact – a bad harvest – may seem to be beyond human election. But the way that fact worked its way out was in terms of a particular complex of human relationship: law, ownership, power. When we encounter some sonorous phrase such as 'the strong ebb and flow of the trade cycle' we must be put on our guard. For behind this trade cycle there is a structure of social relations, fostering some sorts of expropriation (rent, interest, and profit) and outlawing others (theft, feudal dues), legitimizing some types of conflict (competition, armed warfare) and inhibiting others (trade unionism, bread riots, popular political organization) – a structure which may appear, in the eyes of the future, to be both barbarous and ephemeral.

It might be unnecessary to raise these large questions, since the historian cannot always be questioning the credentials of the society which he studies. But all these questions were, in fact, raised by contemporaries: not only by men of the upper classes (Shelley, Cobbett, Owen, Peacock, Thompson, Hodgskin, Carlyle) but by thousands of articulate working men. Not the political institutions alone, but the social and economic structure of industrial capitalism, were brought into question by their spokesmen. To the facts of orthodox political economy they opposed their own facts and their own arithmetic. Thus as early as 1817 the Leicester framework knitters put forward, in a series of resolutions, an under-consumption theory of capitalist crisis:

> That in proportion as the Reduction of Wages makes the great Body of the People poor and wretched, in the same proportion must the consumption of our manufactures be lessened.

> That if liberal Wages were given to the Mechanics in general throughout the Country, the Home Consumption of our Manufactures would be immediately more than doubled, and consequently every hand would soon find full employment.

> That to Reduce the Wage of the Mechanic in this Country so low that he cannot live by his labour, in order to undersell Foreign Manufacturers in a Foreign Market, is to gain one customer abroad, and lose two at home . . .[1]

If those in employment worked shorter hours, and if child labour were to be restricted, there would be more work for hand-workers and the unemployed could employ themselves and exchange the products of their labour directly – short-circuiting the vagaries of the capitalist market – goods would be cheaper and labour better-rewarded. To the rhetoric of the free market they opposed the language of the 'new moral order'. It is because alternative and irreconcilable views of human order – one based on mutuality, the other on competition – confronted each other between 1815 and 1850 that the historian today still feels the need to take sides.

It is scarcely possible to write the history of popular agitations in these years unless we make at least the imaginative effort to understand how such a man as the 'Journeyman Cotton Spinner' read the evidence. He spoke of the 'masters', not as an aggregate of individuals, but as a class. As such, 'they' denied him political rights. If there was a trade recession, 'they' cut his wages. If trade improved, he had to fight 'them' and their state to obtain any share in the improvement. If food was plentiful, 'they' profited from it. If it was scarce, some of 'them'

[1] H.O. 42.160. See also Hammonds, *The Town Labourer*, p. 303, and Oastler's evidence on the handloom weavers, below, p. 329.

profited more. 'They' conspired, not in this or that fact alone, but in the essential exploitive relationship within which all the facts were validated. Certainly there were market fluctuations, bad harvests, and the rest; but the experience of intensified exploitation was constant, whereas these other causes of hardship were variable. The latter bore upon working people, not directly, but through the refraction of a particular system of ownership and power which distributed the gains and losses with gross partiality.

*　　*　　*　　*

The controversy as to living standards during the Industrial Revolution has perhaps been of most value when it has passed from the somewhat unreal pursuit of the wage-rates of hypothetical average workers and directed attention to articles of consumption: food, clothing, homes: and, beyond these, health and mortality. Many of the points at issue are complex, and all that can be attempted here is to offer comments upon a continuing discussion. When we consider measurable quantities, it seems clear that over the years 1790–1840 the national product was increasing more rapidly than the population. But it is exceedingly difficult to assess how this product was distributed. Even if we leave other considerations aside (how much of this increase was exported owing to unfavourable terms of trade? how much went in capital investment rather than articles of personal consumption?) it is not easy to discover what share of this increase went to different sections of the population.

The debate as to the people's diet during the Industrial Revolution turns mainly upon cereals, meat, potatoes, beer, sugar and tea. It is probable that *per capita* consumption of wheat declined from late eighteenth-century levels throughout the first four decades of the nineteenth century. Mr Salaman, the historian of the potato, has given a convincing blow by blow account of the 'battle of the loaf', by which landowners, farmers, parsons, manufacturers, and the Government itself sought to drive labourers from a wheaten to a potato diet. The critical year was 1795. Thereafter war-time necessity took second place to the arguments as to the benefits of reducing the

poor to a cheap basic diet. The rise in potato acreage during
the Wars cannot be attributed to wheat shortage alone: 'some
deficiency there was, but unequal division between the different
classes of society consequent on inflated prices was a far more
potent factor . . .' The great majority of the English people,
even in the north, had turned over from coarser cereals to
wheat by 1790; and the white loaf was regarded jealously as a
symbol of their status. The southern rural labourer refused to
abandon his diet of bread and cheese, even when near the
point of starvation; and for nearly fifty years a regular dietary
class-war took place, with potatoes encroaching on bread in
the south, and with oatmeal and potatoes encroaching in the
north. Indeed, Mr Salaman finds in the potato a social stabilizer
even more effective than Halévy found in Methodism:

> . . . the use of the potato . . . did, in fact, enable the workers
> to survive on the lowest possible wage. It may be that in this
> way the potato prolonged and encouraged, for another
> hundred years, the impoverishment and degradation of the
> English masses; but what was the alternative, surely nothing
> but bloody revolution. That England escaped such a violent
> upheaval in the early decades of the nineteenth century . . .
> must in large measure be placed to the credit of the potato.[1]

Nutritional experts now advise us that the potato is full of
virtue, and certainly whenever standards rose sufficiently for
the potato to be an added item, giving variety to the diet, it
was a gain. But the substitution of potatoes for bread or oatmeal was felt to be a degradation. The Irish immigrants with
their potato diet (Ebenezer Elliott called them, 'Erin's root-fed
hordes') were seen as eloquent testimony, and very many
Englishmen agreed with Cobbett that the poor were victims of
a conspiracy to reduce them to the Irish level. Throughout the
Industrial Revolution the price of bread (and of oatmeal) was
the first index of living standards, in the estimation of the
people. When the Corn Laws were passed in 1815, the Houses
of Parliament had to be defended from the populace by troops.

[1] R. N. Salaman, *The History and Social Influence of the Potato* (Cambridge, 1949).
esp. pp. 480, 495, 506, 541–2. J. C. Drummond and A. Wilbraham, the historians
of *The Englishman's Food* (1939), also see this as a period of decline.

'NO CORN LAWS' was prominent among the banners at Peterloo, and remained so (especially in Lancashire) until the anti-Corn Laws agitation of the 1840s.

Meat, like wheat, involved feelings of status over and above its dietary value. The Roast Beef of Old England was the artisan's pride and the aspiration of the labourer. Once again, *per capita* consumption probably fell between 1790 and 1840, but the figures are in dispute. The argument turns mainly upon the number and weight of beasts killed in London slaughterhouses. But even if these figures are established, we still cannot be sure as to which sections of the people ate the meat, and in what proportions. Certainly, meat should be a sensitive indicator of material standards, since it was one of the first items upon which any increase in real wages will have been spent. The seasonal workers did not plan their consumption meticulously over fifty-two Sunday dinners, but, rather, spent their money when in full work and took what chance offered for the rest of the year. 'In the long fine days of summer,' Henry Mayhew was told,

> the little daughter of a working brickmaker used to order chops and other choice dainties of a butcher, saying, 'Please, sir, father don't care for the price just a-now; but he must have his chops good; line-chops, sir, and tender, please – 'cause he's a brickmaker.' In the winter, it was, 'O please, sir, here's a fourpenny bit, and you must send father something cheap. He don't care what it is, so long as it's cheap. It's winter, and he hasn't no work, sir – 'cause he's a brickmaker.'[1]

Londoners tended to have higher standards of expectation than labourers in the provinces. In the depth of the 1812 depression, it was the impression of an observer that the London poor fared better than those of the north and the west:

> The Poor of the Metropolis, notwithstanding the enormous price of the necessaries of life, are really living comparatively in comfort. The humblest labourer here frequently gets meat (flesh meat) and always bread and cheese, with

[1] Mayhew, op. cit., II, p. 368.

beer of some sort, for his meals, but a West Country peasant can obtain for his family no such food.[1]

There was, of course, a variety of inferior 'meats' on sale: red herrings and bloaters, cow-heel, sheep's trotters, pig's ear, faggots, tripe and black pudding. The country weavers of Lancashire despised town food, and preferred 'summat at's deed ov a knife' – a phrase which indicates both the survival of their own direct pig-keeping economy and their suspicion that town meat was diseased – if forced to eat in town 'every mouthful went down among painful speculations as to what the quadruped was when alive, and what particular reason it had for departing this life'.[2] It was not a new thing for town dwellers to be exposed to impure or adulterated food; but as the proportion of urban workers grew, so the exposure became worse.[3]

There is no doubt that *per capita* beer consumption went down between 1800 and 1830, and no doubt that *per capita* consumption of tea and of sugar went up; while between 1820 and 1840 there was a marked increase in the consumption of gin and whisky. Once again, this is a cultural as well as dietetic matter. Beer was regarded – by agricultural workers, coal-whippers, miners – as essential for any heavy labour (to 'put back the sweat') and in parts of the north beer was synonymous with 'drink'. The home-brewing of small ale was so essential to the household economy that 'if a young woman can bake oatcake and brew well, it is thought she will make a good wife': while 'some Methodist class-leaders say they could not lead their classes without getting a "mugpot" of drink'.[4] The decline was directly attributed to the malt tax – a tax so unpopular that some contemporaries regarded it as being an incitement to revolution. Remove the malt tax, one clerical magistrate in Hampshire argued in 1816, and the labourer

would go cheerfully to his daily employ, perform it with manly vigour and content, and become attached to his house,

[1] *Examiner*, 16 August 1812.

[2] E. Waugh, *Lancashire Sketches*, pp. 128–9.

[3] See J. Burnett, 'History of Food Adulteration in Great Britain in the Nineteenth Century', *Bulletin of Inst. of Historical Research*, 1959, pp. 104–7.

[4] J. Lawson, op. cit., pp. 8, 10.

his family, and, *above all*, his country, which allows him to share, in common with his superiors, in a plain wholesome beverage, which a poor man looks up to, more, indeed, than to any thing that could possibly be granted them by a British Parliament.[1]

The additional duty upon strong beer led to widespread evasion: and 'hush-shops' sprang up, like that in which Samuel Bamford was nearly murdered as a suspected exciseman until he was recognized by one of the drinkers as a *bona fide* radical 'on the run'.

The effect of the taxes was undoubtedly to reduce greatly the amount of home-brewing and home-drinking; and, equally, to make drinking less of a part of normal diet and more of an extra-mural activity. (In 1830 the duty on strong beer was repealed and the Beer Act was passed, and within five years 35,000 beer-shops sprang up as if out of the ground.) The increase in tea-drinking was, in part, a replacement of beer and, perhaps also, of milk; and, once again, many contemporaries – with Cobbett well to the fore – saw in this evidence of deterioration. Tea was seen as a poor substitute, and, with the increased consumption of spirits, as an indication of the need for stimulants caused by excessive hours of labour on an inadequate diet. But by 1830 tea was regarded as a necessity: families that were too poor to buy it begged once-used tea-leaves from neighbours, or even simulated its colour by pouring boiling water over a burnt crust.[2]

All in all, it is an unremarkable record. In fifty years of the Industrial Revolution the working-class share of the national product had almost certainly fallen relative to the share of the property-owning and professional classes. The 'average' working man remained very close to subsistence level at a time when he was surrounded by the evidence of the increase of national wealth, much of it transparently the product of his own labour, and passing, by equally transparent means, into the hands of his employers. In psychological terms, this felt very

---

[1] *Agricultural State of the Kingdom* (1816), p. 95.

[2] For an indication of some of the points at issue here, see the articles on the standard of living by T. S. Ashton, R. M. Hartwell, E. Hobsbawm and A. J. Taylor cited above.

much like a decline in standards. His own share in the 'benefits of economic progress' consisted of more potatoes, a few articles of cotton clothing for his family, soap and candles, some tea and sugar, and a great many articles in the *Economic History Review*.

The evidence as to the urban environment is little easier to interpret. There were farm labourers at the end of the eighteenth century who lived with their families in one-roomed hovels, damp and below ground-level: such conditions were rarer fifty years later. Despite all that can be said as to the unplanned jerry-building and profiteering that went on in the growing industrial towns, the houses themselves were better than those to which many immigrants from the countryside had been accustomed. But as the new industrial towns grew old, so problems of water supply, sanitation, over-crowding, and of the use of homes for industrial occupations, multiplied, until we arrive at the appalling conditions revealed by the housing and sanitary inquiries of the 1840s. It is true that conditions in rural villages or weaving hamlets may have been quite as bad as conditions in Preston or Leeds. But the size of the problem was certainly worse in the great towns, and the multiplication of bad conditions facilitated the spread of epidemics.

Moreover, conditions in the great towns were – and were felt to be – more actively offensive and inconvenient. Water from the village well, rising next to the graveyard, might be impure: but at least the villagers did not have to rise in the night and queue for a turn at the only stand-pipe serving several streets, nor did they have to pay for it. The industrial town-dweller often could not escape the stench of industrial refuse and of open sewers, and his children played among the garbage and privy middens. Some of the evidence, after all, remains with us in the industrial landscape of the north and of the Midlands today.

This deterioration of the urban environment strikes us today, as it struck many contemporaries, as one of the most disastrous of the consequences of the Industrial Revolution, whether viewed in aesthetic terms, in terms of community amenities, or in terms of sanitation and density of population. Moreover, it took place most markedly in some of the high-wage areas where 'optimistic' evidence as to improving standards is most well based. Common sense would suggest that we must take both kinds of evidence together; but in fact various arguments in mitigation have been offered. Examples have been found of improving mill-owners who attended to the housing conditions of their employees. These may well lead us to think better of human nature; but they do no more than touch the fringe of the general problem, just as the admirable charity hospitals probably affected mortality rates by only a decimal point. Moreover, most of the serious experiments in model communities (New Lanark apart) date from after 1840 – or from after public opinion was aroused by the inquiries into the Sanitary Conditions of the Working Classes (1842) and the Health of Towns (1844), and alerted by the cholera epidemics of 1831 and 1848. Such experiments as antedate 1840, like that of the Ashworths at Turton, were in self-sufficient mill villages.

It is also suggested that worsening conditions may be somehow discounted because they were no one's fault – and least of all the fault of the 'capitalist'. No villain can be found who answers to the name of 'Jerry'. Some of the worst building was undertaken by small jobbers or speculative small tradesmen or even self-employed building workers. A Sheffield investigator allocated blame between the landowner, the petty capitalist (who offered loans at a high rate of interest), and petty building speculators 'who could command only a few hundred pounds', and some of whom 'actually cannot write their names'.[1] Prices were kept high by duties on Baltic timber, bricks, tiles, slates; and Professor Ashton is able to give an absolute discharge to all the accused: 'it was emphatically not the machine, not the Industrial Revolution, not even the speculative bricklayer or carpenter that was at fault'.[2] All this may be true: it is notorious that working-class housing provides illustrations of the proverb as to every flea having 'lesser fleas to bite 'em'. In the 1820s, when many Lancashire weavers went on rent-strike, it was said that some owners of cottage property were thrown on the poor-rate. In the slums of the great towns publicans and small shopkeepers were among those often quoted as owners of the worst 'folds' or human warrens of crumbling mortar. But none of this mitigates the actual conditions by one jot; nor can debate

[1] G. C. Holland, *The Vital Statistics of Sheffield* (1843), pp. 56–8.
[2] *Capitalism and the Historians*, pp. 43–51.

as to the proper allocation of responsibility exonerate a process by which some men were enabled to prey upon others' necessities.

A more valuable qualification is that which stresses the degree to which, in some of the older towns, improvements in paving, lighting, sewering and slum clearance may be dated to the eighteenth century. But, in the often cited example of London, it is by no means clear whether improvements in the centre of the City extended to the East End and dockside districts, or how far they were maintained during the Wars. Thus the sanitary reformer, Dr Southwood Smith, reported of London in 1839:

> While systematic efforts, on a large scale, have been made to widen the streets . . . to extend and perfect the drainage and sewerage . . . in the places in which the wealthier classes reside, nothing whatever has been done to improve the condition of the districts inhabited by the poor.[1]

Conditions in the East End were so noisome that doctors and parish officers risked their lives in the course of their duties. Moreover, as the Hammonds pointed out, it was in the boom towns of the Industrial Revolution that the worst conditions were to be found: 'what London suffered [in the Commercial Revolution] Lancashire suffered at the end of the eighteenth and at the beginning of the nineteenth century'.[2] Sheffield, an old and comparatively prosperous town with a high proportion of skilled artisans, almost certainly – despite the jerry builders – saw an improvement in housing conditions in the first half of the nineteenth century, with an average, in 1840, of five persons per house, most artisans renting a family cottage on their own, with one day room and two sleeping rooms. It was in the textile districts, and in the towns most exposed to Irish immigrations – Liverpool, Manchester, Leeds, Preston, Bolton, Bradford – that the most atrocious evidence of deterioration –

---

[1] *Fifth Annual Report of the Poor Law Commissioners* (1839), p. 170. See also *Fourth Report* (1838), Appendix A, No. 1.

[2] See M. D. George, *London Life in the Eighteenth Century*, ch. 2; *England in Transition* (Penguin edn), p. 72; Hammond, *The Town Labourer*, ch. 3 and Preface to 2nd edition; Dr R. Willan, 'Observations on Disease in London', *Medical and Physical Journal*, 1800, p. 299.

dense overcrowding, cellar dwellings, unspeakable filth – is to be found.[1]

Finally, it is suggested, with tedious repetition, that the slums, the stinking rivers, the spoliation of nature, and the architectural horrors may all be forgiven because all happened so fast, so haphazardly, under intense population pressure, without premeditation and without prior experience. 'It was ignorance rather than avarice that was often the cause of misery.'[2] As a matter of fact, it was demonstrably both; and it is by no means evident that the one is a more amiable characteristic than the other. The argument is valid only up to a point – to the point in most great towns, in the 1830s or 1840s, when doctors and sanitary reformers, Benthamites and Chartists, fought repeated battles for improvement against the inertia of property-owners and the demagoguery of 'cheap government' rate-payers. By this time the working people were virtually segregated in their stinking enclaves, and the middle classes demonstrated their real opinions of the industrial towns by getting as far out of them as equestrian transport made convenient. Even in comparatively well-built Sheffield,

> All classes, save the artisan and the needy shopkeeper, are attracted by country comfort and retirement. The attorney – the manufacturer – the grocer – the draper – the shoemaker and the tailor, fix their commanding residences on some beautiful site . . .

Of sixty-six Sheffield attorneys in 1841, forty-one lived in the country, and ten of the remaining twenty-five were newcomers to the town. In Manchester the poor in their courts and cellars lived,

> . . . hidden from the view of the higher ranks by piles of stones, mills, warehouses, and manufacturing establishments, less known to their wealthy neighbours – who reside chiefly in the open spaces of Cheetham, Broughton, and Chorlton – than the inhabitants of New Zealand or Kamtschatka.

[1] G. C. Holland, op. cit., p. 46 *et passim*. An excellent account of the working man's urban environment in mid-century Leeds is in J. F. C. Harrison, *Learning and Living* (1961), pp. 7–20.
[2] R. M. Hartwell, op. cit., p. 413.

'The rich lose sight of the poor, or only recognize them when attention is forced to their existence by their appearance as vagrants, mendicants or delinquents.' 'We have improved on the proverb, "One half of the world does not know how the other half lives," changing it into "One half of the world *does not care* how the other half lives." Ardwick knows less about Ancoats than it does about China . . .'[1]

Certainly, the unprecedented rate of population growth, and of concentration in industrial areas, would have created major problems in any known society, and most of all in a society whose rationale was to be found in profit-seeking and hostility to planning. We should see these as the problems of industrialism, aggravated by the predatory drives of *laissez-faire* capitalism. But, however the problems are defined, the definitions are no more than different ways of describing, or interpreting, the same events. And no survey of the industrial heartlands, between 1800 and 1840, can overlook the evidence of visual devastation and deprivation of amenities. The century which rebuilt Bath was not, after all, devoid of aesthetic sensibility nor ignorant of civic responsibility. The first stages of the Industrial Revolution witnessed a decline in both; or, at the very least, a drastic lesson that these values were not to be extended to working people. However appalling the conditions of the poor may have been in large towns before 1750, nevertheless the town in earlier centuries usually embodied some civic values and architectural graces, some balance between occupations, marketing and manufacture, some sense of variety. The 'Coketowns' were perhaps the first towns of above 10,000 inhabitants ever to be dedicated so single-mindedly to work and to 'fact'.

[1] G. C. Holland, op. cit., p. 51; W. Cooke Taylor, *Notes of a Tour in the Manufacturing Districts of Lancashire* (1842), pp. 12, 13, 160.

7 The Standard of Living, 1780–1844: a Regional and Class Study

R. S. NEALE

[This article was first published in the *Economic History Review*, 2nd series, vol. XIX, no. 3, 1966.]

I

The re-opening of the debate on the standard of living, 1780–1850, has provided an opportunity for much extravagant writing, the introduction of more sophisticated economic and sociological terminology into the discussion, a growing recognition that economic advance does not preclude working-class discontent, and a plea for more industrial and regional research. Writing in 1949, T. S. Ashton said, 'It is important to distinguish between the period of the war, the period of deflation and re-adjustment, and the succeeding period of economic expansion . . . We require not a single index but many, each derived from retail prices, each confined to a short run of years, each relating to a single area, perhaps to a single social or occupational group within an area.'[1] The last sixteen years has brought forth little of this kind of evidence. Instead, fashions have changed. There has been a move away from price and wage indices, related to specific regions and groups, through indirect indicators of less specific applicability, like unemployment, mortality rates, and *per capita* consumption, to the current belief in the usefulness of the macro-economic approach based on estimates of population, national income, national product and price deflators. Such a development, however, leaves the economic historian hovering on the brink of repeating the sociological error made by Marx, that is, viewing labour during the period 1780–1850 as 'Labour', an homogeneous class experiencing and participating in the process of industrialization as

[1] T. S. Ashton, 'The Standard of Life of the Workers in England, 1790–1830', *Capitalism and the Historians* (ed. Hayek), pp. 133, 152.

a whole. The present paper is an attempt to avoid this error and to meet some of the requirements set out by Professor Ashton.

Before doing so, however, it is advisable to look at two considerations of a general nature influencing the conclusion, which rarely receive sufficient attention. One is whether the post-war period should be compared with the years immediately before the war or with the wartime period. The other is whether one should study the experience of particular generations, or age cohorts of labourers, instead of 'Labour'.

The choice of the base year with which comparisons are to be made is crucial. Those who argue strongly for improvement in living standards argue from 1800. Those who employ other years, as the base year for comparison, generally observe that the admittedly uneven post-war recovery, to the mid-1840s, was barely sufficient to restore the position in existence before the war.[1] Indeed, the choice of 1800 as a base has no deep rationale. It is true that the beginning of the century coincided roughly with the first fairly reliable estimates of national income, and with the first census, and thereby permits a rough calculation of income per head, yet it marks neither the end nor beginning of any trend, cyclic period or stage of growth conventionally adopted. In the area with which the main body of this paper is concerned, the city of Bath, the year 1800 and the winter of 1800–1 were disastrous.[2] The harvest month of September 1799 had 8·8 inches of rain, and the price of wheat at Warminster rose from 82s. per quarter in January to 160s. by the end of June 1800. In Bath, in the same six months, the penny loaf of best wheaten bread fell in weight from 5 to 2½ ounces. Rents were stable, but other prices were high. Coal was 10d. per cwt., and meat 8d. or 9d. per lb. The earnings of labourers remained unchanged until May 1801. During July imports from abroad – wheat from Europe, flour and rice from

[1] E. J. Hobsbawm writes of the period 1790–1850, S. Pollard 1745–55 to 1840–50, A. J. Taylor 1780–1850, T. S. Ashton 1790–1830, R. M. Hartwell 1800–50. See particularly S. Pollard, 'Investment, Consumption and the Industrial Revolution', *Economic History Review*, December 1958, p. 221, note 1.

[2] R. S. Neale, 'Economic Conditions and Working Class Movements in the City of Bath, 1800–1850' (unpublished dissertation for M.A. degree, Bristol University Library). All references to Bath are based on chs. I to V of this dissertation.

America – helped to reduce wheat to a low point of 86*s.* and to increase the weight of the penny loaf to 4·4 ounces. But, from then on, in spite of the increase in marketable corn from the home harvest, the price of wheat rose steadily to 144*s.* in December 1800, and the penny loaf finished the year a third lighter than when the year started. Prices remained high throughout the first months of 1801 and by February wheat reached 184*s.* per quarter. In March the quartern loaf, at 1*s.* 11*d.*, was one halfpenny dearer than in London and was fivepence more than a day's pay for an unskilled labourer.

The resultant famine conditions precipitated violent rioting and arson. To alleviate the worst consequences rice was bought and rationed out at reduced prices to half the city's population of 33,000, a woollen manufacturer baked bread to sell at a 24 per cent reduction in price to his workmen, poor relief expenditure rose by 50 per cent and a minimum of £13,000 was publicly spent on relief and charity in one year. Thus it would not be difficult to show that real incomes for most classes were higher in every other year between 1780 and 1850 or, indeed, during the rest of the century. *A fortiori* the choice of almost any other year between 1780 and 1800 as a base year makes it doubtful whether real incomes did remain stationary during the war years and whether the immediate post-war improvement in real incomes was sufficient to make good the wartime deterioration. On the other hand, the decade 1780–90, before the house and canal building locally associated with the early 1790s got under way, and before the Napoleonic Wars, was a period of stability in wage-rates, earnings and prices. Thus for a broader perspective the year, against which comparisons will be made, will be 1780.

The importance of the age-cohort approach to the experience of members of the labour force can best be appreciated, given the following: the working life of an adult male was about thirty years, the bulk of working men, in the early nineteenth century, reached their maximum earnings early in life and could expect their earnings to decline during the final third of the working life,[1] the rise in real wages between 1780 and 1850,

[1] See Richard M. Titmus, *Essays on the Welfare State*, for a discussion of this during the more recent past; Neil J. Smelser, *Social Change in the Industrial*

or between 1800 and 1850, was interrupted by periods of stagnation and deterioration.[1] Then, leaving aside the problems of regional and industrial deviations from the average, and redistribution of income,[2] and looking at the labour-force as a succession of cohorts moving through employment from different starting points and at different relative rates of change in money incomes, it becomes possible to argue that large groups of workers could pass through working lives of thirty years, within a period of 50 or 60 years, the terminal point of which indicates a rise in average real income, experiencing a below-average rise or no rise at all. That is, there is no reason to suppose that the evidence of a general rise in *per capita* income, between 1800 and 1850, based on national estimates for discontinuous years, rules out the existence of real economic

---

Revolution, pp. 195–220, on the changing position of the adult male worker; *Men Without Work*, Report to the Pilgrim Trust, 1938, pp. 119, 212–20; Seebohm Rowntree, *Poverty; A Study in Town Life*, pp. 169–71, for a variant of this argument.

[1] The phasing from 1800 acceptable to T. S. Ashton, R. M. Hartwell and P. Deane is something like the following; 1800–12/17, stagnation; 1812/17–1830, improvement; 1830–40, deterioration; 1841 onwards, improvement. T. S. Ashton, op. cit.; R. M. Hartwell, 'The Rising Standard of Living in England, 1800–1850', *Econ. Hist. Rev.* April 1961, p. 398; P. Deane, 'Contemporary Estimates of National Income in the First Half of the 19th Century', *Econ. Hist. Rev.* April 1956, p. 253. Hobsbawm, however, argues that stagnation 1822–42 is the most favourable interpretation for these years, 'The British Standard of Living, 1790–1850', *Econ. Hist. Rev.* August 1957, pp. 60–1. The Tucker and Schumpeter/Gilboy Indexes suggest a decline in real wages for the period 1780–1800, Schumpeter, 'The Cost of Living and Real Wages in Eighteenth-Century England', *Review of Economic Statistics*, vol. 18 (1936), pp. 134–43; R. S. Tucker, 'Real Wages of Artisans in London, 1729–1935', *Journal of the American Statistical Association*, vol. 31 (1930), pp. 73–84. See also S. Pollard, op. cit.

[2] Hartwell argues the probability of a constant wage/income ratio for 1800–50 from the fact of a long period constant wage/income ratio after 1870 (*Econ. Hist. Rev.* August 1963). Yet Phelps Brown, although arguing that changes in real wages due to distributive shifts have been small over long periods, also observes, 'we notice here the upward shifts (in the wage/income ratio) of 1870–1873 and 1888–1891, and the downward shifts of 1903–1906 and 1926–1928: these were not reversible cyclical swings, but moved the wage earnings/income ratio to a new level'. 'The General Level of Wages', *The Theory of Wage Development*, ed. J. T. Dunlop, p. 54. Clearly there is nothing here ruling out the possibility of shifts in real wages associated with shifts in the wage/income ratio during the period 1780–1850 or the possibility of shifts in distribution within the wage sector itself. See also W. A. Lewis, 'Economic Development with Unlimited Supplies of Labour', *The Economics of Under-Development*, Ed. Argawala and Singh, pp. 416–20.

distress, caused by a fall in real wages for many workers, particularly if this age-cohort approach is linked with the social consequences of structural changes in the economy.[1] Only detailed work on lines suggested by Ashton can help to resolve this problem for individual regions, industries and classes.

II THE EXPERIENCE OF BATH

Traditionally the city of Bath is held to be outside the main stream of eighteenth-century and early nineteenth-century development. The appeal of its history – literary, architectural, genteelly erotic – has diverted the attention of historians away from its essential economic substructure. And few recognize that, as the Miami of the eighteenth century, its creation, construction and operation depended on widespread entre-preneurial activity and considerable investment; that the multiplier effect stimulated the building industry, the development of extensive stone quarries, the growth of industrial villages, the construction of tramways and the canalization of the river Avon, all before the middle of the eighteenth century. Thereafter continued building, re-building and a high level of expenditure on high-quality consumer goods attracted a heavy concentration of craftsmen, tradesmen and non-agricultural labourers. By the beginning of the nineteenth century the city, with a resident population of 33,000, was one of the largest in the country. It continued to increase in population, during the first two decades, at a rate comparable with that of the country as a whole and by 1831 had a population of 50,000.

Between 1800 and 1830 there was incipient industrialization with the establishment of steam-powered manufactories in brewing, glass and soap-making. Stothert's ironmongery developed into ironfoundry, woollen mills were established on the Avon at Twerton, coal-mining was attempted at Batheaston and a railway company projected to connect Bath with Bristol. Thus in one sense the city of Bath is an example of an isolated region with a leading sector – a quality entertainment industry having some backward linkages – brought into existence by concentrated and sustained aristocratic expenditure. This

[1] Neil J. Smelser, *Social Change in the Industrial Revolution*, pp. 196-9, 205-9.

luxury expenditure, however, made little contribution to the development of the surrounding complex of industrial villages whose course and decline was determined by the main current of economic development. Consequently, and as fashion changed, the city failed to 'take off' and after a period or re-adjustment replaced its highly profitable growth industry with one which continued to use the existing stock of social over-head capital but produced little stimulus to further investment.[1]

Table I shows the occupational distribution of the adult male population in 1831 and the extent to which employment de-pended on manufacturing, building and the retail trade.

TABLE I   *Occupational distribution of males in the City of Bath, 1831*

Occupation	No. of males over 20 years of age
Capitalists, bankers and other educated men	1,196
Building trades	1,074
Labouring (non-agricultural)	1,480
Retail (includes some craftsmen)	2,797
Domestic service	670
Shoemaking	529
Furniture and coachmaking	351
Tailoring	349
Labouring	110
Total	8,556

Census of Population, 1831.

The growth of the city also placed concentrations of population under local administration by parish officers, and stimulated the newspaper industry: two developments important for this article. The first led to attempts to systematize the administration of the parish of Walcot, which had a population of 26,000 in 1831.[2] This resulted in a good series of wage-accounts kept

[1] R. S. Neale, op. cit. chs I, II and V, also 'The Industries of the City of Bath in the First Half of the Nineteenth Century', *Somersetshire Archaeological and Natural History Society Proceedings*, vol. 108 (1964), pp. 132–44, and 'An Equitable Trust in the Building Industry 1794', *Business History*, July 1965.

[2] See 'The Report of the Committee Appointed to Examine into and Control the Receipts and Expenditure of the Parish of Walcot to the Parishioners Assembled in Vestry', 1817, *Poor Rate Books*, Bath Reference Library.

by the Overseer of Highways from 1780 to 1851.[1] The second provided the opportunity for the weekly publication of a selection of retail prices in Bath market.[2]

III EARNINGS

The first point to be emphasized in this section is that unlike all other wage-series for the late eighteenth and early nineteenth centuries the Bath series is compiled entirely from records of actual weekly earnings. The Highway Accounts record the number of men employed each week, their weekly earnings, the number of days or half days worked and the daily rate. The index, based on 1780 = 100 = 8s. per week for a six-day week, shows the average earnings of all men employed on the Walcot highways for the first week in January, May and September each year. Unfortunately the numbers employed in the earlier years are smaller than in the later period, consequently the average is probably more meaningful for the period 1832–51. Where possible the annual earnings or wage experience of individual labourers has been traced over several years, and all figures are supplemented by wage-rates. The data for the index is tabulated in the statistical appendix[3] and, in Table II, is simplified into an annual index.

It is probable that the movement of wages for this group of highway labourers indicates the direction and magnitude of wage movements for the whole group of 1,480 non-agricultural labourers who, in 1831, constituted approximately 20 per cent of the adult male work-force in the city.[4] These were men who earned 8s. per week in the 1780s, between 7s. and 9s. in the 1830s and 10s. to 12s. 6d. in the 1850s.[5] There is some evidence

---

[1] Account Books of Overseer of Highways 1780–1851, Bath Reference Library. Accounts missing 1809 to 1832.

[2] There were five weekly newspapers, *The Bath Herald, The Bath Chronicle, The Bath Journal, The Bath Guardian* and the *Bath and Cheltenham Gazette.* All prices are from the latter from 1812 to 1844.

[3] Appendix C.   [4] See below pp. 161–3.

[5] There is, however, some evidence to suggest that, during the 1830s and 1840s men regularly employed by local authorities were a favoured group and, therefore, that the index exaggerates the level of earnings, e.g. 1831, 354 men earned 6s. to 8s. per week through the Bath Employment Society (*Bath and Cheltenham Gazette,* 20–12–1831, 11–1–1831, 25–1–1831, 5–4–1831); 1833,

for 1865 to show that about 42 per cent of 600 outpatients at the United Hospital then earned less than 12s. per week, and to suggest that the size of this class did not decline after 1830 even though the census returns for 1851 record only 10 per cent of males as labourers.[1]

TABLE II *Average weekly earnings of non-agricultural labourers in the City of Bath, 1780–1851*

(1780 = 100)

(a) 1780–1809								
	Rate	Earnings		Rate	Earnings		Rate	Earnings
1780	100	100	1789	100	96	1801	113	119
1781	100	92	1790	100	95	1802	150	120
1782	100	102	1791	100	108	1803	113	113
1783	100	83	1792	113	114	1804	113	119
			1793	113	101			
1786	100	101	1794	113	102	1807	125	120
1787	100	100	1795	113	114	1808	125	125
1788	100	96	1796	113	118	1809	125	117
(b) 1832–51								
	Rate	Earnings		Rate	Earnings		Rate	Earnings
1832	—	96	1839	141	103	1846	141	138
1833	—	97	1840	141	128	1847	141	132
1834	—	86	1841	141	127	1848	141	136
1835	—	95	1842	141	134	1849	141	142
1836	—	98	1843	141	134	1850	141	137
1837	100*	95	1844	141	137	1851	141	141
1838	100	98	1845	141	134			

* After 1837 rates varied between 1s. 4d and 1s. 5d per day. After 1839 between 1s. 5d and 2s. The index averages maximum and minimum rates.
Source: Highway Accounts, Walcot.

1780–1809. Wage-rates and earnings remained fairly constant from year to year from 1780 to May 1792, when wage-rates

masons previously earning 21s. reduced to 6s. on road works (*Bath Journal*, 13–4–1833); 1841, 36 masons employed at labourers rates (*Bath and Cheltenham Gazette*, 9–2–1841); 1845, an average of 150 men employed by Bath Employment Society for three months at an average wage of 5s. 8d. per week. In one week the average take-home pay of 222 men was 4s. 6d. (*Bath Chronicle*, 20–3–1845).
[1] Report of the Committee of Investigation on the Bath United Hospital 1866, *Bath Pamphlets*, vol. VI in Bath Reference Library, also R. S. Neale, op. cit. p. 53.

were increased 13 per cent to 1s. 6d. per day. Earnings, however, had begun to increase in 1791, and in the early part of 1792, through much overtime working of six and a half and seven-day weeks. Subsequently, in 1793 and 1794, earnings fell to only one or two points above the 1780 level. After 1795 earnings began to rise again and received a boost from a rise in rates of 33 per cent from 1s. 6d. to 2s., during the period May 1801 to May 1803. Consequently, average earnings, 1801–4, were 18 per cent higher than in 1780. In May 1803 rates fell again to 1s. 6d., the level prevailing from 1792 to 1801. There was a further rise to 1s. 8d. in 1807, but in 1809 earnings were only 17 per cent higher than in 1780.[1]

Overall rates rose more than earnings. In eleven years they rose, on average, ten points more, in four years both indices moved to the same extent and in the same direction, and in seven years earnings rose, on average, three points more than rates. Where it is possible to compare rates, weekly earnings and yearly earnings, the evidence suggests that rates rose more than weekly earnings while yearly earnings fluctuated more and tended to rise less, over a long period, than weekly earnings. This point is illustrated in Table III, which, although by no

TABLE III   *Wage rates, average weekly and average yearly earnings 1803–9.*

(1780 = 100)

	Rate	Weekly earnings	Yearly earnings*	No. of weeks worked†
1803	113	113	116	51
1804	113	119	130	52
1807	125	120	103	47
1809	125	117	113	50

* Based on the earnings of one labourer employed from 1803 to 1809 and compared with a full year's earnings of a different labourer in 1780.

† Refers to the number of weeks by the labourer whose yearly earnings are recorded in col. 3.

Source: Highway Accounts, Walcot.

[1] Bowley's index of agricultural wages shows a doubling of annual average wages 1780–1810 A. L. Bowley, *Journal of the Royal Statistical Society*, vol. 62, September 1899. Data given in Appendix B, p. 250.

means conclusive, serves as a reminder of the problems of determining actual income, and ultimately real wages, from evidence of rates of pay or even average weekly earnings.

1832–51. It is difficult to establish an index of rates for these years, since rates were not recorded from 1832 to 1837. Thereafter they varied from employee to employee. Between 1837 and 1839 the range, from 1*s.* 4*d.* to 1*s.* 5*d.*, was much the same as for the period 1780–92. After 1839 the range was from 1*s.* 5*d.* to 2*s.*

Apart from the high earnings in September 1832, average earnings 1832–9 fluctuated at a level 5 to 10 per cent below the base year 1780. This could have resulted from the employment of large numbers of unemployed skilled workmen on road construction and it could be supposed that earnings were depressed in consequence.[1] However, it has been argued above that numbers of labourers and craftsmen earned less than those employed by the parish. Consequently the figures for the 1830s probably minimize the decline in the earnings of non-agricultural labourers after 1809. Rates were increased in May 1839 and average earnings increased 20 per cent. Thereafter earnings rose more slowly until by 1843 they were between 30 and 40 per cent higher than for the early 1830s. The wage experience of two long-serving men (Table IV) illustrates most clearly the course of earnings between 1836 and 1851.

TABLE IV   *Average weekly earnings of two labourers, 1836–51*

Year	1836	'37	'38	'39	'40	'41	'42	'43	'44	'45	'46	'47	'48	'49	'50	'51
Rose	←——7s.——→		←—8s.—→	←	←			——9s. 6d.——			→	←———	—10s.———			→
Slade	←8s. 9d.→	←9s. 6d.→	←11s.→	←	——12s.——		→	←———	—12s. 6d.——			→

Source: Highway Accounts, Walcot.

One point that is clear, both from the index of average earnings and from Table IV, is that earnings rose rapidly between 1839 and 1843. Such a rise which appears to be unequalled elsewhere

[1] The average number of men employed by the Walcot Overseer of Highways was swollen by the employment of large numbers on relief works: average number employed, December to January 1830, 103; 1831, 101; 1832, 87.

and in other industries[1] merits explanation. It may well have been the intention of the Assistant Surveyor of Highways to pursue a policy of high or higher wages in order to build up a permanent and reliable labour force able to work well without supervision, or at least with less supervision than was required with the hundred or so men employed in the early 1830s. There is some evidence that this might have been so. The status of the foreman was reduced by reducing the differential between his salary and the weekly earnings of labourers, men were rewarded with higher wages for particular jobs and dismissals for bad work or drunkenness were recorded.[2] Yet it is difficult to believe that a public body, open to popular criticism from year to year, could pursue for long a policy of paying wages greatly in excess of those paid for similar work elsewhere in the parish and the city, particularly since it is possible to suggest an alternative explanation of the initial rise in 1839 and 1840.

In the early part of 1839 work on the construction of the G.W.R. railroad in the neighbourhood was begun. By midsummer work was under way on a viaduct, alterations to the approach road from Wells and on the permanent way. By the end of the year the Kennet and Avon canal was turned from its original course, and the construction of tunnels, cuttings, the skew bridge and the station were begun with the result that, 'The contractors appeared to put an embargo upon all the disposable labour of the city and its suburbs.'[3] It is also possible to suggest that wages in Bath were unduly depressed throughout the 1830s, even when compared with agricultural wages in neighbouring counties, and that the lift given to wages in 1839–40 by railway construction restored the early urban advantage which remained to the end of the period.[4]

[1] Gayer, Rostow and Schwarz, *The Growth and Fluctuations of the British Economy, 1750–1850*, II, pp. 949–57; Kuczynski, *Short History of Labour Conditions in Great Britain, 1750 to the Present Day*, pp. 55–60; A. L. Bowley, 'The Statistics of Wages in the U.K. during the last 100 Years', *Journal of the Royal Statistical Society*, LXI, Part IV, LXIII, Part III of reprint; R. S. Neale, op. cit. pp. 39–42.

[2] Proceedings of the Waywardens of Walcot, 1839–43. Bath Reference Library.

[3] *Bath and Cheltenham Gazette*, 1–9–1840.

[4] A. L. Bowley, loc. cit.; R. S. Neale, op. cit. p. 44, Table X. See Statistical Appendix A.

PRICES

Only three budgets were discovered for the period 1800–50. One was for a Bristol artisan in 1842, one was a minimum estimate for a labourer's family in 1831, the third was a pauper dietary for 1836.[1] They largely support each other as indicators of the proportion of income spent on different commodities. The budget for 1831 shows the following:

'The Charge Per Week for Keeping a Poor Man, Wife and Two Children, with Nothing Superior to Gaol Allowance'

	s.	d.	Percentage
Subsistence for man, wife and two children	7	9	64·5
Beer		8	5·5
Clothing and shoes	1	4	11·1
Washing, soap, candles		3	6·2
Fuel		6	
Rent	1	6	12·5
	12	0	99·8

The pauper dietary in 1837 suggests that a weekly subsistence diet, i.e. the item 'subsistence' to which 65 per cent of expenditure was allocated in 1831, for a family of four, would have consisted of: 33½ lb. of bread, 1 lb. 11 oz. of meat, 1 lb. 1 oz. of bacon, 4¼ lb. of cheese and 6 lb. of potatoes. The cost of this basket of goods in Bath market at the lowest retail prices in 1837 was 8s. 10¾d. Prices were slightly higher in 1831, consequently the 7s. 9d. then allocated to subsistence, would have purchased considerably less.

Labourers' wages rarely rose above 8s. per week throughout the 1830s and only reached 12s. in a very few cases in the 1840s, consequently it was decided that an index, weighted very much in favour of food, is to be preferred to a more general index incorporating a wide range of manufactured products.[2] Thus

---

[1] *Bath Journal,* 17–1–1831; *Bath and Cheltenham Gazette,* 13–12–1836, 13–12–1842; *Bristol Gazette,* 15–12–1842.

[2] The harshness of this picture would possibly be modified by taking into account family income rather than the income of one wage-earner. This, however, is an impossible task, for while there is some evidence that wives and children could earn sufficient to meet the cost of their own subsistence there is other evidence pointing to long-term unemployment for men, and of wives supporting whole families out of earnings and/or poor relief. R. S. Neale, op. cit. pp. 47–53, 118–29.

the price index is based on six items; the retail prices of bread, potatoes, mutton, pork and coal, and the rent of housing. Prices for potatoes, mutton and pork are minimum quotations. Those for bread are for the best quality wheaten loaf and, as for coal, are either the only or maximum quotations. Bread prices are continuous from 1800 to 1844, all others from 1812 to 1844 with the exception of potatoes which run to 1832 after which cheese is substituted in 1834.[1] The disadvantage in using maximum prices for bread and coal is that the price may not reflect the absolute cost to this group of workers. There is, however, some reason to suppose that the cheaper brown household loaf was held to be greatly inferior to white bread and that all classes considered it better value to pay an extra 1*d.* or 2*d.* for a quartern of white bread rather than save on an inferior brown bread. In addition all bread prices moved in the same direction while remaining in a constant relationship with each other. In Bath the difference between the wheaten and standard loaf was always 1*d.* on a quartern. The difference between the wheaten and the household loaf was always 2*d.* Thus the movement of maximum bread prices indicates the movement of all bread prices. The advantage in using maximum prices is that other prices were frequently not quoted at all. In the case of coal the maximum is often quoted as including the cost of transport from the weighing engine to the city outskirts. Since working-class areas, with one exception, were on the out-skirts of the city the maximum price can be regarded as representing the retail price of coal plus transport costs.

Rents were estimated for eighty-one working-class houses in Avon Street, at five-yearly intervals, from the poor and highway rate books.[2] Of the rate assessments four were based on rent, the remainder on annual value. In 1841 and 1845 the rate was based on estimates of rent and annual value. In both cases the rent estimates were generally more than those for annual value. Thus annual value probably underestimates the level of rent.

---

[1] This means that for the period in which the retail price index is used to calculate real wages the price relative used is that for cheese. See below, p. 169, and Statistical Appendix D.

[2] Rateable values for thirty artisan houses in Morford Street rose rather higher than those in Avon Street, 1800–10.

There is also some scatter of evidence to suggest that the poundage of the rate assessments reflected the level of rents actually paid for whole houses. Rate assessments, however, do not reveal the extent of sub-letting, the cost of a single room or part of a house, or the degree of bed sharing.[1] Nevertheless, it seems likely that the movement of rate assessments is a reasonable indication of the movement of rents.[2]

In order to attempt the construction of an index of real wages for non-agricultural labourers it was decided to use 1838 as the base year for prices and to allocate the following weights: bread 12, potatoes 3, pork 2, mutton 1, coal 2, rent 3. For the period 1832–44 it is possible to construct an index of real wages entirely from local material. The lack of price data prevents this for the earlier period. Nevertheless, Table V includes an index of real wages for the period 1780–1812 compiled with the aid of the Schumpeter–Gilboy Consumer Goods (*a*) Index.[3] Unfortunately it is not possible to bridge the crucial twenty-three-year gap between 1809 and 1832 for although local price data exist after 1812 there is no local wage data of any kind for non-agricultural labourers.[4]

REAL WAGES

1780–1812. After 1780 real wages fluctuated at a level slightly lower than in the base year and it was only in 1792 that they rose above the level of 1780 as a result of much overtime

[1] R. S. Neale, op. cit. pp. 66–70.

[2] See Statistical Appendix D.

[3] The Schumpeter–Gilboy Index, although suffering from the defect of representing recorded institutional prices in London, measures the movements of 35 commodities, and weights the major components in the following way which nearly corresponds to the weighting in the Bath Index.

| Schumpeter– Gilboy: | Bread/flour 40%, | Animal products 20%, | Rent/fuel 15%. |
| Bath: | Bread   52%, | Animal products 13%, after 1834, Rent/fuel 22% | 26%   when using cheese |

Where there is overlap, i.e. 1812–23, both indices move in the same direction by approximately the same amount. Elizabeth Gilboy in *Review of Economic Statistics*, XVIII (1936), pp. 134–43.

[4] See below, pp. 168–70, for an attempt to compare 1780–1812 with 1832–50.

working and a 13 per cent increase in wage-rates in the middle of the year. From then on, in spite of the rise in rates, real wages fell to 1801, improved slightly to 1804–5 then fell again to 1812 to a level 50 per cent lower than 1780.

1812–32. In order to provide what can only be a tenuous link between the earlier period and 1832–44 it is assumed that the average wage for 1807–9 equals the wage for 1812. This appears legitimate on two grounds. One, the accounts for the years 1810–11, although confused and unsuitable for inclusion in the index, do not show any increase in earnings. Two, it is certain, from literary evidence, that the years 1809 to 1813 in Bath were marked by stagnation, unemployment and special measures of relief similar in extent to those of 1800. Thus the 1807–9 average is more likely to over- than under-estimate the actual level of earnings in 1812. Given this assumption it is possible to derive two estimates of real wages for 1812. The first, using the Schumpeter–Gilboy Index (1780 = 100), gives a figure of 53 and indicates a decline in real wages of nearly 50 per cent from 1780. The second, using the Bath Index (1838 = 100) and a different basket of goods, results in a figure of 64 (67 including rent). This second index indicates a rise of over 60 per cent in real wages by 1832 (index 106 or 103 including rent). This can only serve as the roughest of guides to the movement of real wages over a very long period and, of course, indicates nothing about the movement of real wages during the period 1812–32.

All that local data can show for this period is the movement of retail prices. In spite of a rise between 1815 and 1817, retail prices fell after 1812 from 182 (173 including rent) to 95 in 1822–3 (119 including rent in 1820). Thereafter prices fluctuated between 14 and 34 points above this level – except for 1827–8 – until 1832 when a further downward drift of prices brought them, in 1837–42, to the low level prevailing in the early 1820s.[1] Calculations of the mean monthly deviation from the annual average price of the quartern loaf for five-year periods between 1800 and 1844 also suggest that this low level of prices, after 1832, was accompanied by a reduction in the sharp price fluctuations which were characteristic of the years

[1] See statistical Appendix D.

TABLE V *Earnings and real wages, non-agricultural labourers, in the City of Bath, 1780–1812*

(1780 = 100)

Year	Average weekly earnings	Sch./G.* Consumer goods (a)	Price of quartern loaf	Real wage	Annual real wage	Year	Average weekly earnings	Sch./G. Consumer goods (a)	Price of quartern loaf	Real wage	Annual real wage
1780	100	100	100	100	100	1794	102	123	—	83	—
1781	92	105	—	88	—	1795	114	133	—	86	—
1782	102	105	—	97	—	1796	118	140	—	84	—
1783	83	117	—	71	—	1800	—	192	360	—	—
						1801	119	207	278	55	—
1786	101	108	—	94	—	1802	120	158	154	76	81
1787	100	106	—	94	—	1803	113	141	141	80	89
1788	96	100	—	86	—	1804	119	146	146	82	—
1789	96	106	—	91	—						
1790	95	112	—	85	—	1807	120	169	175	72	61
1791	108	110	100	98	90	1808	125	185	191	67	—
1792	114	110	—	104	—	1809	117	192	229	61	58
1793	101	117	—	86	—	1812	117	215	303	53	—

* Schumpeter-Gilboy.

Source: Highway Accounts, Walcot. Elizabeth Boody Schumpeter, 'English Prices and Public Finance 1660–1822', *Review of Economic Statistics*, XX (1938).

of high prices earlier in the century.[1] Consequently, labourers' experience of a rapid decline in real wages within a short period of months, or sometimes weeks, became less common. This might well be a factor easing the impact of the downward drift of real wages between 1835 and 1838 noted in the following section. Widespread unemployment, however, continued to bring the shock of a rapid fall in real income to many.

TABLE VI   *Earnings and real wages, non-agricultural labourers, in the City of Bath, 1832–44.*

(1838 = 100)

Year	Average weekly earnings (1780 = 100 = Sept. 1838)	Bath retail prices	Price of quarter loaf	Real wage	Real wage of Rose	Real wage of Slade
1812	117	182	191	64		
1832	96	90	94	106		
1833	97	85	84	114		
1834	86	82	84	105		
1835	95	78	73	122		
1836	95	90	84	109	91	—
1837	95	102	94	93	86	92
1838	98	100	100	98	100	100
1839	103	101	105	102	99	115
1840	128	105	105	92	112	110
1841	127	103	100	123	114	113
1842	134	97	94	138	123	130
1843	134	83	78	161	142	152
1844	137	84	84	163	140	150

Source: Highway Accounts, Walcot; *Bath and Cheltenham Gazette.*

1832–44. In the years 1832–5 real wages averaged 112 and were about 70 per cent higher than in 1812. Between this and

[1] The mean monthly deviation from the annual average price of the quarter loaf was:

1800–5	1·48d.	1826–30	0·51d.
1806–10	0·69d.	1831–5	0·17d.
1811–15	1·09d.	1836–40	0·53d.
1816–20	1·14d.	1841–4	0·49d.
1821–5	0·68d.		

The average price in 1801 was 16¾d., the mean deviation 4·09d., in 1844 the average price was 8d., the mean deviation 0·33d.

the subsequent period, 1836–9, they fell by 12 per cent to 100 so that real wages were approximately 60 per cent higher than in 1812. A renewed rise began in 1839 and by 1840 real wages were approximately double the level of 1812. The wage experience of two regularly employed labourers shows that their rise in real wages was below that of the average, which was calculated by including the earnings of men less regularly employed. Nevertheless they too had increased their real wages 50 per cent between the mid-1830s and the mid-1840s.[1]

Although these calculations for the two periods, 1780–1812 and 1832–44, based as they are on different baskets of goods, do not permit a direct comparison between the levels of real wages they do suggest: (*a*) real wages declined between 1790 and 1812, (*b*) a rise in real wages between 1812 and 1832 which probably more than restored the labourer to the position reached in the 1790s, (*c*) real wages fell throughout the 1830s and only remained above the pre-war level in the 1840s. Table VII, however, includes a third calculation of real wages for the whole period 1780–1850 using the Bath index of labourers' earning and Silberling's cost of living index.[2] The index of real wages thus calculated moves in much the same way as the Bath–Schumpeter/Gilboy Index, 1780–1812 and the Bath Index,

---

[1] The downward drift of real wages in the second half of the 1830s is supported by evidence of the decline in wheat yield between 1834 and 1839.

Southern circuit	Yield (bushels/acre)
1834	44·1
1839	31·2

Similarly the rise in real wages after 1839–40 is supported by evidence of a dramatic increase in average wheat yield for the period 1839–50 after a twenty-five-year period, from 1815, during which yields rose at an average rate of rather less than 1 per cent per year. A five-year moving average of the yield figures suggests that there was no sustained upward trend in yields between 1815 and 1830 and that the bulk of the improvement in yields was concentrated in the period after 1840. See M. J. R. Healy and E. L. Jones, 'Wheat Yields in England, 1815–59', *Journal of the Royal Statistical Society*, A (General), vol. 125, Part 4 (1962), pp. 574–9.

[2] Silberling's index, although extending from 1780 to 1850, is a less satisfactory index than Schumpeter/Gilboy. It measures price movements of 15 commodities, the bulk of which are wholesale prices and bases its weighting partly on the budgets of all classes of workers in the late 1880s. Weights are: wheat 26%, animal products 30%, fuel 7%. N. J. Silberling, *Review o Economic Statistics*, October 1923, pp. 233–6.

1832–44.[1] In doing so it confirms the impression that the rise in real wages after the Napoleonic Wars did not permanently restore the labourer to the real wage obtaining between 1780 and 1790 until the early 1840s even though the real wage was then double what it had been in 1812.

TABLE VII   *Real wages of non-agricultural labourers in the City of Bath, 1780–1850*

	Bath–Schumpeter/ Gilboy (a) (1780 = 100)	Bath (a) excluding rent (b) including rent (1838 = 100)		Bath–Silberling (1838 = 100)
1780–3	89			118
1786–90	90			123
1791–6	90			115
1801–4	73			94
1807–9	66	(a)	(b)	90
1812	53	64	67	77
1832–5	—	112	111	106
1836–9	—	100	—	100
1840–4	—	141	(Av. of 1840 +1844, 144)	150
1845–8	—	—	—	156
1849–50	—	—	—	194

The application of the age-cohort approach would then suggest that very few labourers entering the labour market in the 1780s could have received a higher real wage at the end of a thirty-year working life. On the other hand, men starting work in the 1790s would probably have experienced a rise in real incomes during the 1820s while others, starting in the first decade of the eighteenth century, would almost certainly have benefited from an early and rapid improvement in real wages only to have had their experience of falling real wages and unemployment deepened by the fact of advancing age during the 1830s. By 1821 about one-third of the city's male population was aged between 20 and 40 years of age, and labourers in this age-group as they moved into the 1830s ten years later, approaching 40 or 50 years of age, would certainly have been able to contrast their middle and old age with a more prosperous youth, while

[1] Statistical Appendix B.

only men aged about 20 in 1821 would have benefited from the steep rise in real wages of the early 1840s when they would have been 40 years of age. Younger men starting work in the 1820s, in relatively favourable circumstances, would also have experienced unemployment and a cut in real wages in the 1830s and then, in the last third of life, particularly as labourers, would have shared in the general improvement to a lesser extent than those ten or twenty years younger whose first work experience began in the middle 1830s.

IV   SUMMARY AND CONCLUSION

It has been argued that, in the discussion on the standard of living during the Industrial Revolution, wage and price data should relate to specific classes and regions and enable comparison to be made with the pre-Napoleonic period. A further suggestion was that the real impact and meaning of movements in real wages, for those classes and regions studied, could be clarified further if, to the consequences of differences between the experience of workers in different regions and industries, and to the consequences of possible shifts in income distribution and of development in technology, is added an awareness of the role of the age-cohort approach in focusing attention on the wage and life experience of people. This was followed by an attempt to explore the experience of non-agricultural labourers in Bath. The approach was made through the construction of an index of weekly earnings and an index of retail prices, both of which were new and firmly based on local wage, retail price, rent and budgetary data relevant to the real experience of these non-agricultural labourers. The general conclusion was: a decline in real wages from 1790 to 1812 followed by a rise to 1832, which restored the labourer to the real-wage position of the same class of labourers in 1780–90. This was followed, in the 1830s, by a decline in real wages which was made worse by unemployment although partially offset by a reduction in price fluctuations. Rising earnings and falling prices after 1839–40 meant that by 1850 real wages were about double what they had been in the period 1801–4 and 50–60 per cent higher than in the pre-war period.

Although lack of data on the relationship of earnings to unemployment, age-structure and family size prevented a more rigorous discussion of the age-cohort approach, it was suggested that the experience of different generations or age-cohorts of labourers, within the seventy-year period, varied according to the way in which the phasing of the movement of real wages was imposed on the rhythm of their earnings experience.

Thus it is held that at least some of those requirements set out by T. S. Ashton have been fulfilled in a way which sheds much light on the experience of one group of the lowest class of urban workers, and in a way which offers a further possibility of reconciling the fact of a rise in real wages over a long-term with the short-term experience of men.

University of New England, N.S.W.

APPENDIX A

Earnings of labourers in Bath, Somerset, Wiltshire and Gloucestershire in selected years, 1767–1860

	Bath*	Somerset †	Wiltshire †	Gloucestershire †
1767–70	—	6s. 5d. ††	7s.	6s. 9d.
1780	8s.	—	—	—
1790	7s. 7d.	—	—	—
1795	9s. 1d.	7s. 3d.	8s. 4d.	7s.
1801	9s. 6d.	—	—	—
1809	9s. 4d.	—	—	—
1824	—	8s. 2d.	7s. 6d.	9s. 3d.
1831	—	9s.	9s. 5d.	10s.
1832	7s. 6d.	8s. 6d.	9s. 1d.	9s. 6d.
1833	7s. 9d.	8s. 4d.	9s. 2d.	9s. 3d.
1834	7s. 2d.	—	—	—
1837	7s. 7d.	8s. 7d.	8s.	9s.
1840	10s. 3d.	—	—	—
1850	11s.	8s. 7d. ††	7s. 3d.	7s.
1860	—	9s. 10d.	8s. 6d.	9s. 6d.

* Account Books of Surveyor of Highways, Walcot Parish.
† A. L. Bowley, 'The Statistics of Wages in the UK. During the last 100 Years', *JRSS* LXI, Part IV, LXIII, Part III of reprint.
†† Interpolated.

APPENDIX B

Real wages of non-agricultural labourers in the City of Bath, 1780–1850

Year	Bath earnings/ Schumpeter– Gilboy prices 1780 = 100	Bath earnings/ Silberling prices 1838 = 100	Year	Bath earnings/ Bath prices 1838 = 100	Bath earnings/ Silberling prices 1838 = 100
1780	100	133	(1812)	64	77
1781	88	113			
1782	97	120	1832	106	104
1783	71	105	1833	114	108
			1834	105	100
1786	94	138	1835	122	112
1787	94	126	1836	109	101
1788	86	121	1837	93	101
1789	91	120	1838	98	98
1790	85	112	1839	102	99
1791	98	130	1840	122	125
1792	104	127	1841	123	130
1793	86	112	1842	138	149
1794	83	110	1843	161	167
1795	86	104	1844	163	170
1796	84	106	1845		163
			1846		162
1801	55	81	1847		134
1802	76	102	1848		166
1803	80	95	1849		194
1804	82	100	1850		195
1807	72	98			
1808	67	93			
1809	61	78			
1812	53	77			

APPENDIX C

Average weekly earnings of labourers employed by the highway surveyors in the Parish of Walcot in the City of Bath, 1780–1851

Year	First week in January		First week in May		First week in September	
	No. emp.*	Average earnings	No. emp.	Average earnings	No. emp.	Average earnings
		s. d.		s. d.		s. d.
1780	1	8 –	1	8 –	1	8 –
1781	1	8 –	1	8 –	1	6 –
1782	–	—	1	8 –	2	8 7
1783	2	4 8	2	7 6	3	8 –
1786	1	8 8	2	7 6	2	8 –
1787	1	8 –	2	8 –	2	8 –
1788	2	8 –	1	8 –	3	7 1
1789	1	8 –	2	7 2	2	8 –
1790	2	7 8	3	8 5	5	6 7
1791	2	8 –	3	9 –	3	9 –
1792	3	8 –	7	9 8½	5	9 5½
1793	3	6 6	4	9 –	5	8 8
1794	3	8 –	5	8 3	5	8 3
1795	3	9 2½	3	9 2½	2	8 9
1796	2	8 9	2	9 6	1	10 –
1801	2	9 6	3	8 1	2	11 –†
1803	–	—	–	—	2	9 6‡
1804	2	9 6	2	9 6	2	9 6
1807	–	—	–	—	2	9 7
1808	4	10 –	3	10 –	3	10 –
1809	4	10 –	3	10 –	3	8 1
1832	89	5 9	8	6 2	11	10 7
1833	21	8 –	19	7 6	14	7 10
1834	23	7 1	20	7 1	16	7 5
1835	24	7 7	23	7 9	19	7 5
1836	–	—	19	7 9	19	7 11½
1837	21	7 5	18	7 9	18	7 7
1838	22	7 7	20	7 10	18	8 –
1839	22	7 10	7	9 5	6	9 11
1840	14	10 1	9	10 4	7	10 3
1841	11	9 4	5	10 8	5	10 6
1842	9	10 11	5	10 6	4	10 10
1843	6	10 3	6	11 1	4	10 10
1844	6	11 5	4	10 10	4	10 10
1845	4	10 10	3	10 8	3	10 8
1846	7	11 5	4	10 10	4	11 –
1847	7	10 4	4	10 4	4	11 1½
1848	5	10 6	4	11 1½	4	11 1½
1849	4	11 1½	4	11 8	4	11 6
1850	6	11 5	5	11 4	4	10 1½
1851	8	11 10	3	10 11	5	11 4

* Emp. = Employed.   † August.   ‡ October.

Source: Account Books of the Surveyor of Highways.

APPENDIX D

An index of retail prices in the City of Bath, 1812–44
(1838 = 100*)

Year	Mutton	Pork	Potatoes to 1832, cheese after 1834	Bread	Coal	Rent	(a) Without rent	(b) Including rent
							Retail Price Index	
1812	115	141	244	190	118	113	182	173
1813	123	150	222	163	113	—	133	—
1814	123	133	122	126	118	—	123	—
1815	100	108	133	116	109	106	116	115
1816	77	83	177	133	109	—	129	—
1817	77	83	188	179	100	—	157	—
1818	107	100	166	137	100	—	132	—
1819	123	125	133	121	95	—	120	—
1820	123	133	133	116	100	118	119	119
1821	92	100	105	102	104	—	102	—
1822	70	75	111	97	100	—	95	—
1823	85	93	88	97	100	—	95	—
1824	92	117	111	110	104	—	109	—
1825	107	125	211	116	104	113	129	127
1826	107	117	133	100	100	—	107	—
1827	107	108	77	95	100	—	95	—
1828	100	108	66	105	100	—	99	—
1829	100	108	111	116	100	—	112	—
1830	92	83	190	105	95	112	114	113
1831	92	83	190	105	95	—	114	—
1832	92	83	77	95	93	112	90	93
1833	92	83	—	84	91	—	85	—
			Cheese					
1834	92	83	66	84	89	—	82	—
1835	92	83	77	74	91	100	78	80
1836	92	93	111	84	95	—	90	—
1837	100	100	133	95	104	—	102	—
1838	100	100	100	100	100	100	100	100
1839	97	100	89	105	100	—	101	—
1840	100	125	94	105	100	86	105	102
1841	107	108	111	100	100	—	103	—
1842	100	102	100	95	102	—	97	—
1843	84	83	83	79	104	—	83	—
1844	84	83	77	84	104	80	84	83

* Prices in base year: mutton 6½d. per lb., pork 6d. per lb., potatoes assumed 4s. 6d. per sack [average 1827–32 5s. 6d. per sack and the trend of prices downwards], cheese 4½d. per lb., coal 11d. per cwt., bread 9½d. per quartern loaf, rent £13·21 per house per annum.
Source: *Bath and Cheltenham Gazette*, 1812–44; Poor and Highway Rate Books, Walcot Parish, 1800–50.

EDITORIAL NOTE TO ADDITIONAL CONTRIBUTIONS OF E. J. HOBSBAWM AND R. M. HARTWELL

This volume is intended to reflect the wide variety of contributions to the debate on the standard of living. For this reason it was originally intended to include only one essay from any individual participant in the debate. It is generally acknowledged, however, that the essays of Professor Hobsbawm and Dr Hartwell are central to the discussion and, choice having been made of their seminal 1957 and 1961 articles, it seemed appropriate to ask each to summarize their respective views on the progress of the debate since their initial participation in it. The following short essays – which post-date my own introductory essay – are their response to this invitation.

A. J. T.

8.1 The Standard of Living Debate

E. J. HOBSBAWM

I

The original debate between R. M. Hartwell and myself, which will be familiar to numerous university students, concluded in 1963. Both of us have been asked to review the state of the question ten years after. So far as I am concerned this can best be done by summarizing the nature of the original debate and seeing how it differs from the present discussion, by surveying the new material which has come to light and (in so far as they have changed in nature and emphasis) the new arguments brought into play. I propose to confine myself to the period originally under discussion, i.e. that between the outside limits of *c*. 1780 and the middle 1840s. To enter into earlier or later periods would be to enter a new debate rather than to review an old one

The original discussion dealt primarily, indeed almost exclusively, with the movement of the general level of real incomes. I think both of us accepted that this forms only part of the problem of the 'standard of living' even in the sense in which this is material and strictly measurable, but both of us confined ourselves to this aspect of the question, largely because of the earlier history of the controversy in the days between Clapham and Ashton. However, even within these quite narrow limits, the case for and against an 'optimistic' interpretation was made in three different ways, differently emphasized by the two debaters. It rested (i) on theoretical arguments about what might or might not be expected to happen to the standard of living in the early stages of industrialization *a priori*; (ii) on inferences which could (or could not) be legitimately drawn from the movement of aggregate indices about the economy as a whole; and (iii) on actual evidence – direct or indirect – dealing specifically with real incomes or consumption, such as information about wage-rates, earnings, prices, household expenditure, actual consumption and other relevant data such as unemployment etc.

On the whole Hobsbawm rested his case on (iii), dismissing (ii) where data on this kind appeared to conflict with specific evidence, and relying on (i) only to show that theoretical arguments did not make an 'optimistic' interpretation mandatory, at least for the period concerned. Hartwell, while presumably satisfied that (iii) was not incompatible with his view, relied more heavily (though in a negative way) on (i) and, it seems to me, even more heavily on (ii).[1]

It is difficult for a participant to assess the outcome of the debate, but on the whole it seems to have been to narrow the controversy down to the question 'whether there was a small rise, or an actual fall, in the general level of real wages in England' between the relevant dates.[2] As for the answer to what was thus revealed as a relatively trivial question – given that the earlier 'optimistic' contention of a *major* rise in real incomes is put out of court – opinions differ. They will probably continue to differ, since the evidence remains insufficient for conclusive findings. An agnostic position is probably the most tenable and reflected by the leading text-book ('continuing debate today means that probably no marked general change took place').[3] The most balanced estimate on the 'optimistic' side is modest and cautious, and may be quoted:

> There is no firm evidence for an overall improvement in working class standards of living between 1780 and about 1820 . . . On balance average living standards tended to fall rather than to rise. For the period from about 1820 to about 1840 it is difficult to be as definite . . . Perhaps on balance the optimists can make out a more convincing case for an improvement in the standard of living than the pessimists can for a fall. But either case is based largely on circumstantial evidence and there is only one thing that we can take as reasonably certain – and that is that whichever way it went, the net change was relatively slight.[4]

[1] See E. J. Hobsbawm and R. M. Hartwell, 'The Standard of Living during the Industrial Revolution: a Discussion', *Economic History Review*, 2nd series, XVI (1963), pp. 120–48; Hobsbawm, *Labouring Men* (1964); Hartwell, *The Industrial Revolution and Economic Growth* (1971).

[2] J. Hicks, *A Theory of Economic History* (1969), p. 148.

[3] P. Mathias, *The First Industrial Nation* (1969), p. 222.

[4] P. Deane, *The First Industrial Revolution* (1965), p. 250.

The past ten years have brought a number of monographic studies of localities or regions, such as Bath, Glasgow, the Black Country,[1] whose findings vary, as might be expected. However, there have been no striking additions to the evidence which would allow us to assess the *national* movement of real wages. Hence the question about real incomes still stands very much where it did. It therefore remains unaffected by sophistications in the general theoretical argument or inferences from the movement of aggregate indices. Given the absence of conclusive direct evidence, these by themselves can only provide presumption. If based on pure theory such arguments may be totally convincing in the abstract – but only there. If claiming support from the evidence of aggregate indices, such as the movement of national incomes, the arguments are merely appealing to circumstantial evidence as distinct from direct evidence, or to more circuitous evidence as distinct from the less circuitous. Thus, were we to use *only* the movement of national income *per capita* as a guide to the movement of actual real incomes, we might (if we accept the figures of J. E. Williams) be forced into the manifestly implausible position of believing that the standard of living improved more rapidly between 1800 and 1840 than between 1850 and 1890.[2] What seems implausible is not necessarily untrue, but in this instance it can seem plausible, let alone persuasive, only if we put out of our minds most of what we know about the standard of living in both periods and what contemporaries thought about it. In brief, the aggregate data may help us to formulate a hypothesis, but, even when reinforced by the best theory available, they cannot satisfactorily test it. Only direct evidence can do that, and we may therefore leave arguments unsupported by it to discover the necessary support.

[1] R. S. Neale, 'The Standard of Living 1780–1844: a Regional and Class Study', *Economic History Review*, 2nd series, XIX (1966), pp. 590–606; T. R. Gourvish, 'The Cost of Living in Glasgow in the early nineteenth century', *Economic History Review*, 2nd series, XXV (1972), pp. 65–80; G. Barnsby, 'The Standard of Living in the Black Country during the nineteenth century', *Economic History Review*, 2nd series, XXIV (1971), pp. 220–39.

[2] J. E. Williams, 'The British Standard of Living 1750–1850', *Economic History Review*, 2nd series, XIX (1966), pp. 581–90. In the first 40-year period gross national income per head grew by something like 70 per cent, in the second – at constant prices – by not much over 50 per cent.

However, if the question of the general level of real incomes remains much as it was ten years ago, much has been added to our knowledge of certain measurable aspects of working-class life: food, drink, housing and education. The greatest gap in our knowledge concerns the other consumer goods purchased by the working classes: clothing, household furniture and equipment etc., which have not yet been systematically investigated.

Food availability and consumption have been studied both by historians and nutritionists. The main new finding on availability are Fairlie's data on grain production.[1] These (at least for wheat) lead the author to optimistic conclusions for the post-Napoleonic period, with the proviso that the increase seems to have been concentrated in the industrial and urban centres, and an actual decline in *per capita* consumption is possible for the old agricultural areas of the south and east. These data must of course be taken very seriously, though their interpretation may lead to some debate. As for other work,[2] its most interesting results refer to the period after 1850, but what is said of the period under discussion does not suggest excessive optimism. Thanks to Harrison's encyclopaedic labours[3] we now know a great deal about *alcoholic drinks*, but as the author recognizes[4] their relevance to the standard of living debate is complex and obscure.

The serious study of working-class housing has only begun to advance in the past ten years and is greatly to be welcomed. Its results, according to Sutcliffe, seem so far to be mildly favourable to the optimists, but as this survey of the field notes[5] the ground has been covered patchily, and work for the first half of the century has concentrated on the housing of the more prosperous workers, this being easier to investigate.

[1] S. Fairlie, 'The Corn Laws and British Wheat Production, 1829–76', *Economic History Review*, 2nd series, XXII (1969), pp. 88–116, and unpublished data.

[2] J. Burnett, *Plenty and Want* (1966); T. C. Barker, J. C. McKenzie and J. Yudkin, *Our Changing Fare* (1966).

[3] B. Harrison, *Drink and the Victorians* (1971). See also B. Harrison, 'Pubs', in H. J. Dyos and M. Wolff (eds.), *The Victorian City: Images and Realities* (1973), pp. 161–90.

[4] Harrison, *Drink and the Victorians*, p. 34.

[5] A. Sutcliffe, 'Working-class housing in nineteenth-century Britain: a review of recent research', *Bulletin of the Society for the Study of Labour History*, 24 (1972), pp. 40–51.

The question remains pretty well open. Incidentally, the isolated study of housing runs the risk of neglecting the environmental conditions which surround them – water-supply, drainage, street cleaning, pollution etc – which have not attracted very systematic attention recently. Death from tuberculosis, described by Rosen as 'a rather sensitive index of living conditions in a community',[1] do not appear to have begun to diminish appreciably until after 1847,[2] though the absence of good data before 1840 greatly limits the significance of this observation.

The quantitative study of *education* has also made much progress since 1963, largely thanks to the study of parochial records inspired by historical demography. (The statistics of school attendance and availability have been scrutinized for optimistic purposes,[3] but their value remains in serious doubt.) Whatever the nature of the relation between education and the standard of living, we can accept the nineteenth century's own view that its growth marked 'improvement'. Work so far seems to suggest a halt or even a reversal in the long-term progress of literacy during the early industrial period, at least in industrial Lancashire up to the late 1820s. Whether and how this is directly related to industrialization is at present being debated.[4] It seems clear that educational progress resumed strongly in the 1830s and 1840s and had been more than made up by the mid-century.

II

However, the attempt to measure changes in the mean levels of income, consumption etc. is unrealistic in several respects.

[1] G. Rosen, 'Disease, Debility and Death', in Dyos and Wolff, op. cit. p. 648.
[2] T. McKeown and R. G. Record, 'Reasons for the decline in mortality in England and Wales during the nineteenth century', *Population Studies*, XVI (1962), pp. 94–122.
[3] E.g. by E. G. West, 'Resource Allocation and Growth in early nineteenth-century Education', *Economic History Review*, 2nd series, XXIII (1970), pp. 68–95.
[4] M. Sanderson, 'Social Change and Elementary Education in Industrial Lancashire, 1780–1840', *Northern History*, III (1968), pp. 131–54; 'Literacy and Social Mobility in the Industrial Revolution in England', *Past and Present*, 56 (1972), pp. 75–104.

In so far as it concentrates on averages, it neglects dispersion, which may make the simple average virtually meaningless for many of our purposes. What is the significance of mean or even median income in a region where the bottom quartile of the population receives 2·3 per cent of total incomes, the next quartile 10·1, the third quartile 22·8 per cent and the top 5 per cent, 30·5 per cent – to mention an actual, though non-British example from the 1960s?[1] In so far as we divide aggregate data *per capita*, we neglect the actual units of income-getting and spending, namely families and/or households. In so far as we make a series of cross-sectional analyses at successive moments of time, we falsify the actual life experience and expectations of people in ways which are now more familiar than ten years ago. These defects are now better understood and attempts to remedy them constitute the major novelty in the 'standard of living debate'.

The lack of adequate information about the social structure and income stratification of the British people in the first half of the nineteenth century is probably irremediable. But where social history has been most influenced by historical demography, the study of family structure and family incomes has advanced substantially, though blocked by any satisfactory source earlier than the 1851 census.[2] It has thrown light not only on the nature of the family income – at least in a few areas – but especially on the changes of this income during the life-cycle, e.g. on the burdens carried by families with immature children. I am not aware that the burden of poverty has been systematically recalculated for our period in the light of changes in demographic structure. However, it may well be that general calculations of this kind would be less useful than specific local ones such as those attempted by Foster and Anderson for the end of our period. According to Foster, 20 per

[1] J. Gianella, *Marginalidad en Lima Metropolitana* (*Una investigación exploratoria*) (Cuadernos Desco, Lima, 1970). Mimeograph.

[2] M. Anderson, *Family Structure in Nineteenth-Century Lancashire* (1971); J. D. Foster, *Capitalism and Class Consciousness in earlier Nineteenth-Century Oldham* (Cambridge, unpublished Ph.D. Thesis, 1967); 'Nineteenth-century towns – a class dimension', in H. J. Dyos (ed.), *The Study of Urban History* (1968); *Class Struggle and the Industrial Revolution. Early Industrial Capitalism in three English towns* (1974).

cent of the population of Oldham in a good year (1849) and about half in a bad year (1847) would have been below the Bowley revision of the Rowntree poverty line. Only 3 per cent (fourteen) of artisans' families, but 14 per cent (fifty-two) of skilled factory workers' and 35 per cent (seventy-eight) of labourers' families would fall below this line.[1] Anderson brings out dramatically the effect of non-working children on poverty. Fifty-two per cent of the Preston families in this group lived at or below the Rowntree poverty line, as against about 20 per cent of families with wives of child-bearing age but no more than one baby of less than a year, and a mere 5 per cent of wives over forty-five with no children at home, or only one aged twenty and over.[2]

Another attempt to introduce a diachronic element into the analysis has been the cohort approach, suggested by R. S. Neale[3] who has shown that even if we were to grant that the mean level of income was rising slowly (with fluctuations) over the whole period, it would still be possible for the actual experience of most workers to be discouraging. Neither of these attempts leaves the terrain of material and quantifiable fact. Both merely translate statistical abstractions into more concrete and realistic terms. Thus a cohort of men whose working life on full adult wages (say thirty years) brings them no noticeable improvement even if it occurs during a period of rising mean wage-levels, does not *imagine* that there has been no material improvement. For them there has been none. The argument is of course reversible.

A third method of making the abstractions more realistic would be the study of social and occupational mobility within a generation, i.e. in practice the upgrading of workers from lower to higher paid or from more to less irregular work, or the other way round. It has long been suspected that the rise in the mean standard of living between the mid-1840s and the late

[1] Foster, 'Nineteenth-century towns', p. 284; *Class Struggle and the Industrial Revolution*, pp. 95 ff.

[2] Anderson, op. cit. p. 31. The calculation is *not* an estimate of *actual* poverty but of poverty under optimal conditions, i.e. in conditions of full employment for all members of the family working full-time at the normal wages of the respective occupations.

[3] Neale, op. cit., *passim*.

1860s (as measured by consumption) must have been due mainly to such factors, since wage rates themselves show no dramatic improvement. Unfortunately at present it is difficult to see how sufficiently representative data could be collected for the first half of the nineteenth century.

III

At this point the study of objective and material changes passes into that of men's subjective reactions to the changes imposed on their way of life by industrialization. E. P. Thompson[1] stressed this rather than the purely material aspects of the 'standard of living' problem, thus returning to earlier historians' emphasis on qualitative rather than quantitative changes. Conversely, 'optimistic' scholars have always been inclined to stress subjective factors ('relative deprivation') to account for the enormous social discontent of the period which they cannot otherwise explain.[2] Qualitative changes and non-material factors are evidently crucial: men do not live by real incomes alone. Current general discussions on 'the quality of life' are now reflected even in the 'optimistic' literature.[3] But it should be observed *first*, that (despite Hartwell's assertion to the contrary)[4] the 'pessimistic' side has not abandoned the quantitative argument, and *second*, that the 'way of life' approach inevitably complicates the debate.

It is difficult enough to strike a balance between what is good for people and what they consider desirable, though nobody will argue that, in terms of the present debate, the standard of living rises when men are forced to abandon the steak they prefer for the more nutritious herring, or cannot afford to buy cigarettes, thus improving their health. It is even more difficult to assign relative weights to incommensurables, including matters which can hardly be measured at all. As we now know in the light of our greater information about such matters as

[1] E. P. Thompson, *The Making of the English Working Class* (1963).

[2] Hartwell, *The Industrial Revolution and Economic Growth*, pp. 341 ff.; also in A. Seldon (ed.), *The Long Debate on Poverty. Essays on Industrialisation and the 'Condition of England'* (1973).

[3] Seldon, op. cit. pp. 207-9.

[4] Hartwell, *Industrial Revolution and Economic Growth*, p. xx.

housing and education, even the weighting and combination of more readily measurable aspects of the standard of living pose more complex problems than were allowed for in the earlier debate.

Suppose, for instance, we were to consider the variable 'independence' which was clearly important to such workers as enjoyed it, in spite of Bythell's attempt to dismiss it for the handloom weavers.[1] We should first have to assess the degree to which some workers maintained or actually increased it, e.g. by *de facto* informal job control, and how many did so. We should next have to measure, if we could, the relative attractions of independence and higher income in so far as these could be isolated; both positively (i.e. what an independent person would accept as compensation for loss of independence, e.g. more than the 100 per cent wage-rise refused by the Irish women weavers cited by Pollard),[2] and negatively (i.e. how low and apparently irreparably income would have to fall before the worker was ready to abandon independence). Such calculations may be impracticable and indeed some would say pointless, and have certainly not been made. But unless or until they are made, a 'standard of living' debate which includes the 'way of life' cannot find common ground with the debate which merely concentrates on real incomes.

The Hartwell–Hobsbawm debate therefore has little in common with the debate as conducted by Thompson, though as it happens Hobsbawm and Thompson would jointly as well as severally oppose the 'optimistic' view. Each debate stands on its own feet, though my personal view is that the question as formulated by Thompson is important, because it raises the whole nature of society and industrialization under capitalist conditions and the changes produced by one in the other, whereas the problem as formulated in the Hobsbawm–Hartwell exchanges is trivial, because the question whether the working people received marginally greater or smaller real incomes in one period of the nineteenth century is in itself not of great

[1] D. Bythell, *The Handloom Weavers* (1969), *passim.* The familiar problem of overcoming the resistance of workers who valued their independence is discussed in Thompson, op. cit. and S. Pollard, *The Genesis of Modern Management* (1965), esp. Chap. V.

[2] Ibid., p. 173.

consequence. Of course, as Hicks has recognized, the question why in this phase of British industrialization the real wages of workers lagged so notably behind the growth in output and productivity *is* important.[1] In so far as it implied clearing away the 'optimistic' views which appeared to deny this fact, the Hobsbawm–Hartwell exchanges of 1957–63 may have been a necessary preliminary to asking an interesting question. More generally, they may have served to clear the ground by demonstrating the inadequacy – from the point of view of the historian, the sociologist and, it may be suggested, the serious economist – of an approach to industrialization which was characteristic of a period when W. W. Rostow's *Stages of Economic Growth* could, however briefly, have been taken seriously as a contribution to understanding the development of modern industrial society. Our debate may also have helped to stimulate further research into what happened to the British people during the industrial revolution. But that is all. Nevertheless, it has not been a waste of time. It has eliminated one hypothesis: that of the extreme 'optimists' of the Clapham–Ashton era. It may perhaps even have helped to inject an element of greater rigour into subsequent discussion.

© E. J. Hobsbawm 1974

---

[1] Hicks, op. cit. p. 148.

8.2 Models of Immiseration: the theoretical basis of pessimism[1]

R. M. HARTWELL and S. ENGERMAN

The debate about the standard of living during the Industrial Revolution in England has a long history, from Macaulay versus Southey to Hartwell versus Hobsbawm.[2] Courses on modern English economic history invariably include 'the condition of England question', and the controversy about living standards has become a staple, also, in courses on historical methodology (an interesting and clear-cut example of historians, on the basis of the same evidence, disagreeing, often acrimoniously, about what happened in the past). If there is inconclusiveness in the continuing debate, it cannot be attributed solely to analytical and data problems; rather, disagreement can be explained partly by the historical concerns of both parties, and to the sensitivity of the political nerves touched by the controversy. This paper, however, will not present new data to convince those who will not be convinced; nor will it reveal further evidence of the ideological content of the debate; its focus, instead, will be pedagogical, to identify the analytical framework in which the pessimists have argued. Nevertheless, in

[1] The origin of this article was in a discussion between the authors about the models of immiseration outlined in Hartwell's essay 'The Standard of Living Controversy: A Summary', in R. M. Hartwell (ed.), *The Industrial Revolution* (Blackwell, Oxford, 1970). Hartwell had suggested that the pessimists' arguments implicitly implied models of the economy which were implausible; in particular he detailed three such models commonly used. Engerman suggested that the immiseration arguments implied a much larger number of models, and this essay is the result of their discussion about these models. When Hartwell was asked by the editor for a 'new' contribution to the debate, it seemed that a comprehensive outline of the 'models of immiseration' would be an interesting and constructive contribution. We were helped by comments made by Michael Mussa on an earlier draft.

[2] The historical debate is summarized in Hartwell, 'Interpretations of the Industrial Revolution in England', *Journal of Economic History*, 1959. For a recent judicious evaluation of the quantitative evidence relevant to the debate see P. Deane, *The First Industrial Revolution* (Cambridge University Press, 1965), chapter 15.

identifying the economic models used by those historians who argue that living standards deteriorated during the industrial revolution, or the models they could have used, and in demonstrating the theoretical and empirical implausibility of several of these models, there will be raised issues about the basis of pessimism. In the past, identification of the models of immiseration has been obfuscated, as has been the whole controversy, by a persistent failure to specify the questions being asked, and by a perverse mixing of questions which has confused the issue. The basic issue being debated seems straightforward. *Did the per capita real incomes of the working classes rise or fall during the Industrial Revolution, say between 1750 and 1850?* But this question has rarely been asked straightforwardly, and it and other questions have been run together in a most confusing fashion. In particular, confusion has occurred in three ways. First, there has been a tendency to mix up questions about *quantitative measures of real income over time* with questions about *the changing quality of life.*[1] Second, there has been a confusion about the historical significance of evidence relating respectively to *individuals* and to *aggregates*. Third, there has been a failure to distinguish between *what was, and what was not, exogenous to the Industrial Revolution* in its effects on the standard of living of the working classes.

In this essay we omit consideration of the quality of life changes that came with industrialization, not because we think that they are unimportant, but because determination of living standards has been a specific, important and central issue of the historical debate, because agreement on quantifiable trends should be possible (even if disagreement continues about the interpretation and importance of those trends), and because the

---

[1] The distinction between 'the standard of living' and 'the way of life' has gradually been made explicit, for example by Hartwell ('The Standard of Living Controversy: A Summary', op. cit.), and 'the way of life' now looks like being the central issue in a continuing debate. Why? Mainly for two reasons: first, the debate about the standard of living, based on quantifiable data, has seemingly favoured the optimists, thus making it desirable for the pessimists to shift ground to other well-discussed problems; second, the present vogue for environmental studies emphasizing the problems of pollution in industrial economies has given further impetus to 'quality of life' arguments generally, and, in particular, to the relevance of urban pollution during the industrial revolution in any summing up of the benefits and costs of English industrialization.

problems involved in analysing and interpreting the quality of life are so complex, and disagreement about them on philosophical and political grounds so profound, that a narrowing of the field of inquiry to the quantifiable would seem to be a necessary starting point for the more difficult inquiry. There is, also, an obvious interdependence between living standards and way of life, with changes in one involving changes in the other. Generally, most historians would argue that the optimists' case for the industrial revolution has causation flowing from living standards to way of life. We also omit detailed consideration of the pessimists' emphasis on the significance of particular statements about individuals in, or sections of, the working classes, in contrast to general statements about the working classes as an aggregate. Statistical generalizations are a way of describing, in statistical terms, the general or average characteristics of a group of individuals, and such generalizations are used constantly and meaningfully by historians and social scientists. An expectation of life at birth of seventy in modern England is not 'disproved' by examples of particular deaths at every age from birth to seventy. Similarly generalizations that the standard of living during the Industrial Revolution was rising or falling are not disproved, on the one hand by evidence that the handloom weaver and the working classes of Bath[1] were becoming worse off, or on the other by evidence that skilled cotton operatives and the working classes of Birmingham were becoming better off. Generalizations about the working classes can be made only by using aggregates and averages, even if implicitly. The identification of individual cases, whatever their particular characteristics, does not vitiate general statistical statements about the larger group to which the individuals belonged, but in which they might have been statistical deviants. The controversy about living standards

[1] See, on the working class of Bath, R. S. Neale, 'The Standard of Living, 1780–1844: A Regional and Class Study', *Economic History Review*, 1966. While clearly it is important to get as much evidence on specific areas as possible, it is necessary to distinguish between growing and declining areas in extrapolating the conclusions to the entire nation. The study of Bath suffers, further, in being based on an extremely small number of observations, and in having a money wage series based upon a nominal wage fixed by the government, so that the labour market adjustment is in terms of quantities not wages, and the real wage measure reflects mainly changes in the price of bread.

exists only because of contrary statistical generalizations, and generalizations about deterioration by the pessimists are as vulnerable to 'the contrary case' as are generalizations about improvement by the optimists, a fact which both groups often conveniently forget or choose to ignore.[1]

The third confusion is less obvious, and generally unrecognized. It seems to us that nobody would get particularly excited about what happened to living standards in England between 1750 and 1850 except for two facts: this century covered the early period of the world's first industrial revolution; generalizations about living standards in this period, and their relationship to industrialization, were featured in much influential nineteenth century writing and created a widely but not universally accepted conventional wisdom about English industrialization and its effects on the working classes (and generally about 'capitalist economic growth' and its social effects).[2] The controversy, therefore, is not so much about the living standards of a *particular* class, in a *particular* country, in a *particular* century, as about capitalist industrialization and its effects on the working classes. This distinction is obvious but nevertheless has important implications for our inquiry, especially as regards the influence of events and factors exogenous to the industrial revolution which have been used by historians to help explain trends in living standards during the industrial revolution. For example, because most historians agree that living standards during the Napoleonic Wars were held back, the problem of disentangling the relationship between industrialization, war and living standards is im-

---

[1] The pessimists argue both that aggregates ('global calculations') are unreal or less reliable than 'direct evidence', and that such generalizations must 'yield to the facts' and are vulnerable to 'contrary presumptions'. (The quotations are from Hobsbawm.) The implications of this seem to be that historical generalizations are impossible: there can be no meaningful statistical generalization about the working classes without a comprehensive survey of all members of the working classes, and any individual deviance from the 'norm' or 'average' makes generalization about the working classes impossible.

[2] The debate today is much influenced by the writings of Marx and Engels, and especially by Engels' *The Condition of the Working Class in England*. Earlier pessimists, however, depended on the classical economists, the parliamentary reports and the works of early social critics like Fielden, Kay, Thackrah, Bray and Thompson.

portant; the extent to which the wars were exogenous to English industrialization, yet affected living standards, becomes a relevant issue in determining the effects of industrialization on living standards.[1] This, indeed, poses an obvious counter-factual, one of many. What would have happened to living standards if there had been no wars? Or slower population growth? Or slower industrialization? For example: in the absence of industrialization, and given the rate of population growth, would living standards have been higher or even lower?[2] Thus in evaluating the consequences of the industrial revolution the question should be *whether, given some set of exogenous changes, the working classes were better off than they would have been in the absence of industrialization.* And this question should be distinguished conceptually from the question *whether, given the Industrial Revolution, it would have been possible for there to have been some set of policies which would have permitted the working classes to have been better off than they actually were.*[3] And these questions are different again from the question *whether the*

[1] Historians might argue that the Napoleonic Wars were the outcome of capitalist–imperialist rivalries, in the way in which historians have argued that the First World War was the outcome of competing imperialisms; but they have not. Historians have argued, since Thorold Rogers, about the damaging effects of the Napoleonic Wars on the British economy. Thorold Rogers, for example, argued that 'thousands of homes were starved in order to find the means for the great war. . . . The resources on which the struggle was based, and without which it would have speedily collapsed, were the stint and starvation of labour, the over-taxed and underfed toils of childhood, the underpaid and uncertain employment of men'. (*Six Centuries of Work and Wages*, London, 1884, p. 505.) For an explicit model analysing the effects of the Napoleonic Wars on the distribution of factor income, see Glenn Hueckel, 'War and the British Economy, 1793–1815: A General Equilibrium Analysis', *Explorations in Economic History*, 1973.

[2] The counter-factual was clearly formulated by T. S. Ashton in *The Industrial Revolution, 1760–1830* (Oxford University Press, 1948, p. 161): 'The central problem of the age was how to feed and clothe and employ generations of children outnumbering by far those of any earlier time. Ireland was faced by the same problem. Failing to solve it, she lost in the 'forties about a fifth of her people by emigration or starvation and disease. If England had remained a nation of cultivators and craftsmen, she could hardly have escaped the same fate, and, at best, the weight of a growing population must have pressed down the spring of her spirit.'

[3] Since most historians have accepted that, in the long-run, industry has been 'a good thing', and that it is doubtful that Britain could have benefited to the same extent from concentration on agriculture (as did Denmark), the crucial issues are concerned with the appropriate timing and the specific nature of the transition to industrialization.

working classes improved their standard of living over the period of the Industrial Revolution, say from 1750 to 1850. But finding out what happens to living standards between 1750 and 1850 does not permit unqualified statements about the impact of industrialization on the working classes, or about the ethics of entrepreneurial behaviour, or about the social efficiency of industrial capitalism, without explicit consideration of the implied counter-factuals.

II

The historians who have argued that working-class living standards in England declined from 1750 to 1850, the pessimists, believe that over a long period of rising gross national production, a rise whose reality is not in question,[1] the mass of the workers became materially worse off. In other words, these historians believe *either* that the Industrial Revolution was a period of rising output but not one of economic growth (economic growth defined as a sustained rise in *average per capita* real income), *or* that it was a period of economic growth during which distribution was skewed continuously against the working classes so that their living standards fell. Implicit in these beliefs are macro-economic models of the English economy during the Industrial Revolution, models which have not been conceptualized explicitly. These models, as we have indicated, fall into two distinct classes. The first explains trends in average *per capita* real income, with unchanged distribution of income; the models here depend on trends in the average of all incomes with the implication that all incomes were affected adversely. The second explains trends in the real income of particular classes because of shifts in distribution; the models here depend on a distributive mechanism such that, with rising *per capita* national income, different classes were differently affected; the model is such that, even with a rising *per capita* real national income, the working classes suffered a decline in their real incomes. Given the economic characteristics of the Industrial Revolution, and given the political attitudes of the

---

[1] No pessimist, to our knowledge, has challenged the increase in production; on the contrary, they generally have stressed it.

pessimists, the second type of model would seem to be the more plausible for the pessimist case. But both types of model have been used, and we shall consider both types.

III

A. Models with unchanged income distribution

(i) 'The Malthusian Trap' model. The best known model of immiseration is that of Malthus in which population growth, in a closed economy with given natural resources, leads to diminishing returns and a decline in *per capita* income. The model could be applied both to a single sector economy (agriculture) as well as to a two-sector economy (agriculture and industry); and further, in either case, to an economy open or closed to international trade.[1] In the closed economy case, with two sectors, increasing population leads to rising agricultural prices and a declining industrial sector, as resources transfer to agriculture. (In an open economy, the same mechanism works through adverse changes in the terms of trade.) The Malthusian Trap model applied to a closed economy has some historical plausibility for three reasons: first, during the Industrial Revolution England was to a large extent independent of imported foodstuffs;[2] second, the classical economists Malthus and Ricardo formulated their theories of population, rent and diminishing returns on the basis of their contemporary relevance;[3] and third, studies of recent underdevelopment tend to regard population as a negative element in growth, and thus

[1] We assume that the model is consistently open or closed during the period of analysis. Thus the issues raised by the Stolper–Samuelson theorem concerning the effects of changing trade barriers will not arise. In any case, were these effects considered, the pattern suggested would be a reduction in the income of landowners, not labourers, so that the Stolper–Samuelson argument could not explain an adverse shift in the workers' standard of living. See W. F. Stolper and P. A. Samuelson, 'Protection and Real Wages', *Review of Economic Studies*, 1941.

[2] Food imports, as a percentage of domestic production, were small up to the 1830s, although bad harvest years resulted in some large grain imports (for example, in 1801, 1810, 1817/18, and 1829/30/31). However, the Napoleonic Wars, and the blockade, coincided with a period of slowly growing dependence on imported food, although there were years up to 1840 when exports of wheat were considerable (for example, 1815/6/7, 1821/2/3 and 1835/6/7).

[3] See R. M. Hartwell, 'Introduction', to David Ricardo, *On the Principles of Political Economy, and Taxation* (Pelican Books, London, 1971).

see a Malthusian Trap in many underdeveloped economies.[1] Most pessimists have used the Malthusian model in their explanations of immiseration; for example, Pollard and Crossley.[2] Unfortunately this application is historically unconvincing, again for three reasons: first, the indices of population growth and aggregate output that have been devised show output to have grown faster than population;[3] second, the classical economists by the 1830s had abandoned the theory that wages were tending towards subsistence;[4] and third, the price of food over the period of the Industrial Revolution, in comparison with money wages and other prices, does not confirm the Malthusian thesis.[5]

(ii) The unproductive investment model. The second model of immiseration is one in which investment leads not only to no current income benefits but also to no higher future income.[6]

[1] See, for example, A. O. Hirschman, *The Strategy of Economic Development* (Yale University Press, New Haven, 1958), chapter 2, the section entitled 'The Forces Corroding Development'.

[2] S. Pollard and D. W. Crossley, *The Wealth of Britain, 1085–1966* (Batsford, London, 1968), pp. 174–5: 'unprecedented growth in total population . . . put great strain on the resources available for consumption and for investment'.

[3] For output there are estimates both of national income and of industrial production (see P. Deane and W. Hoffman); population figures come from censuses held regularly after 1801. But the outstripping of population by output can be seen in almost every production series that has survived or has been devised, and even agricultural production, without imports, seems to have kept pace with population up to about 1830 (see M. J. R. Healy and E. L. Jones, 'Wheat Yields in England, 1815–1859', *Journal of the Royal Statistical Society*, Series A, 1962).

[4] See M. Blaug, *Ricardian Economics: A Historical Study* (Yale University Press, 1958) for an account of the abandoning of Ricardian economics in the 1830s, partly on theoretical grounds, but also in the face of the empirical evidence that wages were not sinking to subsistence. For a different interpretation, see in R. L. Meek, *Economics and Ideology and Other Essays* (Chapman and Hall, London, 1967), 'The Decline of Ricardian Economics in England'.

[5] For prices see A. D. Gayer, W. W. Rostow, and A. J. Schwartz, *The Growth and Fluctuation of the British Economy, 1790–1850* (Clarendon Press, Oxford, 1953), vol. II, chapter IX.

[6] The Ricardian discussion of machinery, as recently presented by J. R. Hicks, (*A Theory of Economic History*, Oxford University Press, 1969, chapter 9 and Appendix) does point to the possibility of a reduced wage during the period of building up the fixed capital stock. Yet this analysis differs from those discussed here in that the subsequent benefits to workers' income resulting from this mechanization are pointed out.

It could be argued that we should ignore investment, since it does reduce consumption, and restrict ourselves ,in comparing standards of living, to consump-

As used by the pessimists the argument generally has been that investment needs during the Industrial Revolution were so large that consumption had to be reduced by so much that living standards fell.[1] Thus formulated the model is similar to that used to explain the slow rise in consumption in some modern economies; the investment needs of heavy industry in the form of capital goods, necessary for future growth, preclude rises in consumption during the period of the x-years plan. But in these cases present sacrifices are made, and explicitly rationalized as such, for the sake of real income gains in the next period, when the capital goods begin to produce consumer goods. The peculiarity of this type of model for the Industrial Revolution, however, is the presumed failure of increased capital accumulation to lead to rises in incomes over a very long period.[2] It is necessary, therefore, to have a model of the Industrial Revolution

---

tion alone; this, for example, is what Williams has done. (J. Williams, 'The British Standard of Living, 1750–1850', *Economic History Review*, 1966.) But if investment was the result of voluntary savings decisions (to provide future income), simply to compare consumption standards would be misleading. Ignoring the investment decision, and its costs, thus involves a redefinition of the relevant concept of welfare. This redefinition would be appropriate, however, to the extent that the savings 'attributed' to the working class were not voluntary, but the result of some forced expropriation by the investing class. Since this expropriation could presumably have been done without any subsequent investments, in some sense any investment would have provided a better outcome than might otherwise have been possible.

The Williams article contains a number of problems of statistical analysis, the most crucial being the failure to link the two independent income series (taken from Deane and Cole) for the year of overlap (1800). If done appropriately, the post-1800 *per capita* incomes are raised about one-third above those calculated by Williams, so that a consistent application of his procedure yields conclusions different from those he drew.

[1] For example, see E. J. Hobsbawm (*Industry and Empire*, Penguin Books, Harmondsworth, 1969, p. 92): 'Industrialism means a relative diversion of national income from consumption to investment, a substitution of foundries for beefsteaks. In a capitalist economy this takes the form, largely, of a diversion of income from non-investing classes like peasants and labourers, to potentially investing ones, namely the owners of estates and business enterprises, i.e. from the poor to the rich'. Similar statements can be found in E. P. Thompson and S. Pollard.

[2] It is difficult to find any historical evidence for such a model. Of early industrial revolution investment, indeed up to the 1830s, the only example of large-scale and widespread investment with, sometimes, a slow pay-off, was the canal. It might be argued that investments yielded negative returns to entrepreneurs, but that would conflict with the arguments about the effects of various innovations.

in which increased capital failed to increase income over a succession of investment periods, and to explain why entrepreneur-investors, in these circumstances, continued to invest. A possible immiseration model would be one in which investment was of very long gestation, fifty years or more, but was continued in the expectation of ultimate profit, or else it was unproductive but was continued because what was seen as the high risk of waste was offset by expected long-term profit. Another model would be one in which investment generated further investment, piling up capital goods but producing no consumer goods.[1] All these models are historically, as well as theoretically, implausible: first, the diversion of resources to investment during the Industrial Revolution was not large as a proportion of national income (estimated at less than 10 per cent up to 1840) and it increased quite slowly;[2] second, Industrial Revolution investment was, generally, both short-term and very productive, with quickly constructed capital goods quickly producing a stream of consumer goods (for example, as with textile factories);[3] third, the savings ratio would have had to have increased from *c.* 5 per cent (the estimated ratio at the beginning of the Industrial Revolution) to 'far above anything that we have any evidence for or can be plausibly assumed' to have provided no growth in *per capita* consumption.[4]

However, a consideration of categories of expenditure during the Industrial Revolution could strengthen the pessimist case.

[1] This seems to be the Pollard model. S. Pollard, 'Investment, Consumption and the Industrial Revolution', *Economic History Review*, 1958. See also, Pollard and Crossley, op. cit. p. 189.

[2] See P. Deane, *The First Industrial Revolution*, op. cit., chapter 10. For more detailed treatment, see P. Deane and W. A. Cole, *British Economic Growth, 1688–1959* (Cambridge University Press, 1962), pp. 303 *et seq.* In his more technical writings Pollard has apparently suggested that the initial requirements of fixed capital for the industrial sector were relatively minor. See S. Pollard, 'Fixed Capital in the Industrial Revolution in Britain', *Journal of Economic History*, 1964.

[3] See, for example, S. D. Chapman, *The Cotton Industry in the Industrial Revolution* (Macmillan, London, 1972), p. 70. See also, M. Blaug, 'The Productivity of Capital in the Lancashire Cotton Industry during the Nineteenth Century', *Economic History Review*, 1961. See also, H. D. Fong (*Triumph of Factory System in England*, Tientsin, China, 1930, p. 67), for productivity figures in the woollen industry.

[4] B. Mitchell, review of Pollard and Crossley, *Business History*, 1970.

An allocation of national income along the lines of recent calculations of economic welfare done by Nordhaus and Tobin, for example, making allowance for 'instrumental expenditures' and 'disamenities of urbanization', might reduce the measured contribution of investment to the increased economic welfare of the working classes.[1] It can be argued, indeed, that some consumption expenditures were to offset worsened environmental conditions (for example, those required to keep growing towns 'clean'), or were necessary to earn a living (for example, educational expenditure or expenditure on particular types of clothing, boots for miners, etc.); similarly there is a case for arguing that government expenditure on war was not part of the income stream to be considered as relevant for comparisons of living standards.

(*iii*) *Insufficient aggregate demand model.* A third and popular model of immiseration is one in which any measured gains in income per employed worker during industrialization were more than offset by persistent and increasing unemployment. The model is usually portrayed in terms of labour unemployment,[2] but it obviously implies the general unemployment of all resources. The model uses short-term Keynesian theory for long-term analysis, the argument being that because aggregate demand during the Industrial Revolution failed to increase as rapidly as resources, there was persistent long-term unemployment of resources such that, for example, unemployment of labour increased so much that the average *per capita* income of the labour force as a whole declined. The implications of such a model are obvious: for the model to work, wages and/or prices must have been persistently inflexible, so that the unemployment of resources could have persisted over long periods without market forces being able to operate effectively to produce appropriate wage-price adjustments. The pessimists have used this model usually in the form of an analysis of the trade cycle,

[1] W. Nordhaus and J. Tobin, 'Is Growth Obsolete?', National Bureau of Economic Growth, Fiftieth Anniversary Colloquium V, General Series 96 (New York, 1972).

[2] For example, E. J. Hobsbawm ('The British Standard of Living, 1790–1850', *Economic History Review*, 1957) argues (p. 56) that 'it is highly probable that the period 1811–1842 saw abnormal problems and abnormal unemployment, such as is not revealed by the general "real wage" indices'.

seen as a consequence of industrialization, with consequent reductions of employment and income. They do not make clear, however, whether the emphasis is on the increased number of unemployed, or the longer periods of unemployment, in each cycle, although they seem to imply that the cycle increased in intensity in both respects.[1]

The model, again, while important in explaining short-run trends, is theoretically implausible and historically unproven when applied to periods of the length under consideration. It hinges on the inflexibility of wages and/or prices, without suggestions as to why such inflexibility should have existed over prolonged periods and without historical evidence of its existence. Indeed historical evidence suggests that both wages and prices were very flexible, with rapid and frequent changes in both at any time, say, between 1780 and 1850.[2] Indeed, the fluctuating price of bread is a good example of market response, and the high price of bread, in contrast to previously lower prices, has often featured in the pessimist literature. Nor is there convincing evidence that the trade cycle increased in duration and amplitude during the Industrial Revolution. The massive study of fluctuations between 1790 and 1850 by Gayer, Rostow and Schwartz argues that there was 'no significant alteration in their typical behaviour' over the period, that average duration 'seems not to have altered significantly', that foreign trade exhibited 'a lesser amplitude of movement after 1816 than during the war years', but, nevertheless, that 'the growing relative importance of capital investment and of the coal and iron industries must have involved an increase in the proportion of the total population affected by business fluctuations'.[3]

A final reservation to the insufficient aggregate demand model is that, as usually presented, it is not consistent with the unproductive investment model. In the latter, investment should

---

[1] Ibid., p. 56: 'doubtless the decades of difficulty and adjustment after the wars tended to make the problem [unemployment] more acute'.

[2] The volumes of T. Tooke's *A History of Prices, and of the State of the Circulation, from 1793 to 1837* (London, 1838) detail price changes over the period of industrialization. A. L. Bowley (*Wages in the United Kingdom in the Nineteenth Century*, Cambridge University Press, 1900) has plenty of evidence of wage flexibility.

[3] A. D. Gayer, W. W. Rostow and A. J. Schwartz, op. cit. vol. II., pp. 570–1.

have generated increased aggregate demand, but provided no 'useful' outputs; in the former, labour was persistently unemployed and in consequence had a lowered average income over time. In one model income did not grow as rapidly as it should have done because capital goods or the wrong goods were produced; in the other, there was less output because resources were not employed. In spite of the difficulty of arguing for the simultaneous occurrence of both of these models, this is exactly what some pessimists have done.[1]

(*iv*) *Deteriorating terms of trade model.* A fourth model used by the pessimists has pictured the economy of Industrial Revolution England as one in which much of the benefit of rising output was lost to the working classes because of deteriorating terms of trade: an increasing outflow of exports was necessary to pay for an inflow of necessary imports.[2] Those historians who have used this model, however, have not always made it clear whether their argument is that living standards declined because less and less imports could be bought by more and more exports, as seen in the calculations of measured income received; or whether the loss of income because of deteriorating terms of trade has not been included in existing calculations of income, so that existing income series are falsely inflated. If national income is computed by measuring imports obtained in exchange for exports, then this latter problem does not arise, since the measurement of the incomes of any period is based on the appropriate terms of trade. If, however, national income calculations use different deflators for exports and imports, or physical indices, then measured income does not reflect changes in the terms of trade. Certainly national income estimates at constant values, using the export and import prices of a

[1] Both Pollard and Hobsbawm have had it both ways. For example, Pollard and Crossley (op. cit., p. 189) use both models in successive paragraphs. Possibly they meant to argue that an investment boom which 'failed' was followed by a period of unemployment.

[2] Thus, Pollard and Crossley argue (op. cit., p. 189): 'Instead of benefiting the producers, the enlarged output . . . was almost wholly absorbed by the need for exports to pay for raw materials and for food, to meet the gap in home food supplies, as well as for capital repatriation and some foreign investment.' See also E. P. Thompson, *The Making of the English Working Class* (Gollancz, London, 1963), p. 204. Also, B. Inglis, 'The Poor who were with us', *Encounter* (September 1971), p. 53.

specific base year, overstate the rise in income levels over time when there is a decline in the net barter terms of trade in comparison with the base year. For the years 1800 to 1850, however, adjusting for this makes little difference to the rate of growth of income.[1]

There is, however, a theoretical argument for the possible relevance of a model of 'immiserizing growth' which has been applied to under-developed countries dependent on international trade.[2] There was for England, in the first half of the nineteenth century, a decline in the net barter terms of trade, the prices paid for imports rising relatively to the prices received for exports.[3] But this did not necessarily mean that the English productive factors were worse off; rather, it is generally supposed (for example, about the cotton industry), that increasing productivity in the export industries (an outward shift in supply curves) was reflected in falling export prices, while factor returns remained the same or, more likely, improved. While it is true that English factors would have been better off (*cet. par.*) if the terms of trade had not declined, nothing of certainty can be said from the terms of trade about whether their incomes were higher or lower in the earlier than in the later period. The effect of this increasing productivity on income can be measured by calculating the single factorial terms of trade (the net barter terms of trade multiplied by the changing productivity of the export sector), which gives a measure of the trade-off between the price of the factor's time and the price of imports. Calculations for the period after 1800 show that, while the commodity terms of trade did decline, the single factorial terms of trade did not.[4] Thus whether the

[1] By adjusting the Deane and Cole *per capita* income estimates for the changing terms of trade (as computed by Imlah) the growth rate of *per capita* income from 1801 to 1851 is reduced from 1·22 per cent per annum to 1·15 per cent per annum.

[2] See J. Bhagwati, 'Immiserizing Growth: A Geometrical Note', *Review of Economic Studies*, 1958.

[3] The net barter terms of trade, according to A. H. Imlah (*Economic Elements in the 'Pax Britannica': Studies in British foreign trade in the nineteenth century*, Harvard University Press, Cambridge (Mass.), 1958), declined quite sharply: with 1880 as 100, the ratio of export to import prices declined as follows: 1801—169, 1811—201, 1821—164, 1831—138, 1841—110, 1851—110.

[4] A crude calculation, using the average output per worker in manufactures, mining and building to measure productivity changes, yields the following

deterioration in the terms of trade was the result of the increasing productivity of the English export industries, or to a rising cost of imports, factor incomes were not, in consequence, reduced.

IV

B.   Models with shifts in the distribution of income

In the second class of models, aggregate *per capita* income increases but distribution changes in such a manner that the incomes of the working classes are reduced absolutely. In such a model, the pessimists argue, the non-working classes (let us call them the capitalists and landlords) benefit from the higher average level of income, as well as from a distributive shift which gives them a larger share. It should be noted, however, that a variety of distributive shifts, with different results for income, are possible: there could be a shift towards the capitalists and landlords, with aggregate *per capita* income rising, which also leaves the incomes of the working classes rising; or, the capitalists and landlords could benefit from a larger share of a lower aggregate *per capita* income (as in some models already discussed); or, the working classes could benefit from a larger share of a rising aggregate *per capita* income, *or* from a larger share of a lower aggregate *per capita* income. All this means that to settle the debate about the effects of distributive shifts during the Industrial Revolution it would be necessary to have accurate figures both of aggregate income and of the distribution of income over time. Instead, there are only a small number of estimates of national income and distribution, which, although plausible, are not accurate enough to be conclusive.[1]

---

factorial terms of trade (1880 = 100): 1801—55, 1811—58, 1821—67, 1831—69, 1841—64, 1851—64.

[1] National income estimates have been systematized by Deane and Cole (op. cit.). For income distribution see L. Soltow ('Long Run Changes in British Income Inequality', *Economic History Review*, 1968), who estimated both Lorenz Curves and Pareto coefficients. C. Clark (*The Conditions of Economic Progress*, Macmillan, London, 2nd edn, 1951, pp. 534, 538) also estimated Pareto coefficients, showing that income distribution was more unequal in 1812 than in 1848. For discussion of income distribution generally, and for an argument that income distribution was becoming less unequal, see Hartwell (*The Industrial Revolution and Economic Growth*, Methuen, London, 1971, pp. 321-4).

We can use the estimates made by Bowley of the distribution of British income in 1880 to suggest that it seems implausible that, in aggregate, the working classes did not benefit from increased incomes in the period of the Industrial Revolution. The inequality of 1880, as measured by Bowley, could not be explained by constant or even falling *per capita* wages between 1800 and 1880. If there had been perfect income equality in 1800, and if thereafter all increases in income had gone to the non-wage-earning classes, the share of the latter would have been greatly in excess of the inequality estimated by Bowley in 1880. If income distribution in 1850 had been as unequally distributed as in 1880, then perfect equality of incomes in 1800 and constancy of the *per capita* incomes of wage-earners thereafter would have been consistent with the 1850 inequality. Because of the complete implausibility of the assumption of perfect income equality in 1800, however, the most plausible inference is that the incomes of the wage-earners rose after 1800, this inference being consistent both with the measured growth of national income and also with the 1880 income distribution.[1] Of course the changes made have been adverse to wage-earners in certain periods, but the data suggest that overall, whatever may have been the shifts in the relative distribution of national income, the absolute incomes of this group rose.

Before discussing particular models, some general points should be made. First, even if there had been a marked shift to a higher savings ratio during the Industrial Revolution, and thus to a higher rate of capital formation, redistribution of income would not have been necessary to have produced this result. Further, higher incomes because of redistribution could have been used for purposes other than capital formation; some pessimists have strongly suggested that higher incomes went, partly at least, to conspicuous consumption rather than to investment.[2] In any case, redistribution resulting in industrial

---

[1] These calculations are based upon the estimates of A. L. Bowley (*The Change in the Distribution of the National Income, 1880–1913*, Clarendon Press, Oxford, 1920), and the national income estimates in Deane and Cole (op. cit. p. 282).

[2] See, for example, a characteristic opinion of Hobsbawm (*Industry and Empire*, op. cit. p. 91–2): 'The very moment when the poor were at the end of their tether – in the early and middle 'forties – was the moment when the middle classes

capital formation could give a favourable outcome for the effects of any income redistribution. Second, even if wages in each sector of the economy had remained constant over time, the average wage level may still have risen as workers moved from low-wage sectors to higher-wage sectors (for example, from agriculture to industry). A gain in average wage levels from structural change was certainly part of the process of English growth.[1] Constancy of wages in both industry and agriculture would have been consistent with an average rising standard of living, with the people who moved being made better-off. The pessimists would argue that these were the only workers who were better off, with all other workers remaining at a constantly low standard of living.[2] Third, the crude division of society into two classes (capitalists and workers), or three (capitalists, landlords and workers), is not appropriate for the historical analysis of changing income levels; such a division would be convincing only if aggregate income had been constant and if shares had changed within that given aggregate. During the Industrial Revolution, however, changes in the capital–labour, capital–land and land–labour ratios, and changes in the number of workers, capitalists and landlords were such that a variety of shares would have been consistent with specified levels of per worker, per capitalist and per landlord income. To use changes in factor shares of national income to infer what happened to the levels of income of particular groups it is necessary to know both the changes in national income and the changes in the number of members in each class.

---

dripped with excess capital, to be widely invested in railways and spent on the bulgent, opulent household furnishings displayed at the Great Exhibition of 1851, and on the palatial municipal constructions which prepared to rise in the smoky northern cities.'

[1] It was Colin Clark (*The Conditions of Economic Progress*, Macmillan, London, 1940, p. 344) who first popularized the concept of structural change and its importance: 'economic progress in any country . . . may take place (*a*) as a result of improvement in real output per head in all or any of these three fields [of industry, agriculture and services], or (*b*) as a result of transference of labour from the less productive to the more productive fields'. The case for England has been argued at length by Hartwell.

[2] As is implicit in 'the labour aristocracy' literature, as developed, for example, by Hobsbawm.

Models depending on distributive shifts in income are the following.

(*v*) *The Malthusian redistribution model.* This model has been used by the modern pessimists,[1] and it had strong support among the classical economists and was implicit in much policy discussion in England in the period before 1850.[2] In it the shift in income favours the landowners, and is at the expense of capitalists as well as wage-earners. There is a rise in the relative price of agricultural commodities in comparison with manufactured goods, the result of diminishing returns in agricultural production, with a consequent rising cost of labour and a profit squeeze. Since there is presumed an elastic supply of labour to agriculture, the result of long-run population response, real wages cannot rise; since there is an equilibrium real wage only at subsistence, real wages thus fall to subsistence. In the Malthus–Ricardo model, the final outcome is the stationary state with constant subsistence real wages, zero profits and a share for rents above the pre-equilibrium level. This was the model of the economy which Ricardo saw threatening during the Napoleonic Wars; and he also saw the obvious remedy, the freeing of trade in agricultural commodities, especially corn. To an important extent the debate about the corn laws in England was a debate about the redistribution of income, with landlords on one side, and workers and capitalists the other. It was the failure of history to confirm Ricardo, however, that led to the decline of Ricardianism in the 1830s: by then it was becoming impossible to accept Ricardo's theory of the relationship between wages and profits and difficult to accept the Malthusian theory of population and the doctrine of the stationary state. Such theories were incom-

---

[1] See Pollard and Crossley (op. cit. p. 179): 'Since this increased output [of agricultural produce, 1760–1815] was obtained at great cost, largely under decreasing returns, the incomes of the agricultural sector, i.e. those of farmers and receivers of rent, increased at the expense of those of other sectors of the community.'

[2] See M. Blaug (*Economic Theory in Retrospect*, rev. edn, Irwin, Homewood (Illinois), 1968) for detailed discussion of the classical economists' theories of growth, especially chapter 3, 'Population, Diminishing Returns and Rent', and chapter 4, 'Ricardo's System'.

patible with observations of the growing economy.[1] During the Wars agricultural prices and rents certainly rose, and there could have been a distributive shift towards landlords; after the Wars, however, when both agricultural prices and rents fell, there was almost certainly redistribution against the landlords.[2] And the freeing of trade, even if it made workers and capitalists both better off relative to landlords, by itself tells us nothing about the trends in real wages between 1800 and 1850.

(*vi*) *The inflationary redistribution model.* The usual pessimist model sees the distributive shift towards the capitalists rather than towards the landowners. In one such model there is inflation, with a lag of wages behind prices, leading to forced savings through a distributive shift to profits. This model was used both by Hamilton and Keynes to explain how the Industrial Revolution financed its growth. It has been severely criticized both on empirical grounds, in which the historical reality of the wage lag in the eighteenth century has been questioned, and on theoretical grounds, on the relationship between monetary and real variables.[3] The model does have some plausibility for the Napoleonic Wars period, but none at all for the period of falling prices after the Wars, when wages fell less than prices. Again, since the rate of inflation is not an exogenous variable, it is necessary to ask why prices rose when they did. If inflation

[1] See M. Blaug, 'The Empirical Content of Ricardian Economics', *Journal of Political Economy*, 1956. It is true, however, that to about 1850 there was some relative rise in the price of agricultural commodities *vis-à-vis* other goods, but the pattern was quite mixed and most of the rise had been achieved during the early period of the Napoleonic Wars, and, it could be argued, in the post-1800 fluctuations in the price ratio, there was no basic trend.

[2] There is a considerable literature on 'the agricultural depression' after the Napoleonic Wars; for example, G. E. Fussell and M. Compton, 'Agricultural Adjustment after the Napoleonic Wars', *Economic History*, 1939. For land values see Norton, Trist and Gilbert, 'A Century of Land Values: England and Wales', *Journal of the Royal Statistical Society*, 1891.

[3] J. M. Keynes, *A Treatise of Money* (Macmillan, London, 1930), vol. II, chapter 30; E. J. Hamilton, 'Profit Inflation and the Industrial Revolution', *Quarterly Journal of Economics*, 1942; R. A. Kessel and A. A. Alchian, 'The Meaning and Validity of the Inflation-Induced Lag of Wages', *American Economic Review*, 1960. See also the criticisms of D. Felix, 'Profit Inflation and Industrial Growth: the Historic Record and Contemporary Analogies', *Quarterly Journl of Economics*, 1956; and J. U. Nef, 'Prices and Industrial Capitalism in Engand and France, 1540–1640', *Economic History Review*, 1937; both suggest that any redistribution would have been in favour of landowners and not industrialists.

was the result of government financing of its expenditures, as during the Wars, then the distributive shift was towards the government, and with falling civilian income nothing could be inferred about the relative shares of capital and labour. If inflation was the result of private sector financing of expenditures through their control of the banking system, then the distributive shift could have been towards the capitalists. It would be necessary to examine bank creation of money in detail to determine the exact short-term and long-term effects on distributive shares. Two other problems remain. Why did the money wage rate remain inflexible in the face of rising prices and increasing labour demands? Since prices went both up and down over time, how is it that presumed real wage losses during inflations were not offset by gains during deflations?

(*vii*) *The tax redistribution model.* Another suggested pessimist model is that which stresses the redistribution imposed by the tax burden in war and peace.[1] Both Adam Smith and Ricardo made explicit the redistributive effects of taxation; Ricardo arguing, for example, that taxes 'are always ultimately paid, either from the capital, or from the revenue of the country'. But it is empirically difficult to estimate the burden of taxation and its incidence, as cost or benefit, among classes. For example, was expenditure on the Napoleonic Wars for the benefit of all classes, or should it be examined rather for its redistributive effects, allegedly raising the incomes of landowners and capitalists at the expense of workers? Should not there have been more taxation, and hence redistribution, for the social infrastructure? Were payments under the poor laws to be taken as evidence of poverty or of progressive tax redistribution? Is the argument that the workers were taxed too much by regressive taxation (based largely on tariffs and

---

[1] See Pollard and Crossley (op. cit. p. 207): 'Legislative action did not on the whole favour the poorer classes. The end of the war saw the immediate repeal of the income tax and the tightening up of the Corn Law, both actions favouring large property owners, while a National Debt of £848 millions represented a substantial shift, year by year, from the poor to the rich, particularly those who had profiteered during the war.' And Thompson (op. cit. p. 304): 'When we discuss the minutae of finance we sometimes forget the crazy exploitive basis of taxation after the Wars, as well as its redistributive function – from the poor to the rich.'

consumption goods), or that the benefits of public expenditure went mainly towards the capitalists and landlords or, at least, that too few benefits went to the workers relative to the taxes they paid?

The historical evidence on the weight of tax-financed redistribution during the Industrial Revolution deserves further study. First, given the importance of debt retirement and interest payments resulting from the Napoleonic Wars, these might be thought to have some impact on income distribution.[1] Second, the effects of some taxes (for example, tariffs) went beyond the revenues they generated. Third, while the real weight of taxation relative to national income was reduced increasingly after the Wars, when national income rose steadily and national budgets remained relatively constant, taxation as a proportion of national income remained as high as 11 per cent in 1851. However, the regressive character of taxation was probably reduced in the period before 1850.[2]

(viii) The innovational bias model. A frequently suggested cause of falling real wages during the Industrial Revolution has been that a consistently capital-using and labour-saving bias of innovations lowered the demand curve for labour and thus the marginal product of employed workers.[3] Such a bias, which should have resulted in a rising capital–output ratio, would have had to have been extreme to have actually lowered real wages.

[1] Thus, in 1821, government expenditures on debt charges amounted to about 55 per cent of budgetary expenditures, and equalled 11 per cent of national income. This share fell over time, but was still 52 per cent of the budget and 5 per cent of national income in 1851. The analysis of the effects of debt purchases and retirements on distribution are complex, and it might be argued that debt issuance permitted war finance to occur with lower taxes upon, and thus less consumption decline for, the lower income groups. Again it is necessary to separate, analytically, the impact of the wars from the impact of the industrialization process.

[2] See Hartwell (*The Industrial Revolution and Economic Growth*, op. cit. pp. 323–4) for a discussion of the redistributive effects of taxation and protective legislation.

[3] See Thompson (op. cit. p. 312): 'the evident fact that technological innovation during the Industrial Revolution, until the Railway Age, did displace (except in the metal industries) adult skilled labour'. And Hobsbawm (*Industry and Empire*, op. cit. p. 93): 'the declining industries and occupations, displaced by technical progress, of whom the half-million handloom weavers are the best known example, but by no means the only one. They starved progressively in a vain attempt to compete with the new machines by working more and more cheaply.'

The empirical evidence, however, suggests that there was no particular factor-saving bias in Industrial Revolution innovation,[1] that the capital–output ratio rose very slowly (and in the initial switch from cottage to factory industry may even have fallen) and in aggregate was relatively low,[2] and that labour continued to migrate into industry (a phenomenon difficult to explain if real wages in industry were consistently falling). And there is a puzzle created if the bias is regarded as a deliberate response to relative factor costs: how is this to be reconciled with the labour abundance so frequently asserted by the pessimists?

(ix) The exploitation models. The most popular models of immiseration used by the pessimists, and those which inspire the greatest moral fervour, are ones in which the workers were consciously exploited by the capitalists.[3] In these models wages were kept below marginal value product by deliberate exploitation. The implications must be, either that capitalists had coercive political power which enabled them to direct labour to work and to collude to determine wage rates, or that the capitalists had monopsony powers in the labour market such that they could set wages over which the workers had no control, either individually or in combination. The former might be interpreted as a case of 'the enclosure model' (discussed below), pointing to actions which increased the labour supply by reducing its alternatives. This model is one in which the collusive class action leads to an increased supply of labour in industrial areas, but does not imply any collusive, cartel-like

[1] See Hartwell (*The Industrial Revolution and Economic Growth*, op. cit. pp. 296–7) for a discussion of factor-bias in innovation during the industrial revolution. On the possible effects of biased innovations on factor incomes see, in particular, W. Fellner, 'Marxian Hypotheses and Observable Trends Under Capitalism: A "Modernized" Interpretation', *Economic Journal*, 1957.

[2] Ibid. op. cit. p. 317: 'Of various possibilities . . . the most likely up to about 1840, was a modest rate of savings and a low capital output ratio. . . . But whereas the productivity of much new industrial equipment was high, its cost was low. Thus the comparatively low savings ratio was not incompatible with rising real incomes.'

[3] The exploitation thesis is most explicitly argued by Thompson (chapter VI, 'Exploitation', in *The Making of the English Working Class*): 'over the same period [1790–1840] there was intensified exploitation, greater insecurity, and increasing human misery'.

action in the actual setting of wages by the industrialists.[1] The implications of the monopsony model are that the individual capitalist had considerable control over his labour market, that there was little migration of labour (in or out of the market), and thus that there was an inelasticity of supply of labour which had no alternative choices of employment. The model is, historically, unrealistic. There was constant migration in England over the course of the Industrial Revolution, and the labour that migrated into industry chose not to return to agriculture (for example, the Irish peasants).[2] The forces behind migration suggest that industry did not worsen a low wage situation; rather that workers moved to industry because of the attraction of higher wages.[3] Moreover, there is evidence of intensive labour recruitment by firms, of the poaching of labour, of the hanging-on to skilled labour, and generally of a range of labour-inducement and labour-retention mechanisms.[4] The highly competitive character of Industrial Revolution industry did not provide the economic conditions in which labour exploitation, in the sense of lowering wages below marginal product, was possible. Moreover it was in this period that the workers were able, for the first time in history, to organize themselves effectively in their own interests.

(*x*) *The enclosure model.* The argument that politically determined enclosures drove the workers off the land and into wage employment resolves one crucial weakness in several models of immiseration, and has a long history including its key rôle in Marx's 'primitive accumulation'.[5] The enclosure model pro-

[1] On this point see S. Engerman, 'Some Considerations Relating to Property Rights in Man', *Journal of Economic History*, 1973.

[2] See A. Redford's study of internal migration (*Labour Migration in England, 1800–1850*, Manchester University Press, 1926).

[3] This phenomenon was obvious throughout the eighteenth century; see E. W. Gilboy, *Wages in Eighteenth Century England* (Harvard University Press, Cambridge (Mass.), 1934). For wage differentials in the first half of the nineteenth century see G. H. Wood ('The Course of Average Wages between 1790 and 1860', *Economic Journal*, 1899) and A. L. Bowley (*Wages in the United Kingdom in the Nineteenth Century*, op. cit.).

[4] See, for example, M. Elsas (Ed.), *Iron in the Making: Dowlais Iron Company Letters, 1782–1860* (Glamorgan County Record Office, 1960), Chapter 2, 'Masters and Men'.

[5] On this model see J. Saville, 'Primitive Accumulation and Early Industrialization in Britain', *The Socialist Register*, 1969; and J. S. Cohen and M. L. Weitzman,

vides an explanation of 'voluntary' migration to industrial areas, with presumably higher wages, consistent with a 'push' due to a forced decline in agriculture incomes rather than a 'pull' of higher industrial incomes. While this model is internally consistent, and of obvious historical relevance, some analytical issues remain to be resolved. First, was the nature of the political process such that the industrialists, in their desire to obtain a labour force, forced enclosure, or was the force behind enclosure the agricultural interest, as frequently argued? While the effects on labour could have been the same, there are implications for what the alternative incomes of the industrial labour force might otherwise have been. Second, even if enclosures could have provided an increased industrial labour force, a thesis about which there has been some doubt following the demographic work of Chambers, it could mean only that workers got less than they otherwise would have, not necessarily that observed wage rates fell over time. Nevertheless it seems clear that the enclosure model remains a basic one in the analysis of income changes during, and before, the period of the Industrial Revolution, having the virtues of plausibility, internal consistency and a basis in class interest, however well it will ultimately fare in empirical testing.

V

The conclusions to be drawn from this exercise are brief. By presenting a list of various pessimistic models it is possible to see which are implausible, which conflict with the limited evidence, and which are inconsistent, as well as those which could provide some basis for a pessimistic position, appropriately presented. It is, of course, not to be expected that the 'standard of living' debate will ever be resolved, no matter how much evidence is ultimately brought to bear on the issue. In part this is because the 'basket of goods' approach, however

'A Marxian Type Model of Enclosures' (Unpublished, 1973). There is some issue concerning whether the important movement occurred prior to or during the period of industrial revolution. For an alternative view of enclosure, which suggests lesser impact on the economy and on the distributions of income, see D. N. McCloskey, 'The Economics of Enclosure: A Market Analysis' (Unpublished, 1972).

important, cannot capture the essence of such sweeping social changes which the process of industrialization entails. Yet, despite the dramatic evidence on the difficulties of transition, we must still ask about the alternatives available to society, as well as note that the 'quality of life' changed in both directions during this period.[1]

But in part the debate remains inconclusive, even as regards the 'quantity' issue, because both optimists and pessimists are asking different questions than what happened to *per capita* income and its distribution between 1750 and 1850. And asking different questions has sometimes backed both sides into strained positions, since both positions can be taken independently of observed changes in wages and incomes. For the optimists, who at times seem to ignore the hardships and human sufferings of this period, the analysis begins with some set of exogenous changes (mainly population growth) which would have had even severer repercussions on the standard of living without the alternative of industrial development. For the pessimists, who at times seem to ignore the problems of no-growth, the analysis generally begins with the proposition that the transition to rapid economic growth could have been achieved with less cost to the working classes. Given that there are two different questions being asked – What would have happened without industrialization? Could industrialization have been achieved at lower social and economic cost to wage-earners? – and that the evidence pertains mainly to a third question – What happened to the level and distribution of wage incomes? – it is no wonder that the broad debate has been, and will remain, somewhat inconclusive.

© R. M. Hartwell and S. Engerman 1974

[1] As a critical evaluation of the benefits and cost of economic growth the appendix to W. A. Lewis, *The Theory of Economic Growth* (Allen and Unwin, London, 1955), remains useful.

Select Bibliography

This bibliography excludes source items (e.g. Porter's *Progress of the Nation*) and collections of statistical data (e.g. Mitchell and Deane, *Abstract of British Historical Statistics*).

ASHTON, T. S., 'The Standard of Life of the Workers in England, 1790–1830', *Journal of Economic History*, Supplement IX (1949).

ASHTON, T. S., 'Changes in Standards of Comfort in Eighteenth-Century England', *Proceedings of the British Academy* (1955).

BARKER, T. C., MCKENZIE, J. C., and YUDKIN, J. (eds.), *Our Changing Fare* (1966).

BARNSBY, G. J., 'The Standard of Living in the Black Country during the Nineteenth Century', *Economic History Review*, 2nd series, XXIV (1971).

BOWLEY, A. L., *Wages in the United Kingdom in the Nineteenth Century* (1900).

BURNETT, J., *Plenty and Want: a Social History of Diet* (1966).

BURNETT, J., *A History of the Cost of Living* (1969).

BYTHELL, D., *The Handloom Weavers* (1969).

CHAPMAN, S. D. (ed.), *The History of Working-Class Housing: A Symposium* (1971).

CHECKLAND, S. G., *The Rise of Industrial Society in England, 1815–85* (1964).

CLAPHAM, J. H., *An Economic History of Modern Britain, Vol. I* (1926, 2nd edn 1939).

COLLIER, F., *The Family Economy of the Working Classes in the Cotton Industry 1784–1833* (1965).

DEANE, P., *The First Industrial Revolution* (1965).

DEANE, P., and COLE, W. A., *British Economic Growth 1688–1959: Trends and Structure* (1968).

DRUMMOND, J. C., and WILBRAHIM, A., *The Englishman's Food* (1939, revised edn 1957).

GASH, N., 'Rural Unemployment 1815–34', *Economic History Review*, 1st series, VI (1935).

GEORGE, M. D., *London Life in the Eighteenth Century* (1925).

GILBOY, E. W., *Wages in Eighteenth-Century England* (1934).

GILBOY, E. W., 'The Cost of Living and Real Wages in Eighteenth-Century England', *Review of Economic Studies* (1935).

GOURVISH, T. R., 'The Cost of Living in Glasgow in the Early Nineteenth Century', *Economic History Review*, 2nd series, XXV (1972).

HAMILTON, E. D., 'Prices as a Factor in Economic Growth', *Journal of Economic History*, XII (1952).

HAMMOND, J. L., 'The Industrial Revolution and Discontent', *Economic History Review*, 1st series, II (1930).

HARTWELL, R. M., 'Interpretations of the Industrial Revolution in England', *Journal of Economic History*, XIX (1959).

HARTWELL, R. M., 'The Rising Standard of Living in England, 1800–50', *Economic History Review*, 2nd series, XIII (1961).

HARTWELL, R. M., 'The Standard of Living Controversy: a Summary', in HARTWELL, R. M. (ed.), *The Industrial Revolution* (1970).

HICKS, J., *A Theory of Economic History* (1969).

HOBSBAWM, E. J., 'The British Standard of Living 1790–1850', *Economic History Review*, 2nd series, XI (1958).

HOBSBAWM, E. J., *Labouring Men* (1964).

HOBSBAWM, E. J., *Industry and Empire* (1968).

HOBSBAWM, E. J., and HARTWELL, R. M., 'The Standard of Living during the Industrial Revolution – A Discussion', *Economic History Review*, 2nd series, XVI (1963).

HUNT, E. H., *Regional Wage Variations in Britain, 1850–1914* (1973).

INGLIS, B., *Poverty and the Industrial Revolution* (1971: paperback edn with new foreword, 1972).

KELSALL, R. K., 'The General Trend of Real Wages in the North of England during the Eighteenth Century', *Yorkshire Archaeological Journal*, XXXIII (1936).

MCKENZIE, J. C., 'The Composition and Nutritional Value of Diets in Manchester and Dukinfield in 1841', *Transactions of the Lancashire and Cheshire Antiquarian Society*, LXXII (1962).

MCKEOWN, T., and RECORD, R. G., 'Reasons for the Decline

of Mortality in England and Wales during the Nineteenth Century', *Population Studies*, XVI (1962).

MARSHALL, J. D., 'The Lancashire Rural Labourer in the Early Nineteenth Century', *Transactions of the Lancashire and Cheshire Antiquarian Society*, LXXI (1961).

MATHIAS, P., *The First Industrial Nation* (1968).

NEALE, R. S., 'The Standard of Living, 1780–1844: a Regional and Class Study', *Economic History Review*, 2nd series, XIX (1966).

PEEL, C. S., 'Homes and Habits', in YOUNG, G. M. (ed.), *Early Victorian England* (1934).

PERKIN, H., *The Origins of Modern English Society 1780–1880* (1969).

PHELPS BROWN, E. H., and HOPKINS, S. V., 'Seven Centuries of Prices of Consumables compared with Builders' Wage Rates', *Economica*, new series, XXIII (1956).

POLLARD, S., 'Investment, Consumption and the Industrial Revolution', *Economic History Review*, 2nd series, XI (1958).

POLLARD, S., and CROSSLEY, D. W., *The Wealth of Britain, 1085–1966* (1968).

SALAMAN, R. N., *The History and Social Influence of the Potato* (1949).

SELDON, A. (ed.), *The Long Debate on Poverty. Essays on Industrialisation and the 'Condition of England'* (1973).

SMELSER, N. J., *Social Change in the Industrial Revolution: an Application of Theory to the Lancashire Cotton Industry 1770–1840* (1959).

SUTCLIFFE, A., 'Working-Class Housing in Nineteenth-Century Britain: a Review of Recent Research', *Bulletin of the Society for the Study of Labour History*, 24 (1972).

TAYLOR, A. J., 'Progress and Poverty in Britain, 1780–1850', *History*, XLV (1960).

THOMPSON, E. P., *The Making of the English Working Class* (1963).

TUCKER, R. S., 'Real Wages of Artisans in London, 1792–1935', *Journal of the American Statistical Association*, XXXI (1936).

WILLIAMS, J. E., 'The British Standard of Living, 1750–1850', *Economic History Review*, 2nd series, XIX (1966).

WOODRUFF, D., 'Capitalism and the Historians', *Journal of Economic History*, XVI (1956).